access to history

Edward VI and Mary: A Mid-Tudor Crisis? 1540–58 THIRD EDITION

access to history

Edward VI and Mary: A Mid-Tudor Crisis? 1540–58 THIRD EDITION

Roger Turvey and Nigel Heard

MERCHISTON CASTLE
SCHOOL
HISTORY DEPARTMENT

HODDER
EDUCATION
PART OF HACHETTE LIVRE UK

The publishers would like to thank the following individuals, institutions and companies for permission to reproduce copyright illustrations in this book: © Bettmann/CORBIS, pages 5, 39, 74, 87, 108; © Corpus Christi College, Oxford, UK/Bridgeman Art Library, page 61; Fotomas Index UK, page 126; Lambeth Palace, London, UK/Bridgeman Art Library, page 105; Mary Evans Picture Library, pages 43, 111; The National Archives, ref. E23/4, page 37; National Portrait Gallery, London, UK/Bridgeman Art Library, pages 57, 96; Private Collection/Bridgeman Art Library, pages 49, 85, 141; Private Collection, The Stapleton Collection/Bridgeman Art Library, page 138; Private Collection, Ken Welsh/Bridgeman Art Library, pages 40, 51.

The publishers would like to thank the following for permission to reproduce material in this book: Cambridge University Press for extracts from *Authority and Disorder in Tudor Times, 1485–1603* by Paul Thomas, 1999, used on pages 31, 68, 147, 166.

The publishers would also like to thank the following: Blackwell Publishing for an extract from *The English* by G.R. Elton, 1992 and *Mary Tudor* by David Loades, 1989; Cambridge University Press for extracts from *The Tudor Monarchies 1485–1603* by John McGurk, 1999 and *Tudor Rebellions* by A. Fletcher and D. MacCulloch, 1997; Harvard University Press for an extract from *Reform and Reformation* by G.R. Elton, 1977; Longman for extracts from *The Emergence of a Nation State 1529–1660* by Alan Smith, 1984 and *Tudor Britain 1485–1603* by R. Lockyer and D. O'Sullivan, 1997; Routledge for an extract from *Tudor Government* by T.A. Morris, 1999.

Every effort has been made to trace and acknowledge ownership of copyright. The publishers will be glad to make suitable arrangements with any copyright holders whom it has not been possible to contact.

Although every effort has been made to ensure that website addresses are correct at time of going to press, Hodder Murray cannot be held responsible for the content of any website mentioned in this book. It is sometimes possible to find a relocated web page by typing in the address of the home page for a website in the URL window of your browser.

Orders: please contact Bookpoint Ltd, 130 Milton Park, Abingdon, Oxon OX14 4SB. Telephone: (44) 01235 827720. Fax: (44) 01235 400454. Lines are open 9.00–5.00, Monday to Saturday, with a 24-hour message answering service. Visit our website at www.hoddereducation.co.uk

© Roger Turvey, Nigel Heard 2006
First published in 2006 by
Hodder Education,
Part of the Hachette Livre UK,
338 Euston Road
London NW1 3BH

Impression number	10 9 8 7 6 5 4
Year	2010 2009 2008

The front cover illustration shows a portrait of Mary Tudor by Moro, reproduced courtesy of AKG Photo, London.
Typeset in Baskerville 10/12pt and produced by Gray Publishing, Tunbridge Wells
Printed in Malta

A catalogue record for this title is available from the British Library

ISBN: 978 0 340 91252 2

Contents

Dedication

Keith Randell (1943–2002)

The *Access to History* series was conceived and developed by Keith, who created a series to 'cater for students as they are, not as we might wish them to be'. He leaves a living legacy of a series that for over 20 years has provided a trusted, stimulating and well-loved accompaniment to post-16 study. Our aim with these new editions is to continue to offer students the best possible support for their studies.

1

A Crisis in Mid-Tudor England?

POINTS TO CONSIDER

This chapter is intended to help you to understand what historians mean by the term mid-Tudor crisis. It explains how the views of historians about mid-sixteenth-century England have changed and how they use the ideas of crisis and the development of the State to explain events. By examining the problems created by political, social, economic and religious change you should be able to come to a firm decision about whether there was a mid-Tudor crisis.

These issues are examined as four themes:

- Mid-Tudor England 1540–58
- The historiographical background
- A crisis of the State: government, politics and foreign policy
- A crisis of the State: social, economic and religious change

Key dates

1534		Henry VIII became Head of the Church in England
1540	June	Fall of Thomas Cromwell
1546		Duke of Norfolk (Thomas Howard) imprisoned
1547	January	Henry VIII died
		Edward VI became king
		Duke of Somerset (Edward Seymour) became Lord Protector
1549	November	Somerset replaced by the Duke of Northumberland (John Dudley) who became Lord President of the Council
1553	July	Edward VI died
		Lady Jane Grey crowned queen and 'reigned' for nine days
		Mary became Queen of England

1 | Mid-Tudor England 1540–58

Henry VIII: faction and rivalry at Court 1540–7

In 1540 the fall of Thomas Cromwell, Henry VIII's chief adviser in the 1530s, heralded a period of increased political instability. There was a growth in the rivalry between factions at court. The main issue lay between the reformists who supported reform in politics and religion, and the conservatives who were opposed to reform. The rivalry between these two factions began in 1534 when Henry broke away from the Roman Catholic Church and made himself Supreme Head of the Church in England. Since then the ruling élites had been split over the issue of whether the English Church should remain essentially Catholic or become more **Protestant**.

The reformists

The reformists were led by Archbishop Cranmer and Edward Seymour, later Duke of Somerset, the uncle of Prince Edward. The reformists were unhappy with the **Anglo-Catholicism** established by Henry VIII and Cromwell in 1534. They wanted the Church in England to become more Protestant.

The conservatives

The conservatives were headed by Thomas Howard, Duke of Norfolk, and Stephen Gardiner, Bishop of Winchester. Some conservatives wanted the Church to return to Roman Catholicism, but the majority were content to continue the Anglo-Catholicism established by Henry VIII. The conservatives were united in opposing a Protestant Church in England.

Disputes between the factions

The disgrace and execution of Cromwell, the architect of the **Reformation**, had been a success for the conservatives. This was confirmed by Henry VIII's marriage to Catherine Howard, the Duke of Norfolk's niece. The conservatives hoped to influence the King and the shaping of royal policy via his new wife. However, Catherine's trial and execution for adultery in 1542 marked a victory for the reformists. In seeking out the evidence to destroy her, the reformists hoped to ruin the reputations of both Norfolk and Gardiner.

For the next five years the two factions strove for supremacy at Court. Henry VIII's final marriage, to Catherine Parr, a committed Protestant, showed that the conservatives were losing ground. In 1546 the reformists gained a decisive advantage when the Duke of Norfolk was arrested and put in the Tower of London on a charge of treason, and Stephen Gardiner was dismissed from the **Privy Council**. It was against this background that Edward VI, brought up as a Protestant, came to the throne in 1547.

Some historians see these disputes between the factions as a sign of increasing dynastic weakness. Others argue that factions were a normal part of Tudor politics, and that such rivalry was necessary for healthy government. Nevertheless, the fact remains

Key question
Who were the major political figures in mid-Tudor England?

Key dates

Henry VIII became Head of the Church in England: 1534

Fall of Thomas Cromwell: 1540

Duke of Norfolk (Thomas Howard) imprisoned: 1546

Key terms

Protestant
Used to describe those who had protested against and separated from the Roman Catholic Church.

Anglo-Catholicism
Used to describe the English Catholic Church set up in 1534 with the King as its head rather than the Pope.

Reformation
Used to describe the religious changes of the sixteenth century in England and continental Europe.

Privy Council
Élite body of councillors drawn from the nobility and more powerful gentry who met the monarch on a regular basis to offer their advice, frame laws and govern the country.

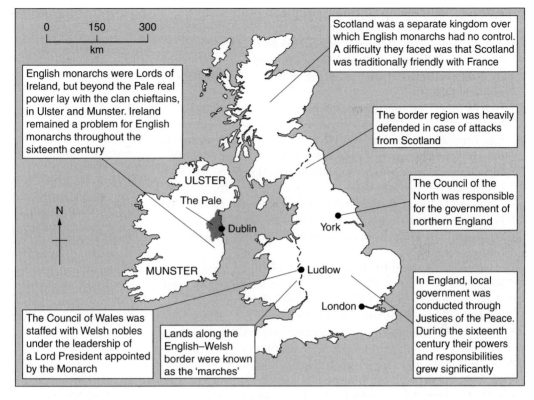

Figure 1.1: The geography of mid-Tudor England.

that Henry VIII's death in 1547 marked the beginning of 11 years of less stable government and this has prompted many historians to see it as a period of crisis.

Edward VI: the Somerset years 1547–9

Henry VIII was succeeded by nine-year-old Prince Edward, his son by his third wife, Jane Seymour. This was a problem in itself because Edward was too young to rule, and periods of **minority government** were often times of potential political unrest. Henry VIII had tried to prevent trouble by establishing a Regency Council led by Edward Seymour, Edward's uncle. Edward Seymour quickly gained control of the Council and, under his new title of Lord Protector Somerset (he had been made Duke of Somerset by his young nephew) ruled the country until 1549. During this time the political situation deteriorated steadily. Whether this was caused by Somerset's lack of ability, or by the numerous difficulties which he had to overcome is hotly debated by historians.

Three major problems were inherited from the policies of Henry VIII:

(1) *Religious policy*. Should the Church of England remain essentially Catholic or become more Protestant? Somerset inherited a divided Church that lacked decisive leadership and a clear direction. Somerset himself was a moderate

reformer, as were most members of the Regency Council, whereas Edward VI, despite his youth, favoured more radical changes. However, powerful politicians such as the Duke of Norfolk and Bishop Gardiner were opposed to change, and such differences only increased the in-fighting among the political factions.

(2) *Foreign policy*. Should the war with France and Scotland begun by Henry VIII in 1542 be continued or stopped? Somerset inherited a war that Henry VIII had hoped would secure the marriage of Edward VI to the young Mary Queen of Scots. Although the government was already bankrupt, Somerset continued the war and thereby further crippled the country's finances. At the same time he strove to continue Henry VIII's policy of keeping on good terms with Charles V, ruler of Spain and the **Holy Roman Empire**, for fear of provoking him into war.

(3) *Economic policy*. Should the economy, which had been neglected by Henry VIII, be reformed or left to repair itself? Somerset inherited an English economy that was in a very weak condition. Population levels had been increasing rapidly since the 1530s, causing prices to rise and making it difficult for young people to find work. The problem was made worse by a fall in demand for English textiles abroad, which caused growing unemployment among cloth workers. By 1549 there was widespread discontent among the mass of the population, leading to large-scale popular uprisings in Norfolk and the West Country.

Although the rebellions were eventually suppressed, Somerset's enemies on the Council seized the opportunity to overthrow him and take power.

Edward VI: the Northumberland years 1550–3

From the ensuing power struggle John Dudley, Earl of Warwick, emerged as the new leader. He was made Duke of Northumberland and Lord President of the Council. He ruled the country as the Lord President Northumberland for the remainder of Edward VI's reign. While Northumberland seems to have adopted more practical policies than Somerset there is some debate as to whether he was any more successful in overcoming the problems that faced the country.

Although the popular discontent had been subdued, Northumberland faced the same problems as his predecessor. These problems were three-fold:

(1) *Foreign policy*. Somerset's fall from power caused a temporary breakdown in military leadership. This enabled the French to gain the initiative in the war and they went on the offensive. This, combined with a lack of money, forced Northumberland to make peace with both France and Scotland. This annoyed many of the ruling élites who thought that this was a humiliating climb-down.

Key term

Holy Roman Empire
Collection of states of varying sizes that covered central Europe (Germany and Austria) and northern Italy, which was governed by an elected ruler, the Emperor.

Key question
What problems did Northumberland face and how did he deal with them?

Key dates

Somerset replaced by the Duke of Northumberland (John Dudley) who became Lord President of the Council: 1549

Edward VI died: 1553

(2) *Religious policy*. At the same time, possibly to secure the support of Edward VI, Northumberland allowed increasingly radical reforms to be introduced into the Church of England. For example, altars were ordered to be removed and the church service was modelled on the Lutheran system of worship. Such a move not only angered the Catholic élites at home, but also antagonised Emperor Charles V, England's major continental ally, who was an active supporter of the Roman Catholic Church.

(3) *Economic policy*. Northumberland had learned from Somerset's mistakes and introduced measures to try to restore stability. The Privy Council and the government were reorganised, finances were reformed, and debts created by the war began to be paid off. Although the economic situation continued to worsen, new **poor laws** were introduced to help the poorest sections of society.

Northumberland and Lady Jane Grey

Whether Northumberland would have succeeded in establishing himself firmly in power is a matter of speculation because Edward VI died in 1553. This created an immediate **constitutional** crisis. Under Henry VIII's will, Mary, the daughter of his first wife, Catherine of Aragon, was to succeed if Edward died childless. However, Mary was a devout Roman Catholic and it was feared

Key question
Why did Northumberland attempt to make Lady Jane Grey Queen of England?

Key terms

Poor laws
Laws to deal with the poor and vagrant in society. Because government did not understand the causes of poverty and vagrancy and they feared rebellion, many of the early poor laws were designed to punish and control the poor. By mid-century some attempt was made to assist the poor by promoting charity and providing work.

Constitution
The rules and regulations that determine how a country is governed.

Lady Jane Grey.

Profile: Lady Jane Grey 1537–54

1537 – Born
1553 – Married Guildford Dudley, youngest son of Lord
       President Northumberland
1553 – Crowned Queen of England. Reign lasted for nine
       days: 6–18 July
1554 – Executed for treason

Lady Jane Grey was the daughter of Frances Brandon, Duchess
of Suffolk and Henry Grey, Marquis of Dorset. Through her
mother, Jane was a granddaughter of Henry VIII's sister Mary.
Because of her royal connections Jane became a victim of Tudor
politics. Edward VI named Jane as his heir because of her
attachment to the Protestant faith. The young King was
determined to prevent his half-sister, Mary, from succeeding to
the throne. In this he was helped by the Lord President
Northumberland and by Jane's mother and father.

Jane was persuaded to marry Guildford Dudley and accept
the crown after Edward VI's death. The Privy Council initially
agreed to proclaim her queen but they soon deserted her when
Northumberland's military expedition to defeat Mary failed. By
the beginning of August 1553 Jane, her husband and father-in-
law were imprisoned. Northumberland was quickly executed but
Mary was reluctant to execute Jane because she recognised her
as an innocent political pawn. However, when Jane's father led
a rebellion against the Crown, Mary felt that she had no choice
but to execute her young cousin.

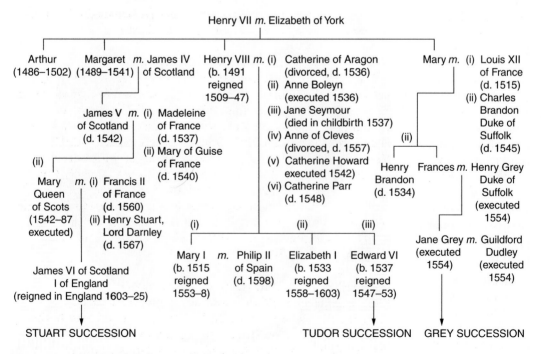

Figure 1.2: The Tudor/Stuart succession.

that she would restore the authority of the Pope and so end the royal supremacy over the Church of England.

In an effort to prevent this, Northumberland tried to change the succession by disinheriting Mary and her younger sister Elizabeth, the daughter of Henry VIII's second wife, Anne Boleyn. Instead, the Crown was to pass to Lady Jane Grey, the Protestant granddaughter of Henry VIII's sister Mary. Moreover, to secure his own position, Northumberland arranged for Lady Jane Grey to marry his son Guildford Dudley.

The plot seemed to have succeeded and Jane was crowned Queen, but the ruling élites, both Catholic and Protestant, rallied to the support of Mary. Whether they did this through dislike of Northumberland or to preserve the legitimate succession is not altogether clear. Northumberland was arrested and quickly executed. Early in 1554 Lady Jane Grey and Guildford Dudley were also executed.

Mary Tudor 1553–8

Until quite recently historians dismissed Mary as lacking political experience and leadership qualities. In addition, she is also accused of being overzealous in her support of Roman Catholicism and Spain. Certainly, by the end of her reign her religious and overseas policies had made her widely unpopular. However, it is now suggested that her reign was not altogether disastrous, and that, but for her early death, her policies might have succeeded.

Mary was widely popular on her accession and had the full support of Parliament. Her two major objectives were:

- to return England to Roman Catholicism
- to create closer links with the **Habsburgs**, her mother's family headed by the Holy Roman Emperor Charles V.

Creating closer links with the Habsburgs

Before Mary could achieve her primary objective of returning England to the Roman Catholic Church she had first to secure an alliance with the most influential ruling Catholic family in Europe, the Habsburgs. Mary believed that an alliance with the Habsburg rulers of the Holy Roman Empire, Spain and the Netherlands would strengthen her religious position both at home and abroad. To achieve this she proposed to marry Charles V's son Philip II of Spain. Although the Council and Parliament somewhat reluctantly agreed to the marriage, there was increasing opposition to the proposal. Many of the ruling élites feared that England would be dominated by Spain and drawn into the Habsburg wars against France.

Returning England to Roman Catholicism

With the Habsburg alliance secured, Mary began the task of restoring the Church of England to Roman Catholicism. In the first year of her reign, Parliament agreed to **repeal** and thereby ignore all the Protestant legislation passed under Edward.

Key date
Lady Jane Grey 'reigned' for nine days: 1553

Key question
What were the main problems facing Mary and how successfully did she deal with them?

Key date
Mary became queen of England: July 1553

Key terms

Habsburgs
Family name of the ruling family of Spain and Austria. The head of the family from 1519 until his retirement in 1555 was Charles V who, as Holy Roman Emperor, also ruled Germany, the Netherlands and parts of Italy.

Repeal
The procedure in Parliament whereby laws are cancelled and removed from the book listing current laws, known as the Statute Book.

Nevertheless, many of the ruling élites had misgivings about such a policy. Some disliked the idea of the royal supremacy over the Church being ended, while others feared that they might have to return the Church lands which had been sold off to the ruling élites during the reigns of Henry VIII and Edward VI. In the end Mary had to compromise, and although papal authority was restored, no attempt was made to reclaim any Church lands that had been sold. At the same time, the **Marian government** began another round of financial reform to reduce costs and increase revenues, and initiated a thorough review of the navy.

Before any benefits could be gained from these reforms the reign was overtaken by events. The persecution and execution of Protestants made Mary increasingly unpopular with all levels of society. Popular discontent was made worse by the steadily worsening economic situation and rising unemployment. Anti-Spanish feelings rose to fever pitch when Philip II, despite his promises to the contrary, involved England in his war with France. As a result, Calais, England's last continental possession, was lost to the French. Mary's death in 1558 was greeted with just as much enthusiasm as had been her accession five years earlier.

Marian government
Term used to describe the government of Mary I.

Key term

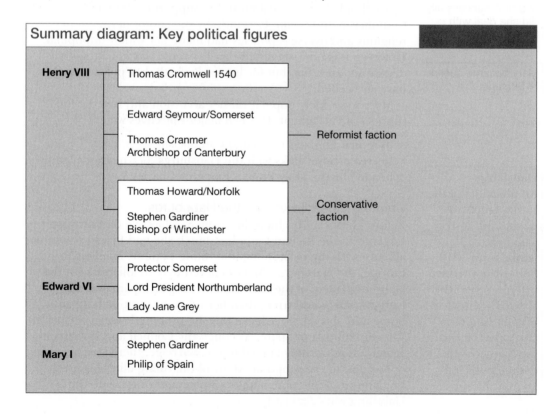

Summary diagram: Key political figures

Henry VIII ── Thomas Cromwell 1540

Edward Seymour/Somerset

Thomas Cranmer
Archbishop of Canterbury ──── Reformist faction

Thomas Howard/Norfolk

Stephen Gardiner
Bishop of Winchester ──── Conservative faction

Protector Somerset
Edward VI ── Lord President Northumberland
Lady Jane Grey

Mary I ── Stephen Gardiner
Philip of Spain

2 | Historiography

Key question
What is meant by 'historiography' and how does it apply to the period 1540–58?

Historiography commonly carries two meanings: it refers to what actually happened in the past, and also to the way in which that past has been written about by historians. Therefore, when historians study a particular event or period in history, mainly through the reading and interpretation of original sources, they naturally record their opinions in print. In this way historical information is compiled alongside historians' opinions which, together, builds into a body of work.

Over time successive generations of historians studying the same event or period in history change their opinions and in doing so they might disagree with or even criticise what previous historians have thought or written. The historians who first study and publish their opinions or interpretations on a historical event or period establish the orthodox or traditional view of that history. The historians who come after and who disagree with their predecessors are usually referred to as **revisionists** because they revise earlier interpretations. It is important to remember that whereas historians generally agree on the facts of history – these do not change unless they are proved to be incorrect – they often disagree on their interpretation of them.

Historiography is the term used to describe the study of this history-writing by taking account of changing ideas and opinions. The historiography referred to in the title to this section deals with the way in which historians have changed their opinions on the mid-Tudor period. Whereas earlier historians firmly believed that there was a mid-Tudor crisis in the period between 1540 and 1558, modern historians are not so convinced. That is why this period of history is a controversial one. It is likely that what historians have thought or written today will be revised in the future.

Key term

Revisionists
Historians who believe that older or more traditional interpretations and ideas in history should be regularly reviewed and changed if necessary.

The Whig interpretation of history

Key question
What is meant by the Whig interpretation of history?

Until the Second World War English historical writing was still largely dominated by the Whig interpretation of history. The middle of the sixteenth century was seen as a 'dead' period between the exciting changes under Henry VIII and the consolidation and expansion of the reign of Elizabeth I. This was because the Whig historians of the nineteenth century did not see any great or 'progressive' events taking place in England at this time. They therefore regarded the reigns of Edward VI and Mary as unimportant. Whig historians assumed that events were shaped by 'great' men (or women). This attitude has created the traditional view of the period, and the years between 1547 and 1558 have tended to be seen in terms of personalities rather than events.

The major and tragic figures have been the dying boy king and the haunted, half-Spanish Mary, driven by love for Philip II and the Catholic religion to commit atrocities against her Protestant subjects. In the background lurked the obscure and slightly sinister figures of the Lord Protector Somerset and the Lord

President Northumberland, one provoking popular rebellion and the other plotting to seize the Crown. These were the people who were thought to have created history and little attention was given to the mass of the population, or to the underlying issues that shaped events.

The revisionist/Marxist debate

During the 40 years following the end of the Second World War historians changed their views about the mid-sixteenth century. There were two broad schools of historical thought: revisionist and **Marxist**:

Key question
What is meant by the revisionist/Marxist debate?

- Revisionist interpretation largely concentrated on the short-term changes in the constitution, politics and foreign policy brought about by the ruling élites.
- Marxist interpretation largely concentrated on the long-term changes in the economy and society.

Not only were the two groups of historians mutually opposed, but members of both schools disagreed among themselves about the causes of change. Nevertheless, both groups saw England as a part of the momentous changes taking place throughout western Europe. To explain these developments they created general theories into which they tried to fit the ever-growing range of conflicting evidence. Of these theories the two with the greatest bearing on mid-Tudor England were those concerning the rise of the State and of crisis.

Marxists
Historians who see historical change as a series of events caused mainly by social and economic tension leading to conflict between the poorer and richer classes.

Key term

General theories concerning the rise of the State and of the idea of crisis

It is particularly important to understand the basis of these theories and how they applied to England in the middle of the sixteenth century. The idea of crisis became very popular among historians in the 1970s. Most revisionist and Marxist historians used these theories to explain the various problems experienced by western European countries. For example, there was:

- the crisis of feudalism in the fifteenth century
- the religious crisis of the sixteenth century.

However, it must be remembered that the so-called mid-sixteenth-century crisis was confined to England and did not form part of a general European crisis.

Defining crisis

A major difficulty for the student trying to understand any theory of crisis is to decide what historians mean by their use of the word. It could be said that a crisis results from an immediate short-term problem such as a foreign invasion, a rebellion or a harvest failure. Equally it could be maintained that a crisis is created by a combination of long-term problems which together threaten the collapse of government or the State. The problems in England during the reigns of Edward VI and Mary combine all these possibilities. Yet, even so, it has to be decided whether the

English State was in serious danger of collapse. Even before trying to answer this question it is necessary to establish exactly what is meant by the sixteenth-century State.

Defining the State

Revisionist and Marxist historians were generally agreed that the **feudal crisis** and chronic anarchy of the late Middle Ages enabled western European monarchs to gain power at the expense of the Church and the aristocracy. There is broad agreement that those monarchs who were able to take advantage of this situation increased their power and became the centrepiece of a new type of State. They achieved this by creating permanent central and local bureaucracies dependent on royal patronage, and by controlling military power. At the same time these monarchs had to maintain a balance between the various sections of their subjects by gaining their acceptance of the legitimacy of royal authority. Thus when historians of either school discussed the sixteenth-century State they were visualising it as the monarch and the permanent machinery of central and local government.

It was generally accepted that, within this broad framework, the states of western Europe were created and developed along different lines depending on their geographical, religious, social, political and economic background.

Finance

Unlike '**absolutist**' states on the continent where, theoretically, the monarch was above the law, had independent sources of taxation and controlled paid officials and mercenary armies, England was more like a **constitutional monarchy**. English monarchs were, to some extent, answerable to Parliament and tended to rule through Statute law. At the same time they had to rely on the revenue from royal estates, and whatever money they could persuade Parliament to grant them. In turn this meant that they could rarely afford to keep a standing army of mercenaries and had to rely on the goodwill of the aristocracy and gentry to raise troops from among their tenants.

Shortage of money also meant that they depended on these same landowners to act as an unpaid bureaucracy to run local government, as **Justices of the Peace** for instance. While this might seem to indicate that the English State was in a weaker position than its more authoritarian counterparts on the continent, this was not true. One could argue that the English taxpayer was getting government on the cheap and was therefore less likely to rebel.

Order

Order was seen as the central problem for the sixteenth-century State. Monarchs had to raise money for the ever-increasing machinery of government needed to maintain peace and security, manage the economy and create social harmony. To achieve this they had to increase their revenue, but extra taxation was

---

Key question
What is meant by the State?

Key terms

Feudal crisis
The breakdown in the relationship between lord and vassal. The relationship changed from one based on rewards of land for service to one based on money payments.

Absolutist/ authoritarian
Similar to dictatorship, where the ruler has absolute power, i.e. unchallenged rule.

Constitutional monarchy
A system whereby a monarch governs the kingdom within the limits of an agreed framework of rules that includes institutions such as the Privy Council and Parliament.

Justices of the Peace
Magistrates, largely landowners, who enforce the State's rules and regulations in local courts of law.

unpopular and likely to provoke rebellion, so leading to the collapse of government. English monarchs depended on the active support of the majority of landowners and the middle classes (described by Marxist historians as the '**bourgeoisie**'), and on the passive obedience of the great mass of the population who had no share in the running of the country. Anything that upset this delicate balance could create a crisis for the English State, if not necessarily for the English people.

The potential for mid-Tudor crises

In terms of these broad theories, the death of Henry VIII in 1547 was seen as a time of crisis. Although Henry had made careful provision for the succession of his young son Edward, the prospect of a minority (see page 3) posed a serious threat to the stability of the government, particularly as the factions at Court were deeply divided over religious issues. This certainly represented a potential crisis for the State, which might have led to civil war, or invasion by a foreign power to restore the Catholic religion.

As well as these political difficulties, England faced a number of long-term socio-economic problems. By the beginning of the sixteenth century the English population had begun to recover from the worst effects of the Black Death of 1349 and the subsequent **plague cycle**. Rising population forced up rents and food prices and made it difficult to find work, causing distress among the urban and rural poor. These difficulties were made worse in the middle of the century by the temporary decline in the English cloth trade, which threw large numbers of people out of work.

Popular unrest was increased by the rapidity of religious changes between 1547 and 1550 – from Anglo-Catholicism to Protestantism – as many people felt that their old, traditional way of life was under threat. This was reflected in the growing tension between **husbandmen** and **cottagers** on the one side and **yeomen** and gentry on the other. The former felt that landowners and richer tenant farmers were using the commercial and religious situation to their own advantage.

So, by 1547, England seemed to be in a precarious position with possible conflict among the ruling élites, the threat of foreign invasion, a failing economy and rising popular discontent.

New approaches to the historical debate

Most historians have recently become suspicious of general theories, particularly of crisis. They have come to the view that history should be seen in terms of separate crises occurring in individual countries or regions at different times without any common linkage or cause. Although this does not necessarily rule out a mid-Tudor crisis, the concept is now no longer fashionable.

Continued research has led to a considerable revision of ideas about all aspects of the reigns of Edward and Mary. Far from a danger of collapse, mid-Tudor government is now considered to show considerable strength in overcoming a series of potentially

Key term

Bourgeoisie
Used by Marxist historians to describe the middle class of lawyers, landowners and merchants.

Key question
Why was the period between 1547 and 1558 seen as being in crisis?

Key terms

Plague cycle
Regular occurrences of plague. For example, the Black Death of 1348–51 was followed by plague outbreaks in 1361–2, 1369 and 1393.

Husbandmen
Peasant tenant-farmers who rented their land from the local landowners.

Cottagers
Poorer peasant farmers who were obliged to work on the landowner's land either for free or for a fixed sum of money.

Yeomen
A social class of richer peasants who may have been as wealthy as some of the gentry but were below them in social class.

damaging difficulties. Religious change is similarly seen as having been achieved with remarkably little disruption when compared with developments on the continent. Although there was popular unrest this is thought to have been caused by economic stresses rather than any weakness on the part of the authorities. The major crisis point is now thought to have been the economy, which suffered not only from government mishandling, but also from a whole range of long- and short-term problems.

These are the issues that will be examined in the following sections to see which, if any, of them constituted a 'mid-Tudor crisis'.

Summary diagram: Historiography

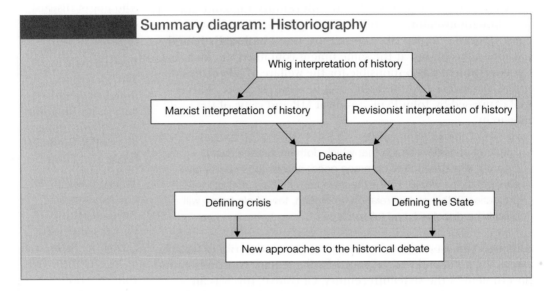

3 | A Crisis of the State: Government, Politics and Foreign Policy

Key question
How and why did the State change during the sixteenth century?

The State

By the early sixteenth century the State was assuming greater responsibility for every aspect of life. In much of Europe government was becoming centralised in capital cities such as London, Paris and Madrid, and growing numbers of civil servants were being employed to administer both central and local affairs. At the same time, the State was trying to take control in areas in which it had had little or no influence during the Middle Ages. As the administration grew in size, statesmen realised that they had to take more control of the economy to ensure that the country was creating the wealth needed to pay the cost of government. Consequently, the government began to pass legislation to try to regulate the economy, and place restrictions on the way in which individual merchants and industrialists could operate.

Many European countries, including Catholic ones, were deciding that religion was such a fundamental concern that it could no longer be left under the control of the Pope in Rome. In England the Henrician Reformation of the 1530s had made the monarch Head of the Church and given Parliament control of religious policy. This meant that religion had become part of the State's social policy, by which the government tried to maintain stability and cohesion. Yet, while the English State had gained great power and influence, it was becoming recognised that the government was responsible for the welfare of all the people in the country. The State expected not only to help the poor by taking over the charitable work previously carried out by the monasteries, but also to find employment for all the able-bodied.

This broad picture of the English State is widely accepted. Although it may appear very much like the creation of the twentieth-century historians using hindsight, it was precisely in these terms that the people of sixteenth-century England saw it as well. **Commonwealth**, or 'commonweal', the word used by contemporaries to describe the country, was a **nationalistic** and patriotic concept, but at the same time it contained the idea that the government was responsible for the welfare of all citizens, just as all citizens had the obligation to serve the State. This is well expressed by John Pym, a radical MP and critic of the monarchy:

> The form of government is that which doth encourage every member of a state to the common good; and as those parts give strength to the whole, so they receive from it again strength and protection. If this mutual relation be broken, the whole frame will quickly be dissolved, and fall to pieces.

Although this was written in the 1620s, Pym is describing what he saw as the good and well-balanced Parliamentary constitution and government of the sixteenth century. Of course, this was an idealistic view of government and society, which only worked partially and for some of the time. The government found it difficult to see all the connections between different parts of the frame. Individuals at all levels of society, like modern historians, had their own biases and priorities. The sixteenth-century English State could only function with the consent of a majority of the people, and the art of government was to achieve as much as was practicable in the circumstances.

The monarchy

Crucial to the delicate structure of checks and balances was the monarch. Although the State was growing in power and becoming more stable with the development of new offices of state and permanent civil servants, it was still dependent on the personality of the king or queen. Much of the thinking concerning the duties of the State was **paternalistic**. Just as a father was head of a family and was responsible for its well-being, so the monarch was to the nation. Equally, just as the father expected obedience from all members of the family, so the monarch expected unswerving loyalty from his subjects. The relationship between the monarch and his people and his place within the State is clearly shown in the **Treason Act** of 1547:

Key terms

Commonwealth
A community of shared interests where everyone, in theory, worked for the common good.

Nationalistic
People who are particularly proud of their country and who might distrust or even hate foreigners.

Paternalistic
The idea that a monarch would govern his kingdom and rule his subjects as a father would his house and family.

Treason Act
Law passed in Parliament to punish those who betray the State and its monarch. Political and religious disloyalty was punishable by death if convicted under the Treason Act.

Key question
What part did the monarch play in the State?

Nothing being more godly, more sure, more to be wished and desired, between a Prince the Supreme Head and Ruler and the subjects whose governor and head he is, than on the Prince's part great understanding and flexibility ... and on the subject's behalf that they should obey rather for ... love of a king and prince, than for fear of his strict and severe laws; yet some times there cometh in the commonwealth problems that make it necessary for the repressing of the insolency and unruliness of men and for the forseeing and providing of remedies against rebellion.

Here is another view of the State which is very similar to John Pym's idealistic picture of the sixteenth-century constitution. Edward VI, although only nine years old, is seen as the father of his people. It is a relationship based on mutual co-operation and love, but the King, like a father, has to punish his children if they become fractious and unruly. In mid-sixteenth-century England the King was seen in these paternalistic terms, and was regarded as the keystone of the constitution.

Key question
Why was the royal succession such a problem?

Key term

Salic Law
A law originating in France and dating from the eleventh century which excluded females from succeeding to the throne.

The succession

Such paternalistic attitudes meant that many members of the ruling élites thought the monarch should be male. Many continental countries recognised **Salic Law**, which excluded women from succession to the throne. Although England did not do this, there was no tradition of female monarchs. Henry VIII's anxiety for a male heir suggest that he considered that a female heir would create dynastic weakness. When Edward VI died in 1553, the Lord President Northumberland tried to exclude the princesses Mary and Elizabeth from the throne on the grounds that they were illegitimate (their mothers' marriages to Henry VIII had been declared invalid so that their father could marry again), and because, as women, they might endanger the security of the State by marrying foreign princes (see page 7). Northumberland did not oppose the idea of a female monarch, which is why he attempted to strengthen his control over the Crown by replacing Mary and Elizabeth with Lady Jane Grey. However, Queen Jane would be a ruler in name only, she would be guided by him and by the advice of an all-male Council. As an additional guarantee of her co-operation Jane was married to Northumberland's youngest son.

Although Northumberland was unsuccessful, it is clear that Mary, after she had overthrown him in 1553, was reminded that there was opposition to the idea of a female monarch, especially one who was unmarried. In 1554 Parliament passed an Act Concerning Regal Power which made it very clear that, within the English constitution, royal authority was 'invested either in male or female, and are and ought to be taken in one as in the other'. Some constitutional historians see this as a very significant piece of legislation which, by removing doubts about the right of women to rule in England, prevented constitutional crises in the future. For other historians, however, the crucial point concerning the succession was not one of gender, but the question of age and ability.

It is widely agreed that if there was to be a constitutional crisis in mid-sixteenth-century England, it was likely to be caused by the succession of the nine-year-old Prince Edward. There is little doubt that England in 1547 could have seen a return to the chaos of the anarchy of the **Wars of the Roses** in the second half of the fifteenth century. That there was no real crisis in either 1547 or 1553 is seen to be the result of the loyalty and support of the majority of the population for the process of legitimacy and law.

The fact that the succession of a minor in 1547 did not cause an immediate crisis does not lessen the potential gravity of the situation. Historians are in broad agreement that a central feature in the development of the State was the struggle for power among the ruling élites. In such circumstances a strong, adult monarch was needed to maintain control, and the accession of a nine-year-old minor clearly opened the way for ambitious men to attempt to gain power.

The key debate: factions and power struggles

Revisionist theory

Early revisionist historians such as Joel Hurstfield and G.R. Elton saw this power struggle within the ranks of the ruling élites as taking two main forms:

- At the court, the centre of government, the courtiers formed groups, or factions, which were constantly striving to gain royal favour. This is not considered to have been particularly dangerous, because factions are seen as a normal part of Tudor government.
- A much greater threat was thought to have been the rivalry between the **'court'** and **'country' parties** (it must be remembered that these were not political parties in the modern sense of the term). Members of the 'country party' were considered to have resented the growth of the central bureaucracy because they thought it was sucking power and wealth into London at the expense of the provinces.

Although this early revisionist theory is now treated with caution, particularly by Alan G.R. Smith and David Starkey, the hostility displayed towards Somerset and Northumberland by many of their fellow members of the ruling élites is thought to have been part of this struggle.

Marxist theory

Marxist historians such as Christopher Hill, E.P. Thompson and Eric Hobsbawm interpreted this struggle for power as part of the class conflict between the old aristocracy and the rising commercial and professional groupings drawn from town and country. It was once fashionable to describe this in terms of 'the rise of the middle class' – a conflict between the new, commercially orientated smaller landowners, merchants and

Key terms

Wars of the Roses
The sequence of plots, rebellions and battles that took place in England between 1455 and 1485. The idea of the warring roses of Lancaster (red) and York (white) was invented by Henry VII after he seized the throne in 1485.

Court party
Seen as consisting of the members of the Privy Council, government officers and courtiers, all of whom held office and enjoyed royal patronage.

Country party
Made up of those among the élites who did not hold office or enjoy royal favour, and generally lived on their estates in the countryside.

professional men, and the old military or feudal aristocracy, for the control of central and local government.

Now it is agreed that these distinctions are much less clear-cut, and that it is often difficult to show the difference between merchants, rising gentry and the old aristocracy. Most Marxist historians came to agree that the conflict was between active reformers and conservatives, who were drawn equally from the ranks of the aristocracy and the new rising groups. This was seen as the beginning of a struggle for power between Protestant commercial interests and the conservative, Catholic forces of paternalism.

Foreign policy

Key question
Why did foreign policy become so important?

Most historians have considered foreign policy to be central to the political development of the State. It is generally agreed that the major problem for the early modern governments was to find fresh sources of revenue to meet their rising costs. Increased taxation was unpopular and might lead to rebellion, while borrowing, or **debasement of the coinage**, was equally dangerous and might result in bankruptcy or high inflation, which merely added to the cost of government. The alternative was for the State to adopt an aggressive foreign policy to acquire land, wealth and trade. Unfortunately, warfare was extremely expensive, particularly because of the rapid changes in military technology. As a result a country waging war, even a successful one, might bankrupt itself.

Key terms

Debasement of the coinage
A process whereby the government tried to preserve its gold and silver reserves by reducing the amount of precious metal that went into making coins.

Valois
Name of the ruling royal family of France between 1328 and 1589.

Hundred Years War
Fought between England and France for control of France between 1338 and 1453.

By the middle of the sixteenth century England was neither strong nor wealthy enough to compete with the great continental powers such as the Holy Roman Empire or France. This meant that it was necessary for England to ally with one or other of her more powerful continental neighbours. Until 1559 western European foreign policy was dominated by the conflict between the **Valois** kings of France and the Habsburg rulers of the Empire and Spain. Several diplomatic considerations made it natural for the early Tudors to ally themselves with the Habsburgs. France had been England's national enemy throughout the Middle Ages. Henry VIII's marriage to Catherine of Aragon in 1509 linked England dynastically with Spain and the Empire. This alliance not only offered more protection against possible French aggression, but it was hoped it might also help the English kings to regain the territories lost to France during the **Hundred Years War**.

Another important consideration was that the Habsburgs ruled the Netherlands, the major industrial centre for textiles in northern Europe. As the English economy was dependent on the export of cloth to the Netherlands, it was essential to maintain good Anglo-Habsburg relations. Although the English Reformation of the 1530s had soured relations with the Catholic lands and Spain, the Anglo-Habsburg alliance was maintained until the death of Mary in 1558.

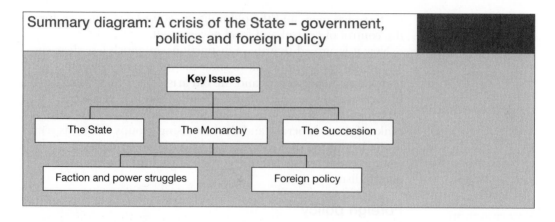

Summary diagram: A crisis of the State – government, politics and foreign policy

4 | A Crisis of the State: Social, Economic and Religious Change

It is widely agreed that fundamental structural changes were taking place in western Europe in the sixteenth century and that these changes were the result of the breakdown of the late medieval economy. Despite differing opinions over detail, it is generally thought that the underlying structural change taking place was a movement away from a self-sufficient rural economy towards a commercial market economy.

Social change

The changes influencing the economy also had a considerable impact upon the structure of society. Medieval society has been described as a feudal pyramid. It was based on the ownership of land, military service and peasant agriculture.

At the top of the pyramid was the king, who was the largest landowner. The military élites were made up of the aristocracy and their families, who held land from the king, and the knights and their families, who held land from the aristocracy. Below them came the great mass of the peasantry, who worked the land and provided food and labour for the élites. The only groups outside this structure were the clergy and the small number of people who lived in towns.

Key question
How did society and the social structure change during this period?

The élites

The economic developments of the late Middle Ages began to change this structure, but it was a very gradual process. It is widely agreed that a highly significant shift among the élites was the rise of 'the gentry', the class of landowners socially just below the aristocracy.

- Revisionists linked this development with the expansion of the State. They considered that the gentry increased in numbers and power because of the growth in royal patronage and in the opportunities to hold government office.
- Other historians, particularly Marxists, saw the gentry rising at the expense of the aristocracy because of their greater ability

and willingness to take advantage of commercial opportunities available after the breakdown of the medieval economy.

It is difficult to choose between these two theories. What is certain is that there were more openings by the sixteenth century than during the Middle Ages for men of initiative to increase their power and wealth.

The gentry are regarded by both contemporaries and historians, as an expanding group ranked below the aristocracy and above the yeomen. They included younger sons from the aristocracy and the upper ranks of the yeomen, as well as wealthy merchants, lawyers and professional men from the towns.

Many Marxist historians saw the English gentry as the rising, capitalistic bourgeoisie, which was in conflict with the aristocracy. This is a difficult argument to sustain because many gentry families were related to the aristocracy, and the ambition of successful gentry families was to join the ranks of the aristocracy. It is certainly true that the gentry, who were becoming increasingly educated through attending university and being trained in law, competed with the aristocracy for offices in central and local government. They are seen also as supplying the capitalistic drive needed to bring about economic expansion, but there is no real evidence to show that the gentry were more commercially motivated than many of the aristocracy.

What can be said is that the ruling élites in general benefited during the sixteenth century from rising prices, and the redistribution of monastic and other Church lands. Only by the

Figure 1.3: Social hierarchy.

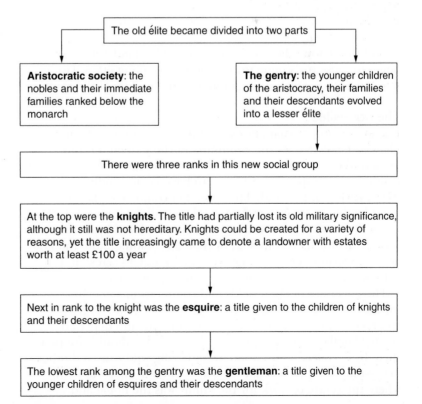

The old élite became divided into two parts

Aristocratic society: the nobles and their immediate families ranked below the monarch

The gentry: the younger children of the aristocracy, their families and their descendants evolved into a lesser élite

There were three ranks in this new social group

At the top were the **knights**. The title had partially lost its old military significance, although it still was not hereditary. Knights could be created for a variety of reasons, yet the title increasingly came to denote a landowner with estates worth at least £100 a year

Next in rank to the knight was the **esquire**: a title given to the children of knights and their descendants

The lowest rank among the gentry was the **gentleman**: a title given to the younger children of esquires and their descendants

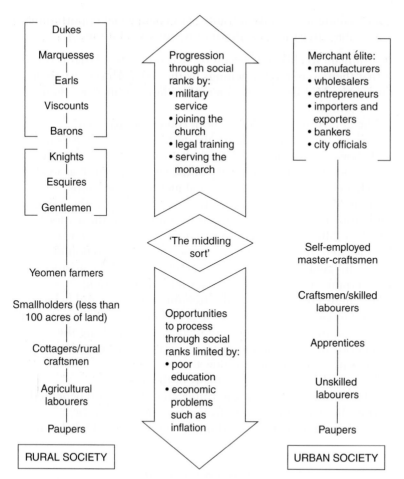

Figure 1.4: The early Tudor social hierarchy c1550.

end of the century did the rising demand for land and titles begin to cause real competition among the ruling élites. However, this process was only just beginning by the middle of the century.

The non-élites

Equally significant changes were taking place among the non-élites or peasantry. By the beginning of the sixteenth century, peasant society, as it was to be found in Scotland, Ireland and continental Europe, is considered to have been rapidly disappearing in England. The spread of commerce placed considerable restraints on the traditional village framework. The generally loose peasant society was being replaced by a more rigid structure. This consisted of yeomen (holding more than 60 acres), husbandmen (farming between 15 and 40 acres) and cottagers (who had a cottage and a small plot of land).

The enclosure of open fields and commons in some areas meant that smallholdings were being absorbed into larger commercial farms. Loss of access to common land deprived poorer families of grazing rights for their animals and stopped them from collecting firewood or gathering wild fruit and other necessities. This meant that the way of life for the rural poor, where the centre of work for the family was the home and smallholding, was being eroded. Those people who could not find work as wage labourers on the large commercial farms run by the gentry, yeomen and husbandmen, or in local rural industry, were forced to move away from the village. Many migrated to the towns where they joined a growing urban population dependent on wage labour.

It must be stressed that changes were generally very slow, and varied widely across the country. A great many villages remained entirely unaltered. Only in the Midlands and around expanding towns, where commercial farming was profitable, were large numbers of people forced off the land. Even so, for a government anxious to maintain the status quo and the traditional village structure, this was not an ideal situation. In an attempt to stop people moving away from the villages the government tried to legislate against enclosure, which they thought was the main cause of depopulation. To stop people moving about the countryside, laws of increasing severity were passed against **vagrancy**. For example, vagrants were to be whipped and branded on their first conviction but executed if caught a second time.

However, what Tudor governments failed to realise was that a rising population and the shortage of job opportunities were the real underlying causes of this problem. It was this situation, worsened by increasingly frequent food shortages, that was the major cause of popular discontent in mid sixteenth-century England.

5 | The Key Debate

Why was there a breakdown in the rural economy?

Marxist theory

Marxist historians saw the breakdown in terms of a 'feudal' crisis caused by a deterioration in the relationships between 'peasant' tenants and their landlords. This resulted in a change from a feudal or self-sufficient 'mode of production' to a capitalist or commercial market 'mode of production'.

These landlords, it was claimed, spent their income on luxury goods, warfare and castle building, and as costs increased they had to raise rents, **tithes** and taxes – a process called 'extra surplus extraction'. As the landlords did not invest their money to improve the efficiency of their estates by improving the quality of their land or introducing new farming techniques, the soil became exhausted and the level of food production fell.

By the end of the Middle Ages there was growing resentment among the tenants who were faced by falling crop yields and rising rents. They began to abandon their farms, to refuse to pay rents and to stage rebellions, for example, the Peasants' Revolt of 1381. Such 'peasant' resistance forced the landlords to lease out their land in larger units to commercial farmers, and this resulted in more tenants being forced off the land to work for wages in agriculture and industry. This was the new and more exploitative

---

Key terms

Vagrancy
Term used to describe the wandering poor who had no permanent work or home.

Tithes
Tax amounting to ten per cent of a parishioner's income (usually paid in goods) levied by the Church.

'mode of production', based on wages, which was spreading in England during the sixteenth century. In turn, this new form of economic relationship caused further resentment, leading to class conflict between the wage-earners and the commercial bourgeoisie in both town and country.

Revisionist theory

While non-Marxist historians agreed that these changes took place, they accounted for them very differently and saw no evidence of class conflict. For them the late medieval economic breakdown came as a result of drastic changes in the level of the population. By the end of the thirteenth century the population growth during the Middle Ages had put great pressure on land and food supplies. This population pressure, combined with inefficient farming techniques, had led to soil exhaustion and a **Malthusian crisis**.

The Black Death solved this problem by reducing the population by about a third. Further outbreaks of bubonic plague maintained a high death rate, so that the population of England had been reduced from about six million in 1300 to about 1.5 million by the middle of the fifteenth century. Such a drastic loss of population led to a deep **recession** which caused a sharp reduction in food prices and rents, but created a demand for labour. As a result, wages rose. While this was very advantageous to the husbandmen and wage labourers, it was disastrous for the great landowners, who lost income from rents and the sale of foodstuffs. Furthermore, they had great difficulty in finding tenants, especially as many of the cottage smallholders found it more profitable to leave their farms to work for wages.

The great landowners were left with no alternative but to rent out all their land cheaply on long leases of up to 99 years to ambitious members of the gentry and prosperous husbandmen, or yeomen. When the population began to recover by 1500 a new group of commercially orientated small landowners – the gentry and yeomen – had emerged. They benefited from the rise in food prices and rent levels, while themselves enjoying low rents because of the long leases obtained in the fifteenth century. The great landowners could not profit from the upturn in the economy until the long leases ran out in the second part of the sixteenth century, while the husbandmen suffered from rising rents, and the wage-earners from increased food prices. The apparent consequence was the rise of this new commercial group at the expense of the great landowners, husbandmen and wage-earners. The lower orders, looking back on what for them was the 'golden age' of the fifteenth century, resented these changes, and this was to be a major cause of popular unrest during the sixteenth century.

Key terms

Malthusian crisis
Socio-economic theory of T.R. Malthus (d. 1834), an English clergyman and economist who argued that when a country's population outstrips food production the result is famine.

Recession
A fall in the demand for goods which leads to a drop in prices and unemployment.

Problems of mid-Tudor agriculture

These two long-term explanations of change (or some combination of them) are still widely accepted as the cause of fundamental structural shifts in England. By the middle of the sixteenth century the government was beginning to face severe economic problems. The population had risen to 2.3 million by the 1520s and had possibly increased to over three million by 1550. This necessitated feeding the extra people – a difficulty made worse because of the drift of the rural unemployed into the towns to find work. As the towns were dependent on the countryside for food this created great problems for the urban authorities.

Many historians consider that continued rural self-sufficiency, whereby many farmers produced only enough to feed themselves and their families, made the situation even more difficult. This can be seen as the basic crisis of mid-century English farming: commercial expansion being severely limited by traditional self-sufficiency. However, there is little evidence that commercial farming was very successful in increasing the levels of food production because many of the gentry and yeomen were more interested in sheep farming in order to benefit from high wool prices.

To improve efficiency and to increase production many commercially orientated landowners fenced off their land from the old open fields. This was the cause of most of the complaints about **enclosure** of land and the eviction of tenants, particularly when former **arable** land was converted to **pasture**. Yet it was necessary to create compact farms and to fence off the common land to bring it under cultivation if farming was to become more specialised and productive. Such was the dilemma facing the government, and by the late 1540s the growing shortage of foodstuffs showed that population was possibly again outstripping food supply. This position was made worse by a growing number of harvest failures – posing the threat of another Malthusian crisis.

Enclosure

The potential danger of widespread starvation presented the authorities with long-term social problems. The government aimed to maintain social stability and order while, at the same time, accepting increased responsibility for poor relief and welfare. The government did not wish to see smallholders evicted or forced to leave the land because they would either drift into the towns or become vagrants, creating a source of riot and unrest.

Enclosures were seen as the major cause of economic distress and social instability, and the government tried to pass laws against the practice. The difficulty was that Parliament, representing the landed interests, often blocked such legislation. Even when anti-enclosure laws were passed, the local magistrates (who were landowners themselves) frequently refused to enforce them. Consequently, not only did the State show itself to be incapable of taking effective action, but it antagonised the landowners by trying to prevent enclosure, and the lower orders by not preventing it.

Urban problems and the cloth industry

Although in the sixteenth century most people lived on the land and depended on agriculture for a livelihood, an increasing minority of the people dwelt in towns and were employed in industry. Here again the government encountered severe difficulties. It is widely accepted that there was an urban crisis in the sixteenth century, which was heightened by a slump in cloth exports. Once again the long-term causes of this situation can be traced back to the late Middle Ages. Early medieval industry was carried out in the towns and was controlled by **craft guilds**. The largest industry was clothmaking, but output was on a small scale: most of the goods manufactured were sold locally. The major international export was wool, which was sold mainly to the Netherlands and Italy.

By the thirteenth century many merchants and industrialists were beginning to leave the towns because of strict guild regulations that restricted the freedom of craftsmen to ply their trade, and the high cost of urban overheads. The result was the establishment of a commercial rural cloth industry, based on the **'putting-out' system**. It produced large quantities of semi-manufactured cloth which were exported to the Netherlands for finishing and sale. The new industry, mainly based in East Anglia and the West Country, continued to expand during the recession of the fifteenth century. This encouraged landowners to convert arable land into sheep pasture to meet the ever-increasing demand for wool.

The transfer of the cloth industry to the countryside caused problems for many towns, and these were made worse by the recession during the late Middle Ages. In addition, because of the very high urban death rate, towns were dependent on migrants from the countryside to maintain, or increase, their population level. The sharp decline in national population during most of the fifteenth century reduced the flow of migrants, and many towns began to shrink in size.

Population levels

When population levels began to recover about 1500, people who could not find work in the countryside drifted into the towns. Consequently, many towns were faced with a new problem of having too many migrants and were unable to feed, house or employ them. In addition, the number of migrants increased because the country-based textile industry was facing growing competition from new types of cloth made on the continent. This meant that from the 1520s there were frequent slumps in demand, and many laid-off workers were forced to go to the nearest town to seek work.

Key question
Why was there an urban crisis and what part did the cloth industry play?

Key terms

Craft guild
Similar to a trade union, formed to protect and promote the particular trade of its members.

'Putting-out' system
Manufacturing system whereby the raw material is sent out for others to finish off.

Antwerp market

By 1550 the Antwerp market had begun to decline, causing widespread unemployment among English clothworkers. Other sources of work were scarce. Although many people were leaving the land and were available for employment in industry, there was little investment in towns to create new jobs. Consequently, the towns faced a very real crisis. The urban authorities had to contend with the problem of housing and feeding large numbers of unskilled migrants with little prospect of finding employment for them.

Discontent

By the mid-sixteenth century the government was threatened by rising discontent in both towns and countryside. The poor agricultural performance meant that the towns had great difficulty in feeding their rising populations and this created the threat of serious bread and unemployment riots. The situation was no better in the countryside. Discontent over enclosures and rising rents was increased by the loss of employment in the rural cloth industry on which many of the agricultural poor relied for subsistence. In these circumstances it is hardly surprising that the Lord Protector Somerset was confronted by widespread popular uprisings in 1549.

Key question
How important was the growth in overseas trade?

Overseas trade

To a large extent these economic problems were outside the control of the mid-Tudor government. To meet the increasing cost of the administration and expand the national economy the English State needed to find new markets both in and beyond Europe to raise national wealth. The exploration of West Africa, Central and South America, carried out mainly by Spain and Portugal in the fifteenth century, is seen as part of this general process of State development. Yet while Spain and Portugal were gaining new markets, colonies and raw materials, and France and the Holy Roman Empire were growing in strength, England was preoccupied with the Wars of the Roses. Far from gaining new territories and trade, she lost all her continental markets apart from the Netherlands.

Clearly, in order to overcome her economic problems England needed to participate in world trade to gain the raw materials and markets to stimulate demand and create new jobs. The first two Tudor monarchs, however, showed little interest in **Atlantic trade**. Henry VIII in particular was much more concerned with his continental ambitions. In any case, England at this stage could not afford to antagonise her Habsburg allies by breaking their **monopoly** of the American trade. Not until after 1550, with the decline of the Antwerp market, did the English government show any serious interest in colonial exploration and the establishment of new markets.

Key terms

Atlantic trade
The triangular trade route between Europe, America and Africa.

Monopoly
Total control of trade by one country to the exclusion of others.

Protestantism and the expansion of trade

The emergence of the expansion of trade is still seen by many historians as being linked with the development of Protestantism. It has been suggested that it was significant that the countries of north-western Europe which were to dominate world trade were all strongly influenced by Protestantism, and especially **Calvinism**, while the more economically backward countries were all Catholic. Consequently the conflicts between the countries of the Reformation and the **Counter Reformation** can be interpreted as economic wars just as much as wars of religion.

Although it is widely agreed that such explanations are too simple to be totally acceptable, they still play an important part in interpretations of western capitalism. In 1550 England was still a backward, off-shore European island and was not to take any significant part in world trade until the end of the sixteenth century. However, some historians accept that the economic and, to a lesser extent, religious changes taking place laid the basis for England's political and economic dominance by the eighteenth century.

Key question
What part did Protestantism play in the expansion of trade?

Religious change

Religious change is still seen by many historians as being very important in this economic and social restructuring. Support for the English Reformation by a large cross-section of the more commercially motivated aristocracy and gentry is interpreted as showing hostility towards the Roman Catholic Church. The break from Rome can be seen as the removal of the 'dead hand' of a Church which, by its opposition to commerce and competition, was slowing the pace of economic development. At the same time the enormous wealth and great territorial possessions of the Roman Catholic Church in England were perceived as unproductive.

The ruling élites

It is suggested that support from the ruling élites for Henry VIII's religious policy was based on their desire to acquire confiscated Church property, which they could use commercially to their own profit. Certainly the seizure and, after 1540, the sale of monastic lands, was the largest redistribution of property since the Norman Conquest of 1066 and enabled an expansion in the number of the land-owning élite. However, there is little evidence to show that the Catholic élites were any less eager to acquire Church property, or were less commercially successful, than their Protestant counterparts. Consequently, while it is possible to say that the Reformation promoted commercial change, it is more difficult to maintain that it was brought about for commercial reasons.

The non-élites

The impact of religious change on the lower orders or non-élites is equally difficult to define. Many among the rural population were opposed to Protestantism, seeing it as a threat to their

Key terms

Calvinism
A term used to describe the influence and religious ideas and teachings of John Calvin of Geneva, a radical Protestant religious reformer who attacked the Catholic Church's wealth and privileges.

Counter Reformation
Catholic reaction against the spread of Protestantism. Led by the Pope, the Catholic Church attempted to reconvert Protestants and bring them back to the Catholic faith.

traditional way of life. Others, especially in the towns, welcomed the ideas of the reformers on the rights of man, equality and the redistribution of Church wealth. These different responses to Protestantism have been cited by many Marxist historians as evidence of the loss of solidarity among the lower orders and of the beginning of the breakdown of community values and mutual support.

Protestantism is perceived as introducing more radical ideas into popular protest or, at least, strengthening those ideas that already existed. Although extreme radical groups among the lower orders in England were always to be a minority, they are seen as playing an important part in increasing social tensions and pressures. For them the Reformation marked the beginning of the millennium, the thousand-year rule of Christ, when all men would be equal and there would be no more hardship, poverty and unemployment.

Obviously such ideas were very attractive in a period of sharply rising prices, food shortages and a lack of job opportunities, and increased the possibility of popular riot and rebellion in years of particular hardship. This was clearly a dangerous situation, and fear among the élites of popular rebellion added to the stresses already being felt within society. Although many of these social, economic and religious changes were only beginning in England by 1550, they can be seen as posing very serious problems to the government and represented a potential crisis for the State.

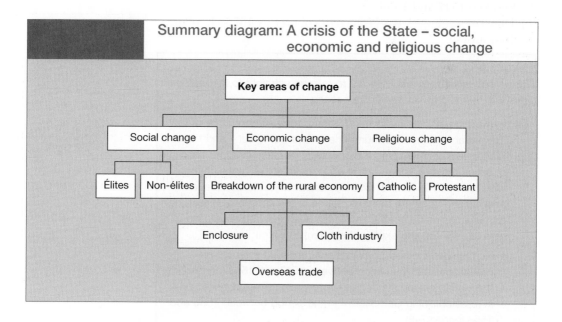

Summary diagram: A crisis of the State – social, economic and religious change

Study Guide

General advice

In examinations marks will only be awarded for answers that are relevant and clearly focused on the exact wording of the question. You will be expected to organise relevant information clearly and coherently. Answers that are descriptive or just made up of a list of points will receive very little credit. Equally, answers that concentrate on one or two aspects and fail to cover the whole question will be penalised.

It is essential to read an examination paper carefully and to make sure you know what the questions are asking before attempting an answer. Examiners can ask questions about a topic in several ways, and each question requires you to organise your material in a way that is relevant to that question. It is essential that you identify the key words and make certain that you fully understand the meaning of a question before attempting to answer it. At the same time, to be sure that you have fully understood the meaning of a question, you should identify any assumptions, misleading or otherwise, that it contains.

AS Questions

In the style of OCR

(a) Compare the importance of the Edwardian and Marian regimes in shaping the course of religious change in England between 1547 and 1558.

(b) How far was England a Protestant country by 1553? Explain your answer.

> ### Exam tips
> The cross-references are intended to take you straight to the material that will help you to answer the questions.
>
> (a) In question (a) you are invited to compare the importance of the Edwardian regime – Northumberland and Somerset – and the Marian regime in shaping the course of religious change. The question requires you to know what the major religious changes were between 1547 and 1558 and expects you to be able to analyse and compare the importance of the contribution that the two regimes made in effecting these changes. You should be able to evaluate and explain the extent to which:
>
> - Northumberland and Somerset succeeded in establishing Protestantism in the period between 1547 and 1553 (pages 2–5)
> - the Marian regime succeeded in reversing these changes and in re-establishing Catholicism in the period between 1553 and 1558 (pages 7–8).
>
> Your evaluation must be balanced and should take into account their respective contributions before a judgement is reached.
>
> (b) In question (b) you are invited to assess how far England had become a Protestant country after six years of Edwardian rule. You will gain very little credit for answering the question by just

making a list of the changes that had taken place. An answer to this question requires a comparison between the degree of Protestantism in England in 1540 and in 1553, a knowledge of how and why changes took place, and an assessment of the extent to which England was more Protestant in 1553. This question contains an assumption on the part of the examiners that England was in fact more Protestant in 1553, and part of your answer will be to test this assumption. As well as assessing the extent to which England was more Protestant in 1553 than in 1540, you will need to analyse the motivations of the major political leaders such as Somerset, Northumberland and Cranmer in making it more Protestant, for example:

- They were Protestant themselves and were determined to continue the religious changes already begun in the 1540s.
- Control of the Church gave them and the government more power (pages 13–14).
- On the other hand, it is important to note that the changes in religion affected the political nation – the gentry and aristocracy – more than the mass of the people.
- Making the state religion Protestant does not necessarily mean that the nation as a whole embraced the new faith. Many people, the élites among them, remained true to Catholicism (pages 26–7).

A2 Synoptic Questions

General advice

As part of your A2 examination you will be expected to answer a synoptic question for which you have to draw your material from a longer time span or a wider range of topics than usual (AQA defines synoptic as drawing on more than one area in their Unit 5 papers). Such questions are designed to test your ability to handle one particular theme over a long period, or a number of themes in relation to one issue over a shorter period. You have to be careful in structuring your answer to such questions because of the amount and diversity of the material that you are expected to handle. For this reason, the introduction and conclusion in answers to this type of question are of crucial importance. For example, your introduction must outline the scope of your answer and put it into a wider context.

In the style of AQA

To what extent had the power of the monarchy been undermined by rivalries between political factions in the period 1540 to 1558?

Exam tips

The cross-references are intended to take you straight to the material that will help you to answer the question.

In this question you are invited to assess the significance of 'faction' and the importance of the role of the monarchy in the period between 1540 and 1558. You should be able clearly to evaluate and explain the extent to which rivalries between political factions – particularly between 1540 and 1552 – affected the power of the monarchy, for example:

- Identify and discuss the nature of the rivalry – reformists and conservatives – and who was involved – Somerset, Northumberland, Norfolk, Gardiner, etc. (pages 2–3).
- Was the rivalry between the noble power-blocs at court so strong that the monarchy could not control them (pages 16–17)?
- Was the rivalry due to: (i) the declining power of an ageing king (Henry VIII); (ii) the sickly nature of a boy-king (Edward VI); (iii) the perceived weakness of a female ruler (Mary)?

On the other hand, it could be argued that:

- Henry VIII maintained almost dictatorial power throughout the remaining seven years of his reign.
- The monarch had the power to deal with any challenge to his/her authority with the axe.
- The fact remains that the monarchy remained intact and the succession, despite attempts to change it, continued unaltered (pages 15–16).

A2 Document Questions

General advice

As part of your AS/A2 examinations you will be expected to tackle document or source questions. The documents or sources have been chosen to test your ability to understand original sources, so that the meaning and significance may not be immediately clear. They will frequently be written in sixteenth century English and this will add to the difficulty of understanding the extracts. This means that it is essential that you read the extracts through several times until you are sure that you know what is being said and that you understand the meaning of all the words. Then you need to analyse the material to identify and note down the main points that are being made. You should develop a system of cross-referring between sources by colour coding or lettering key points. You should also make sure that you are quite clear about when and in what context the extracts were written, so that you have a firm background against which to form judgements about the material. Each question is allocated a number of marks and this indicates the number of relevant points that you are expected to make in answering it.

In the style of Edexcel

Source 1

From: G.R. Elton, The English, *published in 1992.*

Two real crises did occur in the sixteenth century. The first (in the 1540s and 1550s) sprang from a massive inflation of prices, provoked by a repeated debasement of the coinage. The new income from monastic lands in the end did not suffice, and the unrestrained greed of the governing order with neither an effective king nor a Thomas Cromwell to control things produced the economic collapse of the mid-century. The second was the rebellions of 1549 which arose from this complex of economic difficulties and social distress.

Source 2

From: Paul Thomas, Authority and Disorder in Tudor Times 1485–1603, *published in 1999.*

Was there a crisis in religion between 1547 and 1563? Given the confusion, rebellion, plotting and faction that religious change created, it is hard to deny that there was indeed a crisis. It is quite clear that religious change struck at the heart of traditional concepts of authority, at high and low, central and local level.

Source 3

From: Alan Smith, The Emergence of a Nation State 1529–1660, *published in 1984.*

It is doubtful if the Tudor State was ever in quite as serious difficulties as the word 'crisis' implies. Between 1540 and 1558 the throne was occupied successively by a sick and rapidly ageing bully, a boy who was too young to rule and a woman of limited political abilities. In these circumstances what is significant and remarkable is not the weakness of government, but its relative strength.

Source 4

From: instructions issued by King Edward concerning good order and obedience, 1547.

Certain sermons and homilies appointed by the king's majesty to be declared and read every Sunday.

Almighty God hath created all things in heaven, earth and waters in a most excellent and perfect order. In earth he hath assigned king, princes, with other governors under them. Take away kings, princes, rulers, magistrates, judges and such states of God's order, no man shall ride or go by the highway unrobbed, no man shall sleep in his own house or bed unkilled, no man shall keep his wife, children and possessions in quietness.

Source 5

From: Sir William Paget's letter to the Lord Protector Somerset, July 1549.

I told your Grace the truth, and was not believed. Well, now your Grace can see the truth for yourself and what do you see? The use of the old religion is forbidden by law and the use of the new is not yet settled in the stomachs of even one twelfth of the realm. Put no more so many irons in the fire as you have this year – war with Scotland, with France, commissions out for this matter and that, new laws for this, proclamations for that.

Source 6

From: Edward Towne, The Tudor Years, *published in 1994.*

The crisis theory overlooks the fact that the government never lost control, even in 1549. This may have been partly because the two rebellions in 1549 had limited aims and did not intend to topple the government. The Council functioned effectively from 1540 despite undoubted factional turmoil from time to time. The governing élites survived the most dangerous moment in 1553 when they decided to back Mary's legitimate descent.

(a) Using your own knowledge and the evidence of Sources 2, 4 and 5 explain the importance of religion to government in the reigns of Edward VI and Mary.

(b) 'The period between 1540 and 1558 was marked mainly by a crisis in government'.
Using your own knowledge, and the evidence of all six sources, explain how far you agree with this interpretation.

Exam tips

The cross-references are intended to take you straight to the material that will help you to answer the questions.

(a) In question **(a)** you are being asked to explain the importance of religion to government, for example:

- The sources demonstrate how significant religious belief was in determining how people would react to government orders (pages 13–14).
- The people were left confused because of a lack of direction and leadership in the government.
- The Homily of Obedience issued in Source 4 shows how important government considered the Church to be in maintaining law and order (pages 26–7).

(b) In question **(b)** you are invited to evaluate the validity of the interpretation which admits to there being a crisis but in government and not in religion. You must demonstrate that you understand what the question is about by challenging any assumptions contained in the question, for example:

- Is the word 'crisis' appropriate?
- Sources 2 and 6 strongly suggest that there was a crisis in religion. The strength of these opinions is the fact that one is by a highly placed contemporary and the other by a modern historian.
- In your evaluation you must closely compare the information deployed by each historian to support his argument.
- This will show that although they seem to disagree, both Smith and Towne hint at there being some kind of problems in the Tudor state; for example, Smith highlights the weaknesses of the rulers and plays down the seriousness of the problems and Towne talks about 'factional turmoil', 'rebellion' and a 'dangerous moment' when Mary's claim to the throne was challenged (pages 7–8).
- The main disagreement seems to be only in respect of the use of the word 'crisis'.
- You will be able to find enough evidence from your knowledge of the period to support an argument in favour of challenging the interpretation by showing that religious change was also as much a crisis point as government.

On the other hand, the remaining sources suggest that there were problems in government, but you will have to use your own knowledge to decide whether these problems amounted to a crisis.

2 Government, Politics and the State 1540–58

POINTS TO CONSIDER

This chapter is intended to help you to understand the political problems that faced the four regimes that governed England between 1540 and 1558. These included the succession, foreign relations, government finances, changes in religion and the political effects of problems in public order and the economy. By examining the means by which the Tudor regimes dealt with these problems you should be able to come to a firm decision about whether there was a crisis in politics and the State.

These issues are examined as six themes:

- The political situation in mid-Tudor England 1540–58
- Henry VIII and the succession 1544–7
- The Protector Somerset 1547–9
- The Lord President Northumberland 1549–53
- Mary Tudor 1553–8
- Was there a political crisis?

Key dates

1537	October	Birth of Edward
1544		Act of Succession
1546	December	Will of Henry VIII
1547	January	Death of Henry VIII and accession of Edward VI
	February	Edward Seymour created Duke of Somerset and Lord Protector
		Passing of the Treason Act
	December	Passing of the Chantries Act
1549	June/July	Rebellion in East Anglia and the West Country
	October	Fall of Somerset
1550	January	Emergence of John Dudley, Earl of Warwick, as the most powerful man in England
1550	February	John Dudley created Lord President of the Council
1551	October	John Dudley created Duke of Northumberland
1552	January	Execution of the Duke of Somerset

1553	July	Death of Edward VI, brief reign of Lady Jane Grey and succession of Mary I
	August	Execution of the Duke of Northumberland
1554	January	Wyatt Rebellion
	July	Marriage of Mary I and Philip of Spain
1558	November	Death of Mary I

Key question
How have historians changed their views about the political situation in mid-Tudor England?

Key term

State papers
Documents drawn up by ministers that record the decisions made and show the decision-making process undertaken by central government.

1 | The Political Situation in Mid-Tudor England 1540–58

Political history is about an élite of men and women who run the day-to-day affairs of a country. In trying to interpret events, political historians have to rely on written evidence. **State papers** make it easier to discover what happened and at what time. It is more difficult to find out why things happened. This is particularly true for the sixteenth century because many of the documents have been lost or destroyed. However, lack of evidence is only part of the political historian's problem. Successful political leaders tend to manufacture their own history. Being in power they can create evidence which sets their actions in the best possible light. On the other hand, politicians who fail are often unjustly condemned by those who replace them. The 18 years between 1540 and 1558 saw many such shifts in political power. It is for these reasons that political historians continue to re-assess their views about mid-Tudor politicians.

Until the end of the revisionist–Marxist debate (see Chapter 1, page 10) historians generally accepted that the mid-sixteenth century was a time of political conflict and confrontation in England; a period of failure and lack of progress, set between the great achievements of the 1530s and the recovery of the national economy under Elizabeth I. This period of conflict and confrontation was seen to stem from weak political leadership. The result was a contest between Crown and Parliament, and bitter strife between Catholics and Protestants. The four major political figures listed below have been blamed for this failure for various reasons:

- Henry VIII. In his final years Henry was seen as an increasingly weak ruler unable to control the factional disputes that came to dominate the Court.
- Duke of Somerset. Traditionally referred to by some historians as the 'good Duke', Somerset was seen as a moderate reformer, who fell from power because of his tolerant and fair-minded policies.
- Duke of Northumberland. He was considered ruthless and greedy, creating a constitutional crisis by trying to change the succession (see pages 15–16).
- Queen Mary. Mary was condemned for being politically inept, for her obsession with Philip II of Spain and for her devotion to Catholicism.

General theories of crisis and the rise of the State only strengthened the opinion that the mid-Tudor period was one of failure. However, new evidence and research has caused these views to be questioned and revised.

The idea of a mid-Tudor political crisis is no longer popular. Considerable reservations are felt about the theories of the State and the **Tudor revolution in government**. Although there were disruptions in the day-to-day running of the country, the machinery of government continued to operate normally. The period 1547–58 is now seen in terms of co-operation rather than conflict, as a time of definite political and administrative development. In part this change results from revised opinions about the political leaders:

- Although Henry VIII's final years were marked by the King's failing health and power he managed to maintain the authority of the Crown and preserve the unity of the realm.
- The Duke of Somerset is now seen as a Tudor soldier and statesman who was more interested in war than social reform.
- The Duke of Northumberland is still regarded as ruthless and self-seeking, but he is becoming recognised as an able and reforming administrator.
- Although few would claim that Mary was a great queen, her reign is being seen as a time of significant political and administrative progress.

Key term

Tudor revolution in government Theory first put forward in the 1950s by historian Geoffrey Elton to explain the changes that took place in government under the guiding hand of Thomas Cromwell. Elton describes Cromwell's handling of Tudor government during the 1530s as 'revolutionary' because he supervised the emergence of a constitutional monarchy based on parliament and working through bureaucratic departments of State.

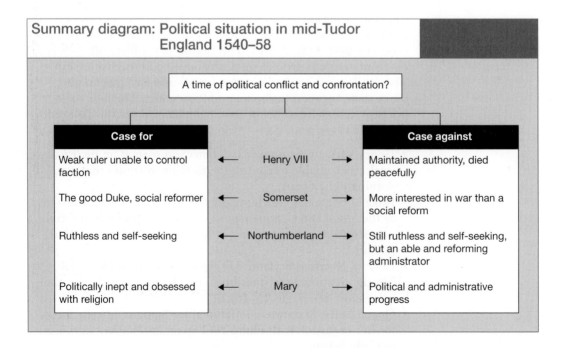

Summary diagram: Political situation in mid-Tudor England 1540–58

A time of political conflict and confrontation?

Case for		Case against
Weak ruler unable to control faction	← Henry VIII →	Maintained authority, died peacefully
The good Duke, social reformer	← Somerset →	More interested in war than a social reform
Ruthless and self-seeking	← Northumberland →	Still ruthless and self-seeking, but an able and reforming administrator
Politically inept and obsessed with religion	← Mary →	Political and administrative progress

Key question
Why was the succession such a problem and how was it resolved?

Key dates

Birth of Edward: 1537

Act of Succession: 1544

Will of Henry VIII: 1546

Key term

Succession Acts
Acts of Parliament passed to clarify and enforce the right of succession to the Crown of England.

2 | Henry VIII and the Succession 1544–7

Apart from the wars with Scotland and France, which had begun in 1542 and 1544, Henry VIII's major concern in his final years was the succession. Since 1527 he had been obsessed with the need to safeguard the dynasty by leaving a male heir to succeed him. The birth of Prince Edward in 1537 had seemed to achieve this objective. By 1546 the king's declining health made it clear that his son would come to the throne as a minor. To avoid any possible disputes Henry made a final settlement of the succession in his will of 1546. This replaced the **Succession Acts** of 1534, 1536 and 1544, although the terms of the will were similar to the Act of 1544.

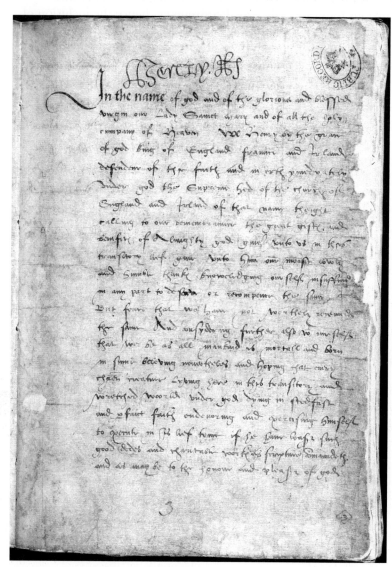

The last will and testament of Henry VIII. Why has Henry VIII's will been described as one of 'extraordinary political significance'?

In the event of Edward dying without heirs, the succession was to pass first to Mary, the daughter of Catherine of Aragon. If Mary died without heirs her sister Elizabeth, daughter of Anne Boleyn, was to succeed. The major change to the previous settlement was that if all Henry's children were to die without heirs, the throne was to pass to his niece Frances Grey.

Lady Frances was the elder daughter of Henry VIII's sister Mary, who first had married King Louis XII of France and then Charles Brandon, Duke of Suffolk. This clause meant that the other possible claimant to the English throne, the infant Mary Queen of Scots, was excluded.

Mary was the descendant of Henry VIII's sister Margaret, who had married James IV of Scotland (see page 6). Henry was anxious to preserve the **royal supremacy**, hence the inclusion of the Protestant Grey family and the exclusion of the Catholic Stuart dynasty. Although the will had replaced the earlier succession settlements, the Acts of 1534 and 1536, which had made Mary and Elizabeth illegitimate to remove them from the line of succession, were not repealed.

Henry's major concern in his will was to secure the peaceful succession of his son and safeguard the royal supremacy. By 1546 it had become clear that the surest way to achieve this, and so prevent a power struggle, was to give authority to Seymour and the reform faction. The disgrace of Howard and Gardiner (see page 2) had secured the position of Seymour and his supporters, and this was strengthened by adjustments to the terms of the will right up to the time of Henry VIII's death. A Regency Council was nominated consisting of Seymour and 15 of his most trusted allies. Members of the Council were to have equal powers, and were to govern the country until Edward reached 18 years of age. In order to secure the loyalty and co-operation of the Council its members were to be rewarded with new titles and lands taken from the monasteries and the Howard family.

Key term

Royal supremacy
The Crown's headship and control of the Church in England.

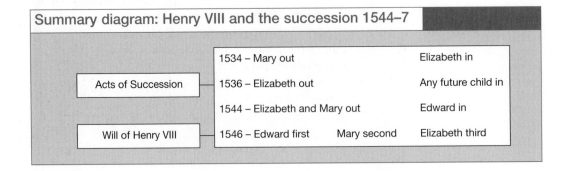

Summary diagram: Henry VIII and the succession 1544–7

Acts of Succession	1534 – Mary out		Elizabeth in
	1536 – Elizabeth out		Any future child in
	1544 – Elizabeth and Mary out		Edward in
Will of Henry VIII	1546 – Edward first	Mary second	Elizabeth third

Key term

Pilgrimage of Grace
Popular rebellion in northern England (1536–7) caused by distrust of Cromwell and discontent over religious changes, particularly the closure of the monasteries.

Profile: Thomas Howard, Duke of Norfolk 1473–1554

1473 – Born
1513 – Fought at the battle of Flodden. Rewarded with the title Earl of Surrey
– Appointed Lord High Admiral (1513–25)
1520 – Appointed Lord Lieutenant of Ireland (1520–22)
1522 – Appointed Lord High Treasurer (1522–47)
1523 – Appointed Warden-General of the Northern Marches
1529 – Contributed to the downfall of Cardinal Wolsey
1533 – Appointed Earl-Marshal
1536 – Presided over the trial of his niece Anne Boleyn
1537 – Put down **Pilgrimage of Grace** with severity
1539 – Supported passing of Act of Six Articles
1540 – Contributed to downfall of Cromwell. With Gardiner led conservative faction at Court
1542 – Disgrace and execution of his niece Catherine Howard damaged his position at Court. Recovered to take command of an army against the Scots
1544 – Appointed Lieutenant-General of the army in France
1546 – Ousted from royal favour by leader of reformist faction, Seymour. Norfolk's son was executed for treason
1547 – Imprisoned in the Tower awaiting execution but spared when Henry VIII died. Remained a prisoner in the Tower throughout Edward VI's reign
1553 – Released from Tower on accession of Mary. Took part in trial and execution of Northumberland
1554 – Served against Wyatt's rebels. Died later that year aged 80

Norfolk was among the most powerful nobles in England. He was well connected having married as his first wife a daughter of Edward IV, and as his second the grand-niece of Edward IV's queen. His Yorkist background counted against him during Henry VII's reign but he gradually proved his loyalty and was rewarded for his service. He actively encouraged his nieces Anne Boleyn and Catherine Howard to become involved with the king but their disgrace and execution damaged his position at Court. His leadership of the conservative faction there brought him into conflict with the reformists under Somerset. The death of Henry VIII saved Norfolk's life but the accession of Edward VI ensured his continued imprisonment. He resumed his career under Mary but he never regained his former high position at Court or in government.

3 | The Protector Somerset 1547–9

Edward Seymour, Duke of Somerset c1502–52

Somerset was the son of a Wiltshire knight, Sir John Seymour, and so came from the middle or gentry class. His father had served both Henry VII and Henry VIII in war and he was personally known to them but he did not secure a permanent place at Court. Somerset's rise to prominence began with his knighthood in 1523 for military service in France under the Duke of Suffolk. The king's chief minister, Cardinal Thomas Wolsey, thought him worthy of promotion and in 1524 he joined the king's service as a member of the Royal Household. He survived Wolsey's fall from power in 1529 by publicly supporting the king in the divorce issue.

His sister Jane's marriage to Henry VIII in May 1536 brought him into the royal family and he was soon showered with honours. Within a week of the marriage he was made Viscount Beauchamp and in 1537 he was created Earl of Hertford. In the same year he became a member of the king's ruling council. In

Edward Seymour, Duke of Somerset.

Key dates

Death of Henry VIII and accession of Edward VI: January 1547

Edward Seymour created Duke of Somerset and Lord Protector: February 1547

1542–3 he became Lord High Admiral and Lieutenant-General in the north in 1544–5 when he waged a successful war against the Scots. On the king's death in January 1547 he became protector of the realm and Duke of Somerset. His younger brother, Thomas, was created Baron Seymour of Sudeley and appointed Lord High Admiral.

In the opinion of some historians Somerset was a kindly and amiable man, but a contemporary who knew him thought him 'dry, sour and opinionated'. His friend and ally, Sir William Paget, described him as a quick-tempered man who was prone to taking the wrong decisions when put under pressure. He was a better soldier than he was a politician and within two years of taking power he had completely lost control of the situation.

Key question
Why was Somerset able to rise to power so rapidly?

Rise to power

In spite of Henry's precautions, it soon became apparent that the plans for the regency were not practical. Even if there had been no tensions between the conservative and reform parties, it is doubtful whether a Regency Council made up of 16 equal members could have operated successfully. The Council system of government in England was designed to function with a chief executive, the monarch, to make final decisions. For the Regency Council to operate successfully it was necessary for one of its members to act as its chief. Somerset quickly emerged as the leader of the Council. He had been high in favour during the last part of Henry VIII's reign and this, coupled with the reputation that he had earned through his successful campaigns in the Scottish war, placed him in a very strong position.

Somerset and his ally and fellow councillor, Sir William Paget, had custody of Henry VIII's will. They kept the king's death secret for four days. This gave them time to take advantage of the weakness of the conservative party and to rally support among the reformers and moderates for the nomination of Somerset as leader of the Council. The reason why he gained power so quickly is not altogether clear, although his being the new king's uncle certainly helped. Clearly, the reformers among the clergy hoped for the introduction of religious reform, and it is likely that many moderates regarded Seymour as the best means of preserving stability and the royal supremacy.

Henry's death and the terms of the will were made known to an assembly of nobles and **higher clergy** at the Tower of London on 1 February 1547. At the same time Lord Wriothesley, the **Chancellor** and new head of the conservative faction, announced that Somerset had been made leader of the Council for 'the better conduct of business'. By the end of February Somerset had secured the firm support of the majority of councillors and was made Lord Protector, with the right to appoint and dismiss members of the Privy Council. These powers made Somerset the undisputed ruler of the country. He was created Duke of Somerset and was given confiscated monastic property to support his new titles. Other members of the Council were given new titles and estates, roughly along the lines laid out in Henry VIII's will.

Key terms

Higher clergy
The bishops and two archbishops of England and Wales.

Chancellor
Senior minister in the royal government who had control of the Great Seal used to authenticate and give legal force to laws.

Somerset's character

Somerset's success in reaching supreme power is often attributed to the support of the very able Paget. Therefore, any valid judgements about Somerset's character and capability have to be based on his achievements, or lack of them, over the ensuing two years if they are to be valid. There are three main views about Somerset's character:

- In the past he has been regarded as a genuine reformer, sympathetic to the plight of the poor.
- More recently, doubts have been expressed about whether he had any interest in social reform and it has been claimed that he was an arrogant self-seeker who refused to accept advice, and who enriched himself with confiscated Church property.
- Using the same evidence, historians currently see him as a Tudor soldier and statesman, whose main interest was the war against Scotland and France.

He is regarded as being no more greedy, and no more sympathetic to the poor, than his fellow aristocrats. Certainly in February 1547 the other members of the Council were just as quick to accept lands and titles as Somerset himself.

System of government

Parliament

Somerset took over a form of administration that had been developed by Henry VII and Henry VIII. Owing to changes introduced by Cromwell in the 1530s (see page 36), Tudor government had come to rest on the principle that the power of the monarch was based in Parliament. Both Houses of Parliament had to approve proposals for taxation and confirm any new laws before they became permanent statutes. On the other hand, the monarch could call Parliament to meet as often, or as infrequently, as he chose.

When Parliament was not in session the Crown could make new laws through **proclamations**, or could suspend existing laws, but these actions had to be confirmed when Parliament met again. Certain things such as diplomacy and the making of war or peace were part of the **royal prerogative**, over which the monarch had complete control. Religion had always been considered part of the royal prerogative until Henry VIII used Parliament to carry through the English Reformation. Under Mary, and later Elizabeth I, religion was to become a matter of dispute between Crown and Parliament.

Privy Council

The day-to-day administration was carried out by the Privy Council. Members of the Council were chosen by the monarch from among the nobles, higher clergy and more important gentry. They were selected for their loyalty and their administrative or military skills, and could be dismissed at will. The work of the Privy Council was supported by a staff of

Key term

Proclamations
The Crown had the power to issue proclamations, which were official or public announcements that included the right to make new laws, especially when Parliament was not in session. The Proclamations Act of 1539 stated that royal proclamations had the same right and power as Acts of Parliament.

Key question
What were Somerset's aims while he was in power?

Key term

Royal prerogative
The rights and privileges that traditionally belonged to the monarch. For example, the monarch had the right to appoint to public office, to dispense justice and regulate trade. In emergencies the monarch also had the power to make war, raise armies and negotiate peace.

Profile: Sir William Paget 1505–63

1505	–	Born in Wednesbury in Staffordshire
1529	–	Entered Parliament as MP
1530	–	Employed by Henry VIII and Archbishop Cranmer to persuade the universities of northern Europe to support the king's divorce from Catherine of Aragon
1541	–	Appointed ambassador to France (1541–3)
1543	–	Appointed to the Privy Council (1543 until his death)
1545	–	Became, with Somerset, Henry VIII's chief adviser (1545–7)
1547	–	Supported Somerset's protectorate, of whom he became a close friend
1549	–	Created Baron Beaudesert. Support Somerset against Northumberland. After initially being arrested was allowed to return to government office
1551	–	Arrested on a charge of conspiring against Northumberland
1552	–	Released from prison and forcibly retired from government
1553	–	Invited to return to government by Northumberland who sought his help in proclaiming Jane Grey queen. Initially supported Jane Grey but soon deserted her for Mary. Appointed to lead Mary's government along with the Earl of Arundel
1554	–	Rewarded for supporting and negotiating Mary's marriage with Philip of Spain
1554–5	–	Refused to support Gardiner's religious legislation, which angered the queen
1556	–	Given the less important office of Lord Privy Seal. Virtually ignored in government
1558	–	Served on the Privy Council of Queen Elizabeth
1560	–	Virtually retired from government
1563	–	Died

Paget was one of the most able and influential men in government. He was trusted by Henry VIII and Somerset but not by Northumberland who distrusted his loyal support of Somerset in the *coup d'état* of 1549. Nevertheless, Northumberland initially employed him for his talent as a minister. His religion was not known to contemporaries who thought him variously a Protestant reformer and a Catholic conservative. The truth is he kept his religious convictions very much to himself. His support of Mary earned her trust and gratitude and his handling of the marriage negotiations won the admiration of Philip of Spain. However, his opposition to what he regarded as extreme religious legislation drawn up by his one-time friend Gardiner, with whom he quarrelled quite violently, led to his losing his leading place in Mary's government. For the final three years of her reign she all but ignored his advice.

permanent civil servants chosen mainly from the gentry, lawyers and minor clergy. The Privy Council was responsible also for the running of local government, with the support of the nobles, higher clergy and gentry. The two parts of the country that were thought most open to rebellion or invasion, Wales and the Scottish border, were administered by the Councils of Wales and of the North. These were regarded as sub-committees of the Privy Council, and were run by members of the local ruling élites chosen by the Privy Council in London.

Local government

Local government in the remainder of England was administered by the nobles and higher clergy in each county. They were expected to maintain order, administer justice, collect taxes, raise troops and carry out instructions from the Privy Council. These duties had to be organised through their own households, and frequently at their own expense. In turn they were supported by the local gentry, who, among other things, acted as Justices of the Peace and commissioners for collecting taxes and assisting the Lord Lieutenants in mustering the **county militias**. The major problem with this system was that if the leading local families did not support the government or did not like the legislation, they often failed to carry out instructions from London. This meant that the central administration had to be careful to maintain the confidence and support of the majority of the landed élites.

County militias
Non-professional military force raised from among the able-bodied local population that lived within the bounds of a county.

Key term

Government under Somerset

There is little evidence to suggest that the administration during the first two years of Edward VI's reign was markedly different from that of the last years of Henry VIII. The Privy Council was made up of men who had risen to power under Henry and who were using the same methods and machinery of government to cope with similar problems. The real differences were the lack of effective leadership, and the fact that existing problems had grown worse. Economic and financial expedients and a half-hearted religious reform policy created confusion and uncertainty among both the landed élites and the general public.

It has been suggested that Somerset was neither more nor less to blame for these problems than his aristocratic colleagues. But whether this was because he was unwilling or unable to change their attitudes is uncertain. While there is no evidence that he tried to corrupt the government, it is equally true that he introduced no reforms. What can also be said is that he failed to show the leadership necessary to compensate for the absence of an adult monarch. Whether this was because of his preoccupation with war, or because of his stubbornness and inability to adjust to new conditions is difficult to judge.

Somerset and the problems of government

Key question
What problems did Somerset face in government?

Short-term problems

The new regime inherited three pressing short-term problems from the previous reign. Decisions had to be made about

- whether or not to continue the wars against Scotland and France
- the question of religious reform
- how to find ways of raising more revenue.

i) War

Whether or not Somerset's main interest was to bring the war against the French and the Scots to a successful conclusion, its continuation (see Chapter 3) was seen as a matter of national pride by most of the aristocracy and gentry. Consequently, any move to end the war would have lost him support among the landed élites. In any case, the Council was bound by Henry VIII's last wishes to arrange a marriage between Edward VI and the infant Mary Queen of Scots to secure the succession. This meant continuing a war based on the ill-founded belief that a military victory would force the Scots to agree to the marriage.

ii) Religious reform

In 1539 Henry VIII had tried to prevent any further religious changes by passing the **Act of Six Articles**, which had laid down doctrines and forms of worship for the Church of England. Since then pressure had been mounting among the Protestant clergy and **laity** for the introduction of reforms along the lines of **Lutheranism** and Calvinism as practised on the continent. Although the Privy Council was made up mainly of moderates, it was anxious to keep the support of influential reformers such as Bishops Ridley and Latimer. For this reason the administration had to make some gesture towards introducing religious reform. If it did not then it would risk losing the support of the Protestant activists and encourage a Catholic revival, which might well have resulted in the administration losing power.

iii) Revenue

Revenue was the most pressing problem. In 1547 the government was virtually bankrupt. The crippling cost of the war was the main reason for this. By 1546 Henry VIII had already spent £2,100,000 on the war, and borrowed a further £152,000 from continental bankers. To pay for this he had sold off most of the monastic lands seized between 1538 and 1540, as well as some Crown lands. By 1547 the annual revenue from Crown lands had fallen to £200,000. This was insufficient to run the country and pay off government borrowing, let alone finance the war. There was an urgent need to reform the taxation and customs systems, and to bring the way that finances were administered up to date. Somerset and the Council did none of these things because of their preoccupation with the war and the concern that if they raised taxes this would be unpopular with the élites and other

Key terms

Act of Six Articles
Passed in 1539, the Act was intended to protect and promote Catholic religious ideas and prevent the further spread of Protestantism in England and Wales.

Laity
Term used to describe the non-clerical general population, the parishioners as opposed to the priests.

Lutheranism
The influence, religious ideas and teachings of Martin Luther of Wittenberg in Germany. His protest against the corruption and wealth of the Catholic Church and criticism of the Pope led to his being thrown out of the Church (1520s), after which he set up his own Protestant Church.

taxpayers. Instead, they fell back on the old expedients of seizing more Church property and debasing the coinage (see pages 188–9).

Long-term problems

As well as these immediate political and administrative difficulties, the government faced a number of serious long-term economic and social problems. Population continued to increase, and this presented a major threat to the government. Increasing population was the main cause of inflation because greater demand for goods pushed up prices. Not only did this add to the cost of administration, but it also threatened most people's living standards at a time when wages were not increasing. In addition, it meant that more people were available for employment. This, in turn, caused more poverty because it also raised the number of vagrants looking for work.

Fortunately, a run of good harvests kept the price of grain stable until 1549. Then a poor harvest made the situation worse, and the level of popular discontent rose (see pages 25 and 127–8). The root causes of these problems were largely beyond the government's control, but continuing high levels of taxation and debasement of the coinage only made the economic situation worse.

The administration was well aware that there was rising popular discontent over the worsening economic conditions. They feared that this might lead to popular uprisings, but they were uncertain how to tackle the economic problems. Therefore, whatever action the government took it was likely to cause as many problems as it solved. In the event, it appears from its actions over the next two years that the government's main objective was to continue the wars. At the same time it cautiously introduced some religious reforms and tried to damp down popular discontent.

Laws and proclamations 1547–8

When the government had established itself in power and decided its **legislative programme**, Parliament was summoned to meet in November 1547. One of its first actions was to pass a new Treason Act. This repealed the old heresy, treason and censorship laws and the Act of Six Articles which had maintained **doctrinal orthodoxy** since 1539.

The removal of the **heresy laws** allowed people to discuss religion freely without fear of arrest, while the ending of censorship on printing and publishing enabled the circulation of books and pamphlets on religion, and the importation of Lutheran and Calvinist literature. A whole mass of unpopular legislation passed during the previous reign was thus swept away.

In the past this has been seen as clear proof of Somerset's tolerant attitude, although it could equally be interpreted as the normal action of a new regime trying to gain popularity by abolishing the oppressive legislation of its predecessor. However, closer examination suggests that the government was clearing the way for religious reforms (see Chapter 4).

Key terms

Legislative programme
The key points of a government's plan to govern the country by passing laws, deciding levels of taxation and controls on trade.

Doctrinal orthodoxy
The traditional or long-held beliefs of, in this instance, the Catholic Church and religion. Because these beliefs and practices (doctrine) had been followed for hundreds of years they had become an accepted (orthodox) part of worship in the Catholic Church.

Key question
Why was it necessary to pass new laws and issue proclamations?

Key term

Heresy laws
Laws to punish those people who reject the state religion and the teachings of the Church.

The Treason Act

Key date

Passing of the
Treason Act: 1547

Whatever prompted the government to pass a new Treason Act, it immediately created problems for itself. The removal of the restrictive laws encouraged widespread debate over religion (see pages 98–9), particularly in London and other towns. Public meetings frequently ended in disorder and riots, with attacks on churches to break up statues of saints and other Catholic images. At the same time, the repeal of the old laws left the county and urban authorities with much less power to deal with such situations. Consequently the government had helped to promote the very disorder that it was trying to avoid. In the process, it had undermined the confidence of the authorities, who now felt themselves powerless to enforce order.

The new Treason Act also repealed the Proclamation Act of 1539 which stated that royal proclamations should be obeyed as if they were acts of Parliament, providing that they did not infringe existing laws. The Proclamation Act had been regarded with suspicion because it was feared that it would allow the monarch to rule without Parliament. It has been suggested that Somerset was trying to give himself more freedom to rule by proclamation by ignoring Parliament.

There is no evidence to suggest that this was his real intention, although there was a considerable increase in the use of proclamations during his period of office. Under Henry VIII proclamations were, on average, used six times a year. During Edward VI's reign they averaged 19 per year, and of these, 77 – well over half – were issued by Somerset. This increase is now seen as a strategy adopted by a government, faced with severe difficulties, which needed to react as quickly as possible to changing circumstances. Certainly contemporaries did not seem to think that Somerset was trying to corrupt the constitution. There is evidence that he lacked the backing of the Privy Council, and there was no sign of protest from Parliament about their use.

The Chantries Act

Key terms

Chantries
Small religious houses endowed with lands to support one or more priests whose duty it was to sing masses for the souls of the deceased founder or members of the founding organisation.

Dissolution of the monasteries
The closure of the monasteries of England and Wales by Henry VIII between 1536 and 1540.

Key date

Passing of the
Chantries Act: 1547

The **Chantries** Act of 1547 can be regarded as another measure of religious reform. Undoubtedly it was a logical step, after the **dissolution of the monasteries**, to close the chantries. Yet, in reality, this Act was a device to raise money to pay for the wars. A similar plan had already been discussed by Henry VIII and his advisers. Commissioners were sent out early in 1548 to visit the chantries, confiscate their land and property, and collect all the gold and silver plate attached to them. The latter was then melted down to make coins. Simultaneously the royal mints were ordered to re-issue the coinage and reduce the silver content by adding copper. The coinage had already been debased in 1543 and there were to be further debasements to 1551, by which time the silver content had been reduced to 25 per cent. Although these measures provided much needed revenue, they created further problems. By increasing the number of coins in circulation the government was adding to inflation. Prices, particularly for grain, rose rapidly, fuelling discontent among the poor.

The Vagrancy Act and Public Order

That the maintenance of public order was very much in the mind of the administration is shown by the Vagrancy Act of 1547. The harshness of this legislation shows little concern for the poor and needy. The earlier Poor Law of 1536 did recognise that the able-bodied were having difficulty in finding work, and ordered parishes to support the **impotent poor**.

The 1547 Act was a savage attack on vagrants looking for work, who were seen by the government as a cause of riots and sedition. Under the new law, any able-bodied person out of work for more than three days was to be branded with a V and sold into slavery for two years. The children of vagrants could be taken from their parents and set to work as apprentices in useful occupations. The new law was widely unpopular, and many of the county and urban authorities refused to enforce it. Although it also proposed housing and collections for the disabled, this measure does little to support Somerset's reputation for humanitarianism.

It is clear that the level of popular discontent had risen by the middle of 1548 because the Privy Council was forced to take measures to appease public agitation. It has been suggested that this legislation formed part of a reform programme put forward by John Hales at the Treasury and the so-called **Commonwealth men**, supported by Somerset. In the light of the evidence now available there are increasing doubts about whether such a group ever existed. It seems more likely that growing discontent over rising prices and local food shortages forced the government to take some piecemeal action. Here again Somerset's reputation as a reformer and a friend to the people is very much open to question.

Enclosure

The trouble was that the government blamed all the economic problems on enclosure. It was felt that the fencing-off of common land for sheep pasture and the consequent eviction of husbandmen and cottagers from their homes were the major cause of inflation and unemployment. Proclamations were issued against enclosures, and commissioners were sent out to investigate abuses. The main effect of these measures was to increase unrest. Hopes were raised among the masses that the government would take some decisive action, which it did not. At the same time, fear grew among the landed élites that the authorities would actually prevent this form of estate improvement. Further measures limiting the size of leaseholds and placing a tax on wool only made the situation worse by increasing these fears. In any case, many of the élites evaded the legislation which, consequently, fell most heavily on the poorer sections of society that it was supposed to protect.

Law and order

It is reasonable to suggest that the government was more concerned with avoiding riot and rebellion than with helping the poor and solving economic problems. This suspicion is supported

Key question
What was the link between vagrancy and public order and how effective was the Vagrancy Act in solving public disorder?

Key terms

Impotent poor
Those who were too old, too young or too sick to work.

Commonwealth men
A group led by John Hales, who was an MP and government minister, concerned with the economic and social welfare of the citizens of the State, especially its poor.

Key dates

Rebellion in East Anglia and the West Country: 1549

Fall of Somerset: October 1549

by three proclamations issued in 1548 aimed specifically at maintaining law and order. A ban on violent sports was rigorously enforced on the grounds that they might end in riots and disorder. It also became an offence to spread rumours, as they were likely to create unrest. Finally, all unlawful assemblies were forbidden. Anyone found guilty of these offences was to be sent for varying periods to the galleys – royal warships propelled by oars. These seem like emergency measures passed by a government which realised that the economic position was getting out of hand, and which feared the consequences.

Fall from power

Key question
How and why did Somerset fall from power?

It appears that these attempts to control the situation were ineffective because in 1549 the country drifted into what was potentially a major crisis. Somerset seemed unable, or unwilling, to take decisive action to suppress well-supported popular uprisings in the West Country and East Anglia (see pages 130–3 and 133–6). His unwillingness to act has traditionally been interpreted as showing sympathy for the rebels. However, it seems more likely that the initial delays were caused by the reluctance of the local ruling élites to intervene without government support. Lack of money made it difficult to raise a new **mercenary army**, and Somerset, as commander-in-chief, was reluctant to withdraw troops from his garrisons in Scotland and France. It was only when the Privy Council realised the seriousness of the situation and provided additional troops that Lord Russell in the West Country and John Dudley, Earl of Warwick, in East Anglia were able to defeat the rebels.

Key term

Mercenary army
Professional troops who serve for pay.

A major consequence of the rebellions was the fall of Somerset, whose colleagues quickly abandoned him as a man who had failed to prevent anarchy and revolution. When his chief rival,

Contemporary illustration showing Protector Somerset's execution at Tower Hill. Why was the execution of Somerset recorded by a contemporary illustrator?

Northumberland, fresh from his victory in Norfolk, engineered Somerset's arrest in October 1549 there was no opposition. Although Somerset was released early the following year and rejoined the Privy Council, within a year he was accused of plotting against the government. He was executed in January 1552.

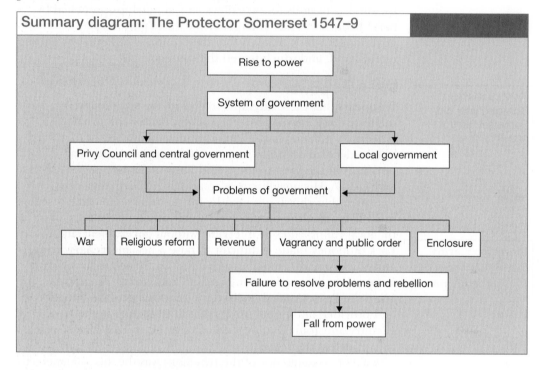

Summary diagram: The Protector Somerset 1547–9

- Rise to power
- System of government
  - Privy Council and central government
  - Local government
- Problems of government
  - War
  - Religious reform
  - Revenue
  - Vagrancy and public order
  - Enclosure
- Failure to resolve problems and rebellion
- Fall from power

4 | The Lord President Northumberland 1550–3

John Dudley, Duke of Northumberland c1504–53

Northumberland was the son of a Sussex gentleman, Edmund Dudley, and so came from the middle or gentry class. His lawyer father had been an MP and Speaker of the House of Commons. He became one of Henry VII's chief councillors and was among the king's most trusted and efficient tax-collecting officers. This made him very unpopular and Dudley was executed for treason by Henry VIII in 1510.

Northumberland's rise to prominence began with his knighthood in 1523 for military service in France under the Duke of Suffolk. He continued to serve in the army and navy of Henry VIII, becoming Lord High Admiral in 1543 (a post he held until 1547) and General in command of the army that took Boulogne in 1544. He also held the posts of deputy governor of Calais in 1538, Warden of the Scottish Marches in 1542 and governor of Boulogne in 1544–6. He was rewarded by the king for his service by being made Viscount Lisle and a member of the Privy Council. In the will of Henry VIII Northumberland was instructed to work with Somerset in ruling the kingdom on behalf of Edward VI.

Key dates

Emergence of John Dudley, Earl of Warwick, as the most powerful man in England: January 1550

John Dudley created Lord President of the Council: February 1550

John Dudley created Duke of Northumberland: October 1551

Execution of the Duke of Somerset: January 1552

John Dudley, Duke of
Northumberland.

The two worked closely together until 1549 when
Northumberland arrested and imprisoned Somerset and took
power for himself.

Northumberland was as able a soldier as he was a politician. He
was intelligent and well educated and although prone to greed
and ruthlessness, was probably one of the most gifted politicians
and one of the ablest rulers of his day. On the other hand, he was
not a man of strong convictions or principles, as may be seen
from the way he used Lady Jane Grey for his own political
purpose and by his hasty decision to renounce Protestantism in
favour of Catholicism in order to save his life when Mary swept to
power in 1553.

Rise to power 1549–51

Key question
How did
Northumberland rise
to power?

Even before his arrest it was clear that Somerset was discredited
and had lost control of the political situation. Many members of
the Privy Council were offended by his aloofness and arrogance.
He had undermined the confidence of the aristocracy and the
gentry because of his inept handling of the popular uprisings,

while his religious reforms (see Chapter 4) had alienated even moderates among the conservative faction.

Power struggle

A power struggle soon developed in which Northumberland was a leading contender. Northumberland crushed the rebel army in Norfolk on 26 August 1549 and returned to London on 14 September. This gave him a distinct advantage because as the commander of the main army in England he controlled the capital. Almost immediately he began to negotiate with Lords Arundel and Wriothesley, leaders of the conservative party. In desperation, on 30 September, Somerset issued a proclamation ordering all troops in England to return to their duties in Scotland and France. On 5 October he issued another proclamation for the recruitment of loyal troops for the defence of the realm. There was no response, and Somerset removed the **Royal Household** from Hampton Court to Windsor Castle for security.

> **Royal Household**
> The living arrangements of the monarch. It consisted of servants who looked after the monarch's person and his financial and political affairs.
>
> *Key term*

   Meanwhile the Privy Council protected its own position by issuing a proclamation blaming Somerset for the rebellions. All parties were anxious to avoid civil war. On 8 October Somerset agreed to negotiate and was arrested three days later.

Northumberland the politician

Northumberland, like Somerset, had risen to political prominence during the final years of Henry VIII's reign. He, too, had gained a good military reputation in the Scottish and French wars. He was a member of the Council named in Henry's will and was ambitious for more power. The events of 1549 gave him his opportunity to take advantage of Somerset's political isolation. By mid-September he had emerged as the major rival for power, and had contrived to have Somerset arrested. At this point Northumberland showed his considerable ability as a politician. By pretending to be a Catholic sympathiser, he successfully conspired with the conservatives. This gave him control of the Council. However, the conservatives – the Earls of Arundel and Southampton and Lords Russell and St John – were secretly planning to seize power and have Northumberland arrested along with Somerset.

Northumberland the tactician

Northumberland plotted too with the reform party, particularly Archbishop Cranmer, who had considerable influence in the Royal Household. With Cranmer's help he gained control over the administration of the Royal Household, which gave him immediate access to Edward VI. This enabled him to win the confidence of the King, and by February 1550 he was in a strong enough position to have the conservatives, Arundel and Southampton, expelled from the Council. To secure his position he became Lord President of the Council. In April he was made General Warden of the North, which gave him military command. However, he only achieved complete power in October 1551 when he had Somerset re-arrested, and assumed the title of Duke of Northumberland. In spite of his continuing reputation for greed and ruthlessness, historians are beginning to recognise Northumberland as an ambitious, but able, politician. In marked contrast to Somerset he introduced a series of significant and lasting reforms.

Maintaining control

Key question
How did Northumberland maintain control?

Northumberland had learned from Somerset's mistakes, and saw that control of the Council was the key to political power. As Lord President he was able to appoint and dismiss councillors at will, and had complete control over procedure. Able supporters of Somerset, such as Paget and William Cecil, who had been arrested, were released and allowed to return to their posts. Under their guidance the Council and its procedures were restored to the pattern established in the period 1536–47.

In order to increase his authority, Northumberland enlarged the membership of the Council to 33, selecting councillors on whose loyalty he could rely. Whenever possible he chose men of military experience, so that in the event of further rebellions, he, unlike Somerset, could be sure of immediate armed support. To make the Council more efficient and stable Northumberland created a smaller, inner committee with a fixed routine to conduct business. Seeing the danger arising from Somerset's frequent by-passing of the Privy Council, Northumberland restored it to the centre of government. For similar reasons he made less use of proclamations, preferring to use Parliament to confirm legislation.

Northumberland and the problems of government

The political difficulties facing the new government were the same as those which Somerset had failed to resolve. Unfortunately for Northumberland, they had become more acute. The most pressing problems were:

- the diplomatic position
- the shortfall in revenue.

Key question
Why was England's diplomatic position such a problem?

i) The diplomatic position

The war situation had deteriorated because the French, taking advantage of England's domestic problems, had declared open warfare in August 1549. This placed Boulogne (see Chapter 3, pages 80–1) under serious threat. Although many of the ruling élites were eager to continue hostilities, Paget and other leading members of the Privy Council had been advocating a peace policy to avoid economic disaster. Possibly it had been Somerset's obsession with continuing the war that had turned influential Privy Councillors against him. Northumberland, very sensibly and in contrast to Somerset, realised that England was in an impossible military and financial position. He ended the war with France and withdrew many of the garrisons from Scotland.

However, while this eased the immediate difficulties, diplomatic relations with Charles V became strained as the Emperor mistrusted England's new position of neutrality towards France. Northumberland was still in the process of gaining supreme power so he allied himself with the more extreme Protestant reformers, such as Bishops Ridley and Hooper. In return for their political support Northumberland had to allow the Church of England to swing towards Calvinism (see page 90). This still further antagonised Charles V, who favoured moderation in the English Church, and England became diplomatically isolated.

ii) The shortfall in revenue

Revenue remained a serious problem. The government was bankrupt in 1549. Somerset had spent £1,356,000 on the war, and sold Crown lands to the value of £800,000. The government even had to borrow to raise the £50,000 a year needed to maintain the Royal Household. Ending the war drastically reduced expenditure, but a number of expedients had to be adopted to keep the government solvent. In May 1551 the coinage was debased for the last time. Although inflation rose still further, the government made a profit of £114,000 to pay immediate expenses and short-term loans. Even so, a further £243,000 had to be borrowed from continental bankers.

Key question
Why was there a shortfall in revenue?

William Cecil, restored as Secretary of State, was put in charge of financial planning. He was assisted by Sir Thomas Gresham from the Treasury. They recommended the sale of chantry lands and Church goods to start paying off loans. The London trading companies agreed to support government debts and more money was raised from the mints and Crown lands. Gresham was sent to the Netherlands with £12,000 a week to manipulate the stock market, restore the value of sterling against continental currencies and pay off loans.

In March 1552 the coinage was called in and re-issued with the silver content restored to that of 1527. This helped to slow the rise in inflation and restore confidence in sterling. Strict economies were made in government spending, and Northumberland paid off the remainder of his mercenary troops. By these means most of the overseas debts were paid off and a 'privy coffer', an emergency fund, was established.

By 1553 the financial situation had been stabilised. Even so, another £140,000 worth of Crown lands had to be sold to replace taxes, voted unwillingly by Parliament, which were not collected because they were so unpopular. However, Northumberland had shown considerable political skill in resolving a serious financial crisis. Unlike Somerset, he had displayed the ability to delegate authority, and in selecting the right people for the task.

At the same time there was a concerted effort to improve the efficiency of the financial machinery. The most pressing need was to streamline the collection of revenue and to find ways of increasing government income. In 1552 a commission began to investigate the five revenue courts which carried out the work of the **Exchequer**. The report recommended that to avoid

Exchequer
The centre of the Crown's financial administration since the twelfth century. It had two functions: (1) to receive, store and pay out money and (2) to audit the Crown's accounts.

Key term

corruption and inefficiency the number of courts should be reduced to two – the Exchequer and the **Office of Crown Lands**. Alternatively all the courts should be merged into the Exchequer. It was also suggested that **custom and excise** rates should be revised. Although these constructive proposals had to be postponed because of Edward VI's death, they were introduced in the reign of Mary.

Economic and social problems

Key question
How serious were the economic and social problems facing Northumberland and how did he deal with them?

The government was faced by equally pressing economic and social problems, for example:

- Population, and with it inflation, was still rising. This meant that the living standards of the masses continued to decline, and that work was more difficult to find.
- By 1550 the growing instability of the Antwerp cloth market was causing widespread unemployment among textile workers in East Anglia and the West Country.
- The debasement of the coinage in 1551 raised inflation still further.
- Grain prices rose rapidly; a situation worsened by poor harvests.
- In 1550 the country was still simmering after the recent popular uprisings and was further unsettled by the political power struggle among the privy councillors.

Consequently, the administration had to act carefully and skilfully if further serious disorder was to be avoided, for example:

- The unpopular 1547 Vagrancy Act and the sheep tax of 1548 were repealed in 1550, and this helped to dispel unrest.
- In the same year a new Treason Act was passed, which restored censorship and gave the authorities more power to enforce law and order.

Initially these measures helped to prevent the widespread popular discontent from turning into actual revolt. Northumberland benefited from the fact that the 1549 rebellions had badly frightened the government, aristocracy and gentry, who drew closer together to avoid further disorder among the masses. At the same time, the administration introduced further measures in 1552:

- It tried to improve the economic situation and relieve poverty and distress.
- The existing anti-enclosure legislation was rigorously enforced, and the unpopular enclosure commissions (see pages 23–4) were withdrawn.
- The revaluation of the coinage halted inflation and reduced prices.
- Acts were passed to protect arable farming, and to stop the charging of excessive interest on debts.

Key terms

Office of Crown Lands
Department set up to manage the estates (most of which had been inherited from previous monarchs) that belonged to the reigning monarch.

Custom and excise
Taxation imposed on the import of goods.

- A new poor law was passed. Although it did nothing to help the able-bodied find work, it did make it easier for the parish and town authorities to support the aged, infirm and crippled.

Again, Northumberland's administration showed a much more positive approach than that adopted by Somerset and although he did little to resolve the underlying economic problems, he did check inflation, and ease some of the worst of the social distress.

The succession

By 1552 Northumberland seemed to be firmly in control, but his power depended on the support of Edward VI. By the end of the year the king's health was deteriorating quickly, and the problem of the succession became a central issue once again. In accordance with Henry VIII's will, Mary was to succeed if Edward died childless. However, it was feared that because of Mary's strong Catholic sympathies she might replace Northumberland and renounce the royal supremacy (see pages 92–3).

To prevent a return to Catholicism, and to retain power, Northumberland, with the full support of the King, planned to change the succession. Lady Jane Grey, the protestant granddaughter of Henry VIII's sister Mary, was chosen to succeed.

Unfortunately for Northumberland, Edward VI died before the plans for the seizure of power could be completed. Queen Jane reigned for only nine days before being removed by Mary. A potential political crisis had been avoided.

Key question
Why did the succession become a serious issue?

Key date
Death of Edward VI, brief reign of Lady Jane Grey and the succession of Mary I: July 1553

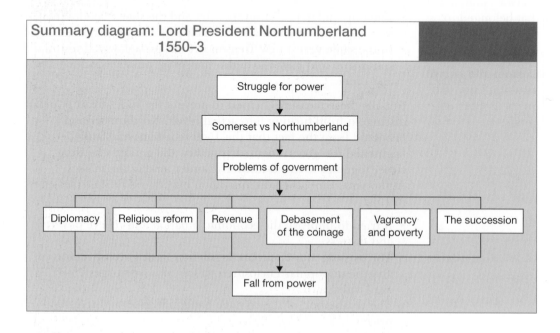

Summary diagram: Lord President Northumberland 1550–3

Struggle for power
↓
Somerset vs Northumberland
↓
Problems of government
↓
Diplomacy | Religious reform | Revenue | Debasement of the coinage | Vagrancy and poverty | The succession
↓
Fall from power

5 | Mary Tudor 1553–8

Mary, the daughter of Catherine of Aragon, was 37 years of age
when she came to the throne. During Edward VI's reign she had
resisted Protestant reform just as strongly as she had under her
father. While Somerset was in power she had been allowed to
follow her Catholic religion in private, and she had remained on
good terms with the Protector and Edward. With the swing
towards Calvinism under Northumberland, increasing pressure
had been put on Mary to abandon Catholicism and to conform to
the Protestant doctrines of the Church of England.

During this difficult period she had received constant support
and advice from her Habsburg cousin, Emperor Charles V. It was
fear of the Habsburgs that had prevented the reformers taking
extreme measures against her. Mary was a proud woman, who
resented the pressures put on her and was embittered by the
treatment of her mother, who had been exiled from the Court
and sent away into the country. This made her mistrust her
English councillors when she became Queen, and lean heavily on
advice from the Habsburg's imperial ambassador, Simon Renard.

Mary Tudor.

When Mary proclaimed herself Queen on 11 July 1553, even Renard and Charles V had thought it a futile gesture. Yet when she entered London at the end of the month she was greeted with enormous enthusiasm. Political prisoners such as the Duke of Norfolk and Stephen Gardiner were released. Following the advice of Charles V, she showed leniency towards her opponents. Only Northumberland and two of his closest confederates were executed. Although some members of Northumberland's Council, such as Cecil, were imprisoned, others, such as Paget, were allowed to join the new Privy Council.

As a devout Catholic, Mary was insistent that England should return to the Church of Rome. At the same time, she was convinced that national safety depended on a close alliance with the Habsburgs. Her policy rested on the achievement of these two aims. Until 1555 this strategy appeared to be prospering, but thereafter Mary's popularity steadily declined until her death in 1558.

Assessments of Mary's character

The cause of this unpopularity has generally been attributed to Mary's own character. Simon Renard's assessment that she was 'good, easily influenced, inexpert in worldly matters and a novice all round' was scarcely a flattering tribute. Elizabethan propagandists were eager to depict Mary as a weak and unsuccessful pro-Spanish monarch in order to highlight the achievements of their own queen. Protestant reformers reviled her as a cruel tyrant trying to enforce Catholicism through torture and burnings. This has produced a popular picture of 'Bloody Mary' – a stubborn, arrogant, Catholic bigot, who burned Protestants and lost Calais to the French because of her infatuation for Philip of Spain.

In a modified form, this has been the view of many historians, but recently there have been attempts to revise this critical appraisal. It has been pointed out that she showed skill and resolution in defeating Northumberland's attempted *coup d'état* (see pages 136–7). Mary has been criticised for indecision in the negotiations over the restoration of Catholicism to England and her marriage to Philip of Spain. This, it has later been suggested, was in fact masterly political inactivity and pretended weakness, designed to win greater concessions from the Papacy and the Habsburgs, similar tactics to those that her sister Elizabeth used so successfully.

Indeed, it is suggested that Mary had the broad support of the majority of the people until 1555. The problem was not the weakness of Mary's character and policies, but her failure to produce an heir to consolidate her position. This, the outbreak of war with France and the declining economic position, was the real cause of Mary's growing unpopularity. On the basis of the existing evidence it is difficult to assess Mary's true character, and the present consensus of opinion lies somewhere between the two extremes.

Key question
What was Mary like as a person?

Key question
How well did the system of government operate under Mary?

Key dates

Wyatt Rebellion: January 1554

Marriage of Mary I and Philip II of Spain: July 1554

System of government

The system of central and local government remained fundamentally unchanged during Mary's reign. The Privy Council continued to be the centre of the administration. One of the main criticisms of Mary's Privy Council has been that it was too large to conduct business effectively. Certainly, at times the membership did reach 43. In addition it has been claimed that the Council contained a few members of no real political ability and administrative experience. The reason for this was that in the first few weeks of her reign Mary was forced to choose councillors from her own Royal Household, and from among leading Catholic noblemen who had supported her. By October several moderate members of Northumberland's Council had been sworn in as councillors, although they were never fully in the queen's confidence. However, they supplied a nucleus of political ability and administrative experience previously lacking. Apart from this, making the Council too large caused strong rivalry between the Catholics, led by the Chancellor, Gardiner, and the moderates, led by Paget.

However, although there was disagreement, these two very able politicians co-operated closely to restore effective government. In any case, affairs of state were soon largely handled by an 'inner council' consisting of those experienced councillors who had reformed the Privy Council under Northumberland. Much of the original criticism of the Privy Council came from Renard, who was jealous of the queen's English advisers and wished to maintain his own influence with Mary. The main problem was that Mary did not appear to exert any leadership or show any real confidence in her Council. Frequently she did not consult the Privy Council until she had already decided matters of policy in consultation with Renard.

It has been maintained that Parliament was strongly opposed to Mary's policies. This view has been modified by recent research. There seems to be little evidence that Mary controlled the House of Commons by packing it with Catholic supporters through rigged elections. She had strong support from the higher clergy in the House of Lords, especially after the imprisonment and execution of Thomas Cranmer, Archbishop of Canterbury, Nicholas Ridley, Bishop of London, and Hugh Latimer, Bishop of Worcester. Apart from the dislike of the Spanish marriage, both Houses seem to have co-operated with the administration throughout Mary's reign. As was the case in the Privy Council, there were lively debates and criticism of policy, but these were generally constructive. As in previous parliaments, the main interest of the members centred on local affairs and the protection of property rights.

Key question
Why was royal marriage such a serious issue during Mary's reign?

The marriage issue

Mary's political inexperience and stubbornness is shown in the first major issue of the reign: the royal marriage. The Privy Council was divided on the matter. There were two realistic candidates for Mary's hand:

- Edward Courtenay, Earl of Devon, who was favoured by Gardiner.
- Philip of Spain, who was supported by Paget.

Courtenay was a descendant of earlier English kings and such a marriage would have strengthened the Tudor dynasty, but Mary favoured a closer link with the Habsburgs through Philip. It was not until 27 October that Mary raised the matter in Council, and then only to announce that she was going to marry Philip. This disconcerted Gardiner, who was blamed by Mary for the petition from the House of Commons in November, asking her to marry within the realm. Mary disregarded all opposition to her plans.

On 7 December a marriage treaty, drafted by Mary, Paget, Gardiner and Renard, was presented to the Council. It was ratified at the beginning of January 1554. Mary had achieved her objective of forming a closer alliance with the Habsburgs. The terms of the treaty were very favourable to England. Philip was to have no regal power in England, no foreign appointments were to be made to the Privy Council, and England was not to be involved in, or pay towards the cost of any of Philip's wars. If the marriage was childless, the succession was to pass to Elizabeth.

In spite of these safeguards Mary's popularity began to ebb, as many people still thought that England would be drawn into Philip's wars and become a mere province of the Habsburg Empire.

By the end of January 1554, anti-Spanish feelings led to rebellion. The rebellion was led by Sir James Croft, Sir Peter Carew and Sir Thomas Wyatt. These men had all held important offices at Court under both Henry VIII and Edward VI. Although they had supported Mary's accession, they feared that the growing Spanish influence would endanger their own careers.

The restoration of Catholicism

Once the rebellion was defeated, the restoration of Catholicism (see pages 109–10) became a political issue. Gardiner had lost Mary's favour over the Spanish marriage. In an attempt to regain it he pressed for religious change. He was opposed in the Council by Paget, who feared that such a policy would cause further unrest. Paget raised the matter in Parliament to try to block Gardiner's proposals.

Key question
Why was the restoration of Catholicism such a serious issue during Mary's reign?

This introduced a serious constitutional issue. Mary thought that religion was still part of the royal prerogative (see page 42). However, she was forced to concede that doctrinal changes could only be made through Parliament. In fact there was only minor opposition in the House of Commons to the restoration of Catholicism, and this was mainly caused by fears over property rights.

Such worries were removed by guarantees that there would be no attempt to take back monastic and chantry lands already sold by the Crown. By 1555 all Henrician and Edwardian religious legislation had been repealed. There was comparatively little opposition to the actual religious changes. However, many historians consider that the policy of Mary and Archbishop Pole of persecuting and burning heretics began to turn even moderate opinion against her (see pages 110–11).

Profile: Stephen Gardiner c1483–1555

c1483 – Born
1520 – Educated at Cambridge University and became doctor of civil law
1521 – Became a doctor of canon law. Appointed tutor to Duke of Norfolk's son
1524 – Appointed secretary to Lord Chancellor Wolsey, Henry VIII's chief minister (1524–9)
1530 – Appointed principal secretary to Henry VIII (1530–4)
1532 – Appointed Bishop of Winchester
1535 – Appointed ambassador to France (1535–8)
1538 – Led resistance to Thomas Cromwell's changes in religion. Fell out of favour with the king
1539 – Promoted Act of Six Articles
1540 – Took part in destruction of Cromwell. With the Duke of Norfolk led Conservative faction at Court
1542 – Became one of Henry VIII's leading ministers (1542–7)
1548 – Forced out of government and imprisoned in the Tower of London for opposing Somerset
1551 – Stripped of his title as Bishop of Winchester
1553 – Restored to all his offices and titles by Mary, who appointed him Lord Chancellor. Led the Catholic counter-reformation and promoted conservative legislation in Parliament
1554 – Married Mary to Philip of Spain
1555 – Died

Gardiner was a talented government minister, and respected thinker and theologian. Although he supported Henry VIII's divorce and break from Rome, he opposed any major changes in religion. He was an able leader of the conservative faction at Court which brought about the downfall of Cromwell. His opposition of Somerset in the final years of Henry VIII's reign ensured his downfall after the king's death. Although Somerset was prepared to work with Gardiner the two could not agree on the religious direction the Edwardian government should take. His downfall was the inevitable result of his refusal to compromise. In spite of his strong Catholic beliefs, he tried to save the leaders of the reformist party, Cranmer and Northumberland, from execution. The accession of Mary rescued his career and although he had supported the break with Rome in 1534 he was willing to restore the Pope as Head of the Church in 1554. He served out the remainder of his life as a trusted adviser to the Crown.

Financial and economic problems

Key question
What were the main financial and economic problems facing Mary?

Financial reforms

The Marian administration was still faced by the financial problems that Northumberland had been trying to solve. To make matters worse, Mary had given away more Crown lands in order to re-establish some monastic foundations. Consequently, it was important both to find new sources of government revenue and to increase the income from existing ones. To achieve this the Privy Council largely adopted the proposals put forward by the commissions in 1552 (see pages 54–5).

In 1554 drastic changes were made to the revenue courts:

- The Exchequer, as the main financial department, took over the work of the Court of First Fruits and Tenths, which had dealt with clerical taxation, and the Court of Augmentations, which had administered income from monastic and chantry lands.
- The Court of Wards, which collected feudal taxation, and the Duchy of Lancaster, administering lands belonging to the monarch as Duke of Lancaster, retained their independence.
- It was planned to remove the large number of debased coins in circulation and to continue the restoration of the silver content of the coinage, but Mary's death meant that the scheme was not put into effect until 1560.
- The 1552 proposal to revise the custom rates, which had remained unchanged since 1507, was implemented. In 1558 a new Book of Rates was issued, which increased custom revenue from £29,000 to £85,000 a year.
- In 1555 a full survey of all Crown lands was carried out. As a result rents and entry fines, a payment made by new tenants before they could take over a property, were raised in 1557.

Mary died before these measures had any real effect, and it was Elizabeth I who benefited from the increased revenue brought about by these reforms.

The economy

Key question
How healthy was the economy during Mary's reign?

During Mary's reign the general economic situation grew worse, with a series of very bad harvests and epidemics of sweating sickness, bubonic plague and influenza. Towns were particularly badly hit, with high mortality rates and severe food shortages. The government's reaction was to continue the policy, started under Henry VIII, of restricting the movement of textile and other industries from the towns to the countryside. This, it was hoped, would lessen urban unemployment and reduce the number of vagrants seeking work. This, however, was short-sighted because what was really needed was an increase in the number and variety of industries in both town and country, which would provide jobs for the growing number of unemployed.

To achieve this the government needed to encourage the search for new overseas markets to replace the trade lost with the decline of the Antwerp market. In 1551 English ships had begun to trade along the north African coast, and between 1553 and 1554 Sir Hugh Willoughby was trying to find a north-east passage to the Far East (see page 83). However, until after 1558, successive English governments were too anxious to avoid offending Spain and Portugal to encourage overseas enterprise. It was not until the reign of Elizabeth I that any real progress was made in this direction.

Key question
How successful were the reforms in the army and navy?

Key date

Death of Mary I:
November 1558

Reform of the army and navy

In spite of the assurance that England would not be involved in Spain's wars, Mary's strong emotional attachment to Philip made it likely that England would be drawn into the continental conflict. As early as 1555 the Privy Council was reviewing the condition of the navy, which had been allowed to decline after Northumberland had made peace with France. A new building programme was started, improvements were made to the dockyards and naval expenditure was increased through a new system of financing.

Equal attention was paid to the army, especially after the outbreak of war in 1557. Arrangements for raising and maintaining the county militias were revised in the Militia and Arms Acts of 1557, which also improved the procedures for supplying arms and equipment. These reforms brought long-term improvements to England's military organisation.

Assessment of Mary's reign

Philip II's visit to England early in 1557, and his success in drawing the country into his war against France (see page 86) intensified Mary's growing unpopularity. The last two years of her reign saw rising anti-Spanish feelings, mounting opposition to religious persecution and discontent with the economic conditions. The war with France and the loss of Calais, England's last continental possession, united the country against the ailing queen. The enthusiasm which marked her death in November 1558 and the succession of Elizabeth to the throne was even greater than that which had greeted Mary's overthrow of Northumberland five years earlier.

Yet, despite its apparent failings, her reign was not one of complete sterility. Important reforms had been made and the institution of monarchy and the State machinery remained intact. Although the loss of Calais was seen as a national disaster, it can be interpreted as the crucial moment when England turned its attention away from fruitless continental conquest towards exploration opportunities in the **New World**. Indeed, some historians would go as far as to claim that Mary's failure was her childlessness and her relatively early death, rather than her policies.

Key term

New World
Used to describe all America.

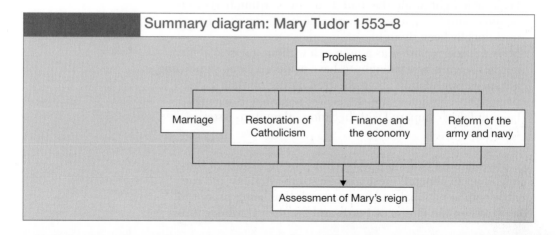

Summary diagram: Mary Tudor 1553–8

6 | The Key Debate

Was there a political crisis?

Great importance has been attached to the potential constitutional and political crisis arising from Henry VIII's failure to leave an adult male heir. With the anarchy of the Wars of the Roses (1455–85) still very much a living memory there were obvious fears that the Tudor State would collapse into chaos. The following key points show why such worries proved to be groundless:

- The permanent machinery of State continued to function without a break after 1547, showing that the overhaul of government under the first two Tudor monarchs had achieved a firm basis.
- At the same time the ruling élites provided great support and loyalty to the legitimate monarchy.
- Although there was considerable rivalry between the political factions under Edward VI, it was no greater than it had been during the reign of Henry VIII.
- At no time, even in 1549 with the fall of Somerset, was there a real political crisis. The most dangerous moment came in 1553 with the death of Edward VI, when Northumberland tried to bar Princess Mary from the succession. Once again the ruling élites were solid in their support for the legitimate descent, and the incident passed without crisis.
- It is true that the political leadership was often inept and indecisive between 1547 and 1558. Even so, the administration continued to function without a check, and some useful measures of bureaucratic reform were passed. When Mary I died in 1558 the Crown was offered peacefully to her sister Elizabeth, a tribute to the strength of Tudor government. Although there is general agreement that there was no serious mid-century political or constitutional crisis, opinions about the political leadership continue to vary.
- The 'good' Duke of Somerset is now seen in a much less favourable light, while the 'bad' Duke of Northumberland is credited with being a much more able politician than has traditionally been thought.
- Mary I is still regarded as a monarch without any real ability, but her reign is now thought to have achieved some significant advances. Speculation about the true nature of Mary's personality continues, and she is now regarded as having been unfairly compared with her more glamorous sister Elizabeth.

Yet, great interest continues to be shown in the nature of the ruling élites in general. Fresh analyses of the nobility and the gentry, both at national and county levels, are being produced. New works on the House of Lords and Stephen Gardiner throw more light on the workings of central government. Particular attention is being paid to the study of individual families and their circle of friends and associates, to reveal the part they played in local and central government. Such research continues to lead to a much greater understanding of the complex motives and ambitions behind the political factions of mid-Tudor England.

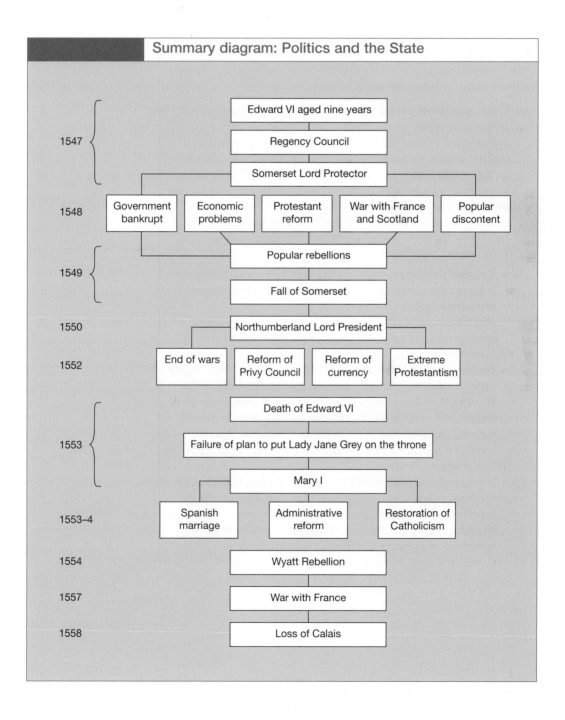

Summary diagram: Politics and the State

1547
- Edward VI aged nine years
- Regency Council
- Somerset Lord Protector

1548
- Government bankrupt
- Economic problems
- Protestant reform
- War with France and Scotland
- Popular discontent

1549
- Popular rebellions
- Fall of Somerset

1550
- Northumberland Lord President

1552
- End of wars
- Reform of Privy Council
- Reform of currency
- Extreme Protestantism

1553
- Death of Edward VI
- Failure of plan to put Lady Jane Grey on the throne
- Mary I

1553–4
- Spanish marriage
- Administrative reform
- Restoration of Catholicism

1554
- Wyatt Rebellion

1557
- War with France

1558
- Loss of Calais

Study Guide: AS Questions

In the style of OCR

(a) To what extent was Northumberland more successful in solving the mid-Tudor political problems than Somerset?

(b) 'The most important reason for Mary Tudor's unpopularity was her weakness of character'. How far do you agree with this view?

Exam tips

The cross-references are intended to take you straight to the material that will help you to answer the questions.

(a) In this question you are invited to compare the political policies of Northumberland and Somerset. You should be able to evaluate and explain the extent to which Northumberland enjoyed greater success than Somerset in solving the political problems that dominated the period between 1547 and 1553. You should indicate what political problems needed to be solved and how successfully each of the rulers dealt with them. Your evaluation must be balanced and should take into account their respective historical reputations before a judgement is reached, for example:

- The main political problems facing both rulers were the system of government, finance, law and order, economic problems and the succession.
- After assessing how each dealt with them you should be in a better position to judge how successful they were in solving them.
- It is important to note that (1) while Somerset may have largely failed to solve the political problems that confronted him, he inherited them from Henry VIII who could not solve them either (pages 35–6 and 49–50); (2) Northumberland benefited from the lessons he learned from Somerset's mistakes. Also it should be pointed out that Northumberland had been part of Somerset's government.
- In conclusion, it is important to mention the fact that although Northumberland was a better ruler than Somerset neither of them truly solved the political problems facing them. Indeed, it might be argued that the succession issue proved to be something of a disaster for Northumberland (page 56).

(b) In question **(b)** the examiner is testing your ability to analyse and evaluate; therefore it is important to remember that marks will be awarded both for the factual content of your answer and for the analytical skills you display. You should be able (1) to evaluate and explain the extent to which Mary's character contributed to her unpopularity and (2) the extent to which other factors contributed, for example:

- The weakness of Mary's character has traditionally been used to explain her unpopularity but you may challenge this in the light of historical/revisionist debate (pages 35–6). Yes there were weaknesses and they did contribute to her unpopularity, but they have been overstated.
- It may be argued that it was her failure to produce an heir, her persecution and public execution of Protestant heretics and a declining economic situation that contributed more to her growing unpopularity after 1555.

Study Guide: A2 Questions

In the style of AQA

Source 1

From: Sir William Paget writes to the Lord Protector Somerset, July 1549.

The King's subjects are out of all discipline, out of obedience, caring neither for Protector nor King. And what is the cause? Your softness, your opinions about doing good to the poor. Look well whether you have either religion or law in the kingdom, and I fear you will find neither. The use of the old religion is forbidden by law. The commons have become king, the foot takes it upon himself the part of the head.

Source 2

From: John McGurk, The Tudor Monarchies 1485–1603, *published in 1999.*

Somerset has been variously judged by historians as an incompetent idealist, inept, and of overweening self-confidence. In fact, Somerset stood for paternal social reforms, but, because he did not combine enlightened aims with statesman-like methods, he seemed to be incapable of implementing them. Although a first-class military man, he put intolerable strains on the treasury by his invasion of Scotland, which in the end only resulted in driving the Scots deeper into the 'Auld Alliance' with France. Somerset's own fall was largely due to his inept handling of the rebellions, and that the work of crushing the rebels had been taken over by his even more ruthless rival in the council, John Dudley, earl of Warwick.

Source 3

From: Paul Thomas, Authority and Disorder in Tudor Times, 1485–1603, *published in 1999.*

The term 'crisis' can be applied with some vigour to a period in which England was ruled, as has been famously and repeatedly paraphrased, 'by a sick and rapidly ageing bully, a boy too young to rule and a woman of limited ability'. From 1540 until, perhaps, 1563 England was faced by a series of disastrous foreign wars, four coup d'état, three serious rebellions, the rule of the above, plus nine days' worth of a teenage female usurper. It also changed the official state religion perhaps six times, suffered several appalling epidemics in which it lost perhaps a fifth of its population, and was ravaged by economic and financial catastrophe. It is significant that, throughout these catastrophic challenges, the Tudor state and its administration struggled on, survived and in some respects even thrived.

(a) **Use Sources 1 and 2 and your own knowledge.**
   To what extent do these two sources agree about Somerset's failings as a ruler?

(b) **Use Sources 1, 2 and 3 and your own knowledge.**
   'The weakness of Mid-Tudor government in the years 1547–58 is explained by widespread religious discontent rather than the inability of the rulers – Somerset, Northumberland and Mary – to govern effectively.' Assess the validity of this view.

Exam tips

The cross-references are intended to take you straight to the material that will help you to answer the questions.

(a) In question **(a)** you are invited to compare and evaluate the opinions contained in two sources about Protector Somerset's alleged failings as a ruler. You must be able to:

- Differentiate between the degree of similarity and difference according to the tone and emphasis of the information deployed in the sources, e.g. both agree that Somerset had serious failings as a ruler but one suggests that it was not all down to him and that he had many fine qualities.
- Evaluate the reliability of the sources, for example, Paget was a contemporary critic while McGurk is a modern historian whose function is to offer a balanced assessment.

(b) In question **(b)** you are required to provide a synoptic view of the central issue – the 'weakness of mid-Tudor government' – in the light of a range of factors, for example, religious discontent and the abilities of the rulers to govern effectively. The examiner is inviting you to challenge the assumptions that:

- there was weakness in mid-Tudor government – this may simply be a myth (as suggested in Source 3)
- religious discontent was at the root of this weakness, rather than the abilities of the rulers.

You must evaluate this interpretation by showing:

- that there were religious problems (pages 45, 47 and 60) – you must decide how significant they were
- that Somerset, and possibly Mary, lacked the ability to rule effectively but that Northumberland was, in the main, an effective ruler (pages 64–5)
- the extent to which many of the problems in government arose because of the policies of Henry VIII (pages 35–6)
- how and with what success each regime reacted to these problems
- that there were other problems which the interpretation does not mention, for example, social and economic problems leading to financial crisis and rebellion (pages 48–9 and 55–6).

It is important to remember that the economic problems were not really political, although they could have political effects, and that public order was only really a major problem in 1549 (pages 49–50).

3

Foreign Policy 1540–58

POINTS TO CONSIDER

The diplomatic position of England during the reigns of Edward VI and Mary was weak. This was due, in part, to the unresolved difficulties they had inherited from Henry VIII. Somerset tried to continue Henry VIII's policies – the conquest of France and the unification of England and Scotland – but he failed. Northumberland largely abandoned the previous policy by seeking peace with both France and Scotland. However, Northumberland's peaceful foreign policy was rejected by Mary, who favoured a more aggressive approach by supporting Spain in her war with France. Did these changes of policy amount to a crisis in foreign affairs?

These issues are examined as six themes:

- Henry VIII's diplomatic legacy 1540–7
- The changing diplomatic scene 1540–58
- The Lord Protector Somerset 1547–9
- The Lord President Northumberland 1550–3
- Mary Tudor 1555–8
- A crisis in foreign affairs?

Key dates

1542	November	English defeated Scots at the Battle of Solway Moss
		Death of James V of Scotland
1543	July	Treaty of Greenwich between England and Scotland
1544	September	Capture of Boulogne by England
1548	July	Mary Queen of Scots taken to France
	September	English defeated Scots at Battle of Pinkie
1549	August	France declared war on England
1550	March	Treaty of Boulogne ended war with France and Scotland
		Boulogne returned to France
1554	July	Mary married Philip II of Spain
1557	June	England and its ally Spain went to war with France
1558	January	French captured Calais
	November	Death of Mary
1559	April	Treaty of Cateau-Cambrensis. Peace made with France and Scotland; Calais given to France

Key question
What diplomatic problems did Henry VIII leave his immediate successors?

Key dates

English defeated Scots at the battle of Solway Moss: November 1542

Death of James V of Scotland: November 1542

Treaty of Greenwich between England and Scotland: July 1543

Capture of Boulogne by England: September 1544

1 | Henry VIII's Diplomatic Legacy 1540–7

England's foreign policy in the mid-sixteenth century, and especially during the reign of Edward VI, was greatly influenced by what had gone before. Until recently many historians considered that Henry VIII had adopted the principle of holding the balance of power in western Europe. It was thought that in order to achieve this he allied with the weaker nations, such as the territories of the princes of northern Germany, against the stronger, such as France and Spain, to prevent any one country from becoming too powerful. Modern historians are sceptical about this theory. It is now believed that Henry allied with whichever side was most likely to win. Henry's foreign policy was based on three main objectives:

- To regain the throne of France and outshine his great rival Francis I.
- To protect English cloth exports to the Netherlands by remaining on good terms with the Holy Roman Empire.
- To gain greater control over Scotland, possibly by uniting the two countries.

Until the 1530s, when the English Reformation had soured relations with the Catholic Empire, the most useful ally in attempting to achieve these aims had been the Emperor Charles V.

By 1542, mutual fears over France had restored good relations between England and the Empire. In particular, Henry VIII had seen the Franco-Scottish alliance, created by the marriage of James V of Scotland and the French Princess Mary of Guise in 1538, as a major threat to English security. Moreover, he had become increasingly concerned over the succession.

Historians are divided about Henry's intentions at this stage, for example:

- A.L. Rowse thought that his main aim was to unite Britain by the conquest of Scotland.
- John Morrill believes that he was more concerned with his earlier ambition of claiming the French throne or, at least, reconquering some of the former English territories on the continent.

War in Scotland

In 1542 an alliance was agreed by which there was to be a joint Anglo-Imperial invasion of France. This alarmed the Scots, who began to launch raids across the border into England. Henry sent a strong army under the Duke of Norfolk into Scotland, and the Scots were decisively defeated at the Battle of Solway Moss in November 1542. This Scottish reverse was followed by the death of James V in December. Mary of Guise was left as regent for the infant Mary Queen of Scots, and was forced to make peace by the Treaty of Greenwich in 1543. Under the terms of the treaty, the Scots had to agree to a future marriage between Mary Queen of Scots and Henry's son Edward.

War in France

Mary of Guise and the Catholic party in Scotland soon rejected the marriage agreement. In 1544 and 1545 Henry sent Somerset (see page 37) to ravage the Scottish Lowlands. This '**rough wooing**' did little to encourage the Scots to support the marriage proposals. Simultaneously, an English army had landed in France to support an invasion by Charles V. This meant that England had to fight a war on two fronts. Consequently, Somerset was given too few troops to do anything effective in Scotland, while the English army in France was too small to do more than capture the port of Boulogne. Even so the cost of the war was enormous, and by 1546 over £2 million, mainly raised by the sale of monastic lands, had been spent.

Charles V withdrew from the conflict and Henry VIII, plagued by ill-health and worried about the cost of the war, was left to make peace with France. It was agreed, under the terms of the Treaty of Campe (sometimes known as the Treaty of Ardres) in June 1546, that England should hold Boulogne for eight years.

Renewal of the Franco-Scottish alliance

When Henry VIII died in 1547 he left behind him a very uncertain diplomatic situation. The uneasy peace with France and Scotland was further undermined by the renewal of the Franco-Scottish alliance, which left England exposed to the danger of invasion from both north and south. England was in a precarious position, especially as the succession of the young Edward VI, a minor, could be exploited by the two main continental powers to strengthen their own positions in their dynastic wars. Furthermore, the Catholic nations were watching with interest to see whether the religious compromise in England would survive the death of Henry VIII.

Lord Paget

Lord Paget, England's ablest diplomat, summed up the whole position very clearly for the new Regency Council. He thought that England was not strong enough to defend Calais and Boulogne against the French. On the other hand, Charles V was a threat because of his support for the Catholic religion. However, Paget felt that it was too dangerous for England to risk assisting the **Lutheran princes** in Germany. Consequently, he recommended that the alliance with Charles V should be maintained, and that all efforts should be made to promote hostility between France and the Holy Roman Empire.

Key terms

Rough wooing
Contemporary term to describe the method used by Somerset to woo or persuade (as one would a lover) the Scots to agree to his marriage proposals.

Lutheran princes
Those rulers of the northern states of the Holy Roman Empire (Germany) who had converted to the Protestant faith established by Martin Luther.

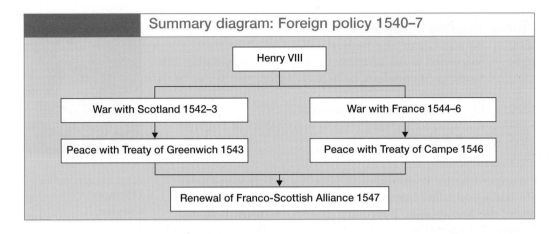

Summary diagram: Foreign policy 1540–7

Henry VIII

War with Scotland 1542–3

War with France 1544–6

Peace with Treaty of Greenwich 1543

Peace with Treaty of Campe 1546

Renewal of Franco-Scottish Alliance 1547

2 | The Changing Diplomatic Scene 1540–58

Changes in English diplomacy

English foreign policy between 1547 and 1558 was unsuccessful and the country's diplomatic position was very fragile. However, it is difficult to maintain that this amounted to an actual crisis because England was never in any real danger of foreign invasion or conquest. A major cause of England's insecurity during this period was thought to be indecisive leadership and governmental weakness. Yet although Somerset and Northumberland can be accused of weak diplomatic leadership, they were faced with situations not of their own making, and with circumstances largely beyond their control. In addition, they had to cope with a deteriorating economic situation and to raise unpopular taxes to sustain the war effort. Equally, Mary, because of her attachment to the Habsburgs, was drawn unwillingly into the final stages of the **Valois–Habsburg wars**.

In 1547 Somerset inherited Henry VIII's ambitious policy of conquest in France, and his plans for the unification of England and Scotland through the marriage of Mary Queen of Scots and the young Prince Edward. Most historians doubt whether Henry VIII, had he lived, would have been successful, because the cost of the war had already crippled the country's finances. Somerset was faced with the problems of:

- establishing a **regency government** for the young Edward VI
- pacifying the religious factions
- finding additional money to continue the war.

After the fall of Somerset in 1550, Northumberland, in addition to having to restore order after the popular uprisings of 1549 (see page 130–6), was confronted with the same difficulties. Furthermore, the economic situation had deteriorated to such an extent that he had little choice but to make peace with France and Scotland, and adopt a policy of neutrality. After 1553, Mary's devotion to the Catholic and Habsburg cause is seen by historians as making it almost inevitable that English foreign policy would be dictated by her forceful husband, Philip II of Spain.

Profile: Charles V 1500–56

1500 – Born in Ghent, the Netherlands
1519 – Succeeded to the territories ruled by his grandfather the Emperor Maximilian, principally Spain, the Netherlands and Austria
1520 – Elected Holy Roman Emperor
1554 – Encouraged his son Philip to marry Mary of England
1555 – Abdicated
1556 – Died

On paper Charles V was the most powerful monarch in Europe. His realms stretched from the Philippines to Peru and included Spain, the Netherlands, Burgundy, Austria, Hungary, Bohemia and parts of Italy along with Germany as Holy Roman Emperor. However, the sheer size of his dominions made them difficult to rule. He opposed Martin Luther and tried to halt the spread of Protestantism. He opposed Henry VIII's divorce from his aunt Catherine of Aragon. He resisted the **Ottoman Empire** in the east and struggled to contain the expansionist ambitions of Francis, King of France. His son's marriage with Mary brought England into an uneasy and short-lived alliance with the Habsburgs. Worn out by the demands of governing such a vast empire, he retired in 1555 and divided up his realms between his son Philip and brother Ferdinand.

> **Key term**
> **Ottoman Empire**
> Islamic empire centred on Turkey that threatened Christian Europe and control of the Mediterranean.

Changes in western European diplomacy

Few historians consider that even without these internal difficulties England could have played anything more than a minor role in mid-sixteenth-century western European diplomacy. As a small off-shore island, England had neither the resources nor the manpower to compete with great continental powers such as France, Spain or the Holy Roman Empire. It is precisely because England was thought by the continental powers to be a weak state that the threat of foreign invasion was regarded as highly unlikely. The Habsburg rulers of the Empire and Spain and the Valois kings of France were so well matched in their struggle for power that neither of them could afford to launch an invasion of England. At the same time, the Scots were not strong enough to pose a serious threat, and the French could not risk diverting enough troops to do more than help the Scots to prevent an English conquest. Thus, an uneasy balance of power maintained the status quo.

In many respects the mid-sixteenth century was a watershed, or turning-point, in western European diplomacy. The **abdication** of Charles V in 1555 brought about the break-up of his empire.

> **Key question**
> What were the key changes in western European diplomacy?

> **Key term**
> **Abdication**
> When a monarch gives up the throne either by force or by retirement.

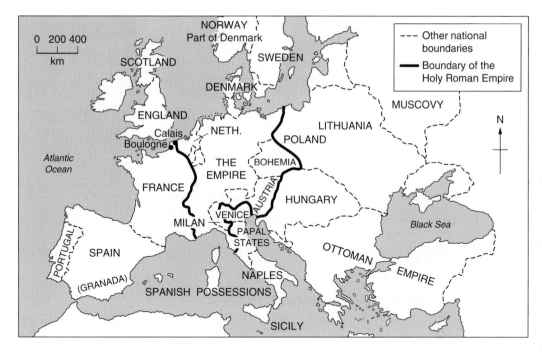

Figure 3.1: Map of Europe c1550.

- To the east of the Rhine, the new emperor, Ferdinand, was preoccupied with the religious quarrel among the German princes and the advance of the Ottoman Turks along the river Danube.
- In the west, Philip II of Spain was to become increasingly concerned about stamping out heresy in his territories and checking the growth of Ottoman seapower in the Mediterranean.

In the 1560s France was to be plunged into religious civil war. The struggle between the forces of the Reformation and the Counter Reformation would soon overshadow the dynastic wars of the first half of the century. In economic terms, the centre of power was moving away from the Mediterranean towards the Atlantic and north-western Europe. The loss of Calais in 1558 effectively ended English hopes of regaining its continental empire. After 1558 English foreign policy began to turn away from continental Europe towards the Atlantic and the colonial empires. A new policy was developing, for which control of the sea was of paramount importance.

Summary diagram: Foreign policy 1547–9

```
              ┌─────────────────────────────────┐
              │ Somerset's leadership qualities  │
              └─────────────────────────────────┘
                              │
                              ▼
                  ┌───────────────────────┐
                  │   Renewal of war with  │
                  └───────────────────────┘
                    │                   │
          ┌─────────┘                   └─────────┐
          ▼                                       ▼
   ┌──────────────┐                        ┌──────────────┐
   │   Scotland   │                        │    France    │
   └──────────────┘                        └──────────────┘
          │                                       │
          ▼                                       ▼
┌──────────────────────────────────┐    ┌──────────────────┐
│ Failure of Anglo-Scottish        │    │ Siege of Boulogne│
│ marriage scheme                  │    └──────────────────┘
└──────────────────────────────────┘             │
          │                                       │
          ▼                                       │
   ┌───────────────────────────────────┐         │
   │ Stalemate in Franco-Scottish war  │ ◄───────┘
   └───────────────────────────────────┘
```

3 | The Lord Protector Somerset 1547–9

Key question
Why did Somerset try to follow Henry VIII's French and Scottish policies and what problems did he face?

The young king's minority created fears over national security and the succession. There were major concerns over the possibility of renewed French intervention in Scotland and the end of the fragile peace. Affairs in Scotland were of paramount importance because of Henry VIII's desire to see his son Edward married to the infant Mary Queen of Scots. Under the terms of his will (see pages 37–8) Henry had set aside the English claim to the Scottish throne. This might be seen as a way of encouraging the Scots to accept the proposed marriage between Edward and Mary. On the other hand, Mary Queen of Scots, as a legitimate claimant to the throne, could be used by either the French or the Habsburgs as a means of gaining control of England in the cause of the Catholic faith.

Renewal of the war with Scotland

Somerset decided to try to isolate the Scots by negotiating with France for a defensive alliance. However, the death of Francis I and the accession of the more aggressive Henry II ended any hopes of a compromise with the French. Somerset strengthened the defences at Calais, Boulogne and Newhaven, and the fleet was sent to patrol the English Channel. Henry II renewed the Franco-Scottish alliance, and in June 1547 sent a fleet of warships with 4000 troops to Scotland. Somerset was left with no alternative but to intervene directly in Scottish affairs on the pretext of arranging the marriage between Edward and Mary, as agreed in 1543.

In September 1547 a joint land and naval invasion of Scotland was launched. Somerset and Dudley led an army to Berwick. They invaded Scotland with 16,000 infantry and 4000 mercenary cavalry, well supplied with cannon. They were supported at sea by a fleet of 30 warships and 50 supply ships under Lord Clinton. In the west Lord Wharton raided into Scotland from Carlisle with 2000 troops supported by 500 cavalry. The Scots under Lord

Key date

English defeated the Scots at Battle of Pinkie: September 1548

Figure 3.2: Map of the Anglo-Scottish border c1550.

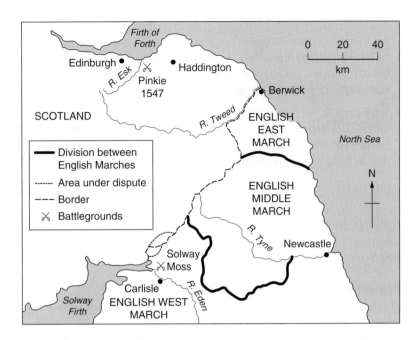

Arran raised an army of 20,000 troops, but it was poorly equipped with cannon and had only 1500 light cavalry.

The main English army occupied Preston Pans and advanced towards Edinburgh to confront the Scots, who held a strong defensive position on the River Esk. On 10 September the Scots crossed the river to attack the English. At the Battle of Pinkie they were cut to pieces by the English cannon and cavalry. After this victory Somerset was able to occupy all of the main border strongholds. This gave England control of the border, but the success was not as decisive as it appeared because the English army was not strong enough to occupy the rest of Scotland. In any case, Somerset was anxious about domestic affairs in England, and left Scotland with the bulk of his army on 18 September.

Key question
Why did the Anglo-Scottish marriage scheme fail?

Failure of the Anglo-Scottish marriage scheme

Defeat united the quarrelsome Scottish nobles, and they supported Mary of Guise in her opposition to England. While Somerset was in London, the Scottish Council met at Stirling and decided to ask the French for more help. It was suggested that, in return for French military aid, Mary Queen of Scots should marry Henry II's eldest son Francis. Meanwhile, England continued to negotiate with France. However, it soon became obvious that war would break out and that France was going to intervene in Scotland. English and French **privateers** attacked shipping in the English Channel and the North Sea, and the French began to build up their forces around Boulogne.

In January 1548 Somerset issued an appeal to the Scots, called the *Epistle of Exhortation*, proposing a union between the two countries:

Key term

Privateers
Professional seamen who sailed for profit by means of trade or piracy, or, if employed by the State, war.

> Who hath read the histories of time past doth mark and note the
> great battles fought between England and Scotland, the incursions,

raids and spoils which hath been done on both parties … [we] think it a thing very unmeet, unnatural, and unchristian that there should be between us so mortal war, … We offer equality and amity, we overcome in war and offer peace, we win [strong]holds and offer no conquest, we get in your land and offer England.

We intend not to disinherit your Queen but to make her heirs inheritors also to England. What greater honour can you seek unto your Queen than the marriage offered? What more meet marriage than this with the King's Highness of England?

For religious and political reasons the Scots preferred to side with the French. In June a French fleet landed an army of 10,000 troops in Scotland, and by August, Mary Queen of Scots had been taken to France to be educated. Henry II proclaimed that France and Scotland were one country.

Stalemate in the Anglo-Scottish war

Meanwhile Somerset remained in London preoccupied with domestic issues. Although Carlisle, Berwick and Haddington Castle, the main English base north of the border (see Figure 3.2), were strengthened, Somerset seemed unwilling to take any decisive action. Lord Wharton, the **Warden of the West March** at Carlisle, and Lord Grey, **Warden of the East March** at Berwick, continued to hold the border with an army of 10,000 troops.

However, without instructions from London, neither of them was prepared to take any initiatives. This encouraged the French troops in Scotland, reinforced with 8000 Scots, to besiege Haddington, which had a garrison of 5000 men. This placed Somerset in a dilemma. He was unwilling to leave London, and was worried by the French build-up of forces around Boulogne. Finally, judging correctly that Henry II would not attack Boulogne for fear of drawing Charles V into the war, he sent the Earl of Shrewsbury north with 12,000 infantry and 1800 cavalry to relieve Haddington.

Shrewsbury succeeded in forcing the besiegers to retreat, but Somerset soon ordered him to withdraw because of the high cost of maintaining his army. The siege was resumed, but after unsuccessfully assaulting the castle in October, the French began to tire of the expense of the war. In any case the Scottish nobles had begun to resent the French presence in Scotland, and Franco-Scottish relations deteriorated.

In January 1549 Somerset decided that Lord Wharton and Lord Grey were failing to take advantage of this situation. They were replaced by Lord Dacre and the Earl of Rutland, while the Earl of Shrewsbury was made Lord President of the **Council in the North**. However, before these changes had had time to take effect, affairs in the north were overshadowed by the peasant uprisings in England (see pages 130–6). Here again Somerset showed indecision. He was unwilling to withdraw troops from the border garrisons, and this delay allowed the situation in England to get out of control.

Key question
Why had the Anglo-Scottish war ended in stalemate?

Key terms

Wardens of the March
Nobles appointed by the monarch to defend and safeguard the eastern and western sections of the northern frontier (March) with Scotland.

Council in the North
Regional council of nobles and gentry based in York to govern northern England on behalf of the monarch.

Finally, in August, he was forced to withdraw troops from the north, and to recall the fleet to guard the English Channel against possible French attack. This caused the English to abandon Haddington and the other strongholds north of the border. Fortunately for England the French had already decided that the war in Scotland was too costly, and had redeployed their forces on the siege of Boulogne. Without support the Scots were too weak to launch any major attack on the north of England.

Somerset's leadership qualities

Key question
Why are historians divided in their opinion of Somerset's leadership qualities?

Opinion among historians in their judgement of Somerset as a diplomat and a military commander is divided. It is widely agreed that although he was a good field general, as a Commander-in-Chief he was indecisive and afraid to delegate authority. He is seen as having failed to take advantage of his victory at the Battle of Pinkie, and as having shown little initiative in pressing home his dominant position along the border. Equally, it is agreed that it was Somerset's military indecision and his unwillingness to redeploy his troops in 1549 that allowed the popular uprisings to get out of hand; not, as it was once maintained, his sympathy for the common people.

However, some historians consider that Somerset was not altogether to blame for the failure of his foreign policy. It is suggested that he had inherited an almost impossible diplomatic and military position in 1547. He was bound by Henry VIII's will to arrange a marriage between Edward VI and Mary Queen of Scots in order to safeguard the English succession from foreign influence or interference. In view of the hostility created by Henry VIII's earlier campaigns against the Scots, it is perhaps inevitable that Somerset would have been forced into war with Scotland to achieve this objective. It is also suggested that, given the Franco-Scottish alliance, England's weak military position in France and the chronic shortage of money, this was a war that could not be won.

Key date
Mary Queen of Scots taken to France: July 1548

In the event, Mary, Queen of Scots was taken to France for her safety.

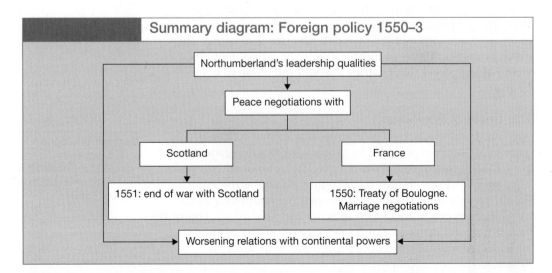

Summary diagram: Foreign policy 1550–3

Northumberland's leadership qualities

Peace negotiations with

Scotland — France

1551: end of war with Scotland — 1550: Treaty of Boulogne. Marriage negotiations

Worsening relations with continental powers

4 | The Lord President Northumberland 1550–3

Key question
Why did English diplomatic relations with Charles V and Scotland worsen?

By the autumn of 1549 foreign and domestic affairs had reached a critical point. The increasing Protestantism of the Church of England (see pages 99–100) had alienated Charles V, and had left England in a very exposed position without a powerful continental ally. Attempts to enforce the agreed marriage between Mary Queen of Scots and Edward VI had not only failed, but had pushed Scotland into a marriage alliance with France. England was committed to a ruinously expensive war on two fronts, the cost of which was adding to the already serious problems at home. Henry II was not slow to take advantage of this situation. He declared war in August and took personal command of the siege of Boulogne. Somerset's failure to deal with all these problems led to his fall, and gave Northumberland the opportunity to seize power.

Peace negotiations with France

War with France

The war had become increasingly unpopular with both the noble élites and the general public. High levels of taxation were undermining the economy and provoking rising hostility towards the government. For some time the Privy Council (see pages 42 and 44), especially Lord Paget, had been advocating peace as a means of restoring financial and economic stability (see page 43). Although Northumberland was much more sympathetic to these views than Somerset had been, during the winter of 1549 he was fully occupied in gaining control of the government.

The French took advantage of this weakness to build up their forces around Boulogne. They were able to break English lines of communication between Boulogne and Calais, which threatened to isolate the garrison of Boulogne under the command of Lord Huntingdon. However, an English fleet decisively defeated a strong force of French galleys in a battle off the Channel Islands. This gave England control of the Channel, and meant that Boulogne could be supplied by sea. As the government was virtually bankrupt, Northumberland was unable to raise an army to lift the siege. Attempts to persuade Charles V to extend the treaty protecting Calais to include Boulogne failed. Even so, Henry II was afraid that Charles V would intervene to help England.

The Treaty of Boulogne

Northumberland was keen to end the war so that he could consolidate his own position. In January 1550 a delegation led by Lord Russell (see page 81) was sent to France to negotiate peace. They proposed that in return for ceding Boulogne the French should pay a sum of money, and re-open negotiations about a marriage between Mary Queen of Scots and Edward VI. Henry II took full advantage of England's weak position and refused to make any concessions. Finally, Northumberland, strongly

Key date

Treaty of Boulogne ended war with France and Scotland; Boulogne returned to France: 1550

Key terms

Dowry
A sum of money paid by the bride's father on her marriage.

Calvinist doctrines
Religious rules and instructions developed by the Protestant leader John Calvin.

Intercursus Magnus
Treaty agreement on trade negotiated by Henry VII between England and the Netherlands.

Edict
A royal decree having the force of law.

Catholic Inquisition
Organisation empowered by the Pope to defend the Church by rooting out enemies such as heretics.

Key question
Why did England's relations with the Holy Roman Empire deteriorate?

supported by Paget, persuaded the Privy Council that they had no alternative but to accept the French terms. The Treaty of Boulogne was signed on 28 March 1550.

Under the terms of the Treaty, the English had to withdraw from Boulogne in return for a sum of 400,000 crowns. At the same time they had to remove their remaining garrisons from Scotland, and agree not to renew the war unless provoked by the Scots. Finally, there was to be an alliance between England and France. Boulogne was handed over to the French on 25 April, and the English garrison was sent to reinforce Calais. Although the Treaty of Boulogne removed the danger of French invasion and ended the crippling expense of the war, the crisis still remained.

Marriage negotiations

The humiliating peace and alliance with a traditional enemy was generally seen as a national disgrace, and added to Northumberland's unpopularity. In spite of this, he negotiated with the French for a marriage between Edward VI and Henry II's daughter Elizabeth. It was agreed that Elizabeth would come to England when she was 12 years of age, and would bring a **dowry** of 200,000 crowns. The alliance was ratified in December 1550 in return for English neutrality in continental wars. England's international position was still very weak, and was made worse because lack of money forced Northumberland to run down both the army and the navy. The Habsburgs remained hostile, particularly as the Church of England was beginning to swing towards more extreme **Calvinist doctrines**.

In many respects England had returned to the position of weakness and isolation which had resulted from the failure of Henry VIII's foreign policy. Certainly the Treaty of Boulogne marked the end of the phase of policy initiated by Henry VIII, during which the reconquest of French territories was a major goal.

Relations with the Holy Roman Empire

England's relations with the Holy Roman Empire deteriorated steadily. Apart from disliking the Anglo-French alliance, Charles V was particularly annoyed by the attempts of the English reformers to force Princess Mary to abandon her Catholic faith. A consequence of this cooling of relations was a breakdown in commercial contacts with the Netherlands, which had been protected by the **Intercursus Magnus** since 1496.

In April 1550 Charles issued an **edict** allowing the **Catholic Inquisition** to arrest any heretics in the Netherlands. This outraged many English merchants. Although the edict was modified to exclude foreigners, it helped to bring about the collapse of the Antwerp cloth market, as many Flemish clothworkers fled to England to avoid persecution. The situation was further complicated by disputes over piracy in the English Channel. It was not until December 1550 that Charles made any attempt to restore good trading relations, and then only from fear that England would be driven into a closer alliance with France.

Anglo-Scottish relations

Anglo-Scottish relationships were in an equally poor state. When Northumberland withdrew the remaining English garrisons from Scotland he left the French in control. However, the Scottish nobles and the **Protestant Lowlanders** were becoming increasingly hostile towards the French, fearing that Scotland would become a mere province of France. The fall of Somerset had left a confused situation on the English side of the border. Lord Dacre and the Earl of Rutland at Carlisle and Berwick had no clear policy to follow. In 1550 Northumberland decided to take personal control of affairs along the border by making himself **General Warden of the North**, with Lord Wharton as his deputy.

To end the constant minor disputes over land which threatened the uneasy peace, Sir Robert Bowen was ordered to survey the border. He reported that an area 15 miles by four miles was under dispute between England and Scotland. After strengthening Berwick and Carlisle, Northumberland returned to London, leaving Lord Dacre to negotiate a settlement of the line of the border with the Scots. Progress was very slow, and it was not until a French fleet landed supplies and troops in Scotland in February 1551 that negotiations began in earnest. Finally, in March 1552, it was agreed that the border was to be restored to the line held before Henry VIII's Scottish campaigns.

Worsening relations with the continental powers

During 1551 Northumberland maintained his policy of neutrality towards the continental powers. Charles V continued to disapprove of the increasing Protestantism of the Church of England, and considered that English foreign policy was unpredictable. It was not until March 1552, when war broke out again between Charles V and Henry II, that Anglo-Imperial relations began to improve. Northumberland resisted French pressure to join in the war against the Holy Roman Empire, and Charles V was more conciliatory over English trade with the Netherlands. Finally, by June 1552, good diplomatic relations were restored between the two countries. Then, when the French invaded Lorraine and the Netherlands, Charles V reminded England that she was bound under treaty obligations to assist the Empire if the Netherlands were attacked.

The garrison at Calais was reinforced, but England still took no active part in the war. Even so, England's relations with France deteriorated. The second half of the money the French had agreed to pay for gaining control of Boulogne remained unpaid and French privateers had begun to attack English shipping. Although England was in no position to take any military action, the French feared an Anglo-Imperial alliance and were careful to avoid open confrontation. In January, Northumberland proposed to act as mediator between France and the Empire. This action was prompted by fears over Edward VI's declining health and the illness of Charles V. The French were not interested in making peace, and in June 1553 the negotiations collapsed.

Key question
Why were Anglo-Scottish relations in such a poor state?

Protestant Lowlanders
Scots who lived in the border region with England and were among the first to be converted to English Protestantism.

General Warden of the North
Nobleman charged with overall responsibility for the defence of the northern frontier with Scotland.

Key terms

At the time, these events were overshadowed by the death of
Edward VI in 1553 and the ensuing constitutional crisis.
Obviously the question of the succession in England was of great
interest to both Charles V and Henry II. The accession of the
Catholic Mary Tudor, with her strong attachment to the
Habsburgs, would probably bring England into the war on the
Imperial side. Charles V was strongly in favour of this solution,
which would enhance his war effort and restore Catholicism in
England. From the French point of view this would have been a
far from ideal situation. Consequently, they favoured a succession
that would leave Northumberland in power, and possibly produce
a situation where they could intervene in favour of the claims of
Mary Queen of Scots. Although the imperial diplomats were
convinced that Mary Tudor's claim to the throne would be
ignored, Northumberland's plans to replace her with Lady Jane
Grey failed because of lack of support among the English
aristocracy and gentry (see pages 136–7).

The beginning of new policies aimed at world trade

The search for new markets

Key question
Why did English
merchants urge the
government to find
new markets?

The decline of the Antwerp cloth market and the breakdown in
commercial relations with the Empire prompted English
merchants to urge the government to find new markets. In 1547
the Italian explorer Sebastian Cabot had been given a pension of
£100 a year to come to England and help to discover new lands.
In 1551 William Hawkins opened up trade in cloth, timber,
saltpetre, iron and sugar along the **Barbary coast**. By 1553
English ships were trading as far as the Gold Coast in West Africa.
However, this was the full extent of the trading effort because,
although English merchants were eager to break into the trade
with the Far East, their ships and their navigation were too poor
to attempt the sea routes around the Cape of Good Hope in
South Africa. In any case, after the death of Henry VII in 1509
successive English governments did not encourage Atlantic
exploration for fear of offending Spain and endangering the
Anglo-Habsburg alliance.

Key term

Barbary coast
Coast of North
Africa, mainly
Morocco and
Algeria.

The search for a north-east passage

To overcome these difficulties the cartographer and geographer
John Dee proposed finding a north-east passage to the East.
In 1552 a company was established with Sebastian Cabot as its
governor, to which city merchants and members of the Privy
Council each contributed £325. In May 1553 Sir Hugh
Willoughby was put in command of three ships, and given sailing
orders drawn up by Sebastian Cabot. The Privy Council gave
Willoughby letters of introduction to the ruler of China.
Willoughby and two of the ships were lost in Lapland in 1554.
His second-in-command, Richard Chancellor, succeeded in
reaching the port of Archangel in the White Sea and established
diplomatic links with Ivan IV, the Tsar of Muscovy. In 1553 the

Muscovy Company was founded to establish trade between the two countries (see page 186). Early English exploration, improvements to the dockyards and the navy, begun in 1555, were to come to fruition later, during the reign of Elizabeth I.

Muscovy Company
Company set up to trade with Russia.

Key term

Northumberland's leadership qualities

Historians have revised their opinion of Northumberland as a diplomat. In the past he was seen in the same light as by his contemporaries, as a man who betrayed the national honour by giving Boulogne back to France.

Recently historians have begun to see him not only as a good soldier, but also as a capable diplomat. They consider that as he was confronted by an impossible military situation and a bankrupt Exchequer, he was taking the only sensible course by making peace. With Mary Queen of Scots safely in France, there would have been little point in prolonging hostilities with Scotland. Furthermore, Northumberland took decisive action by assuming personal control as Lord Warden to investigate the petty disputes along the Scottish border.

Northumberland also possessed the ability to delegate authority, by leaving Lord Dacre, with his wide experience of northern affairs, to reach a final settlement. The return of Boulogne to the French was equally practical and sensible. Historians now consider that, even with the support of the Habsburgs, England would not have been able to hold Boulogne, a town which, apart from being a symbol of national prestige, was of no real value to the country.

Key question
Why are historians divided in their opinion of Northumberland's leadership qualities?

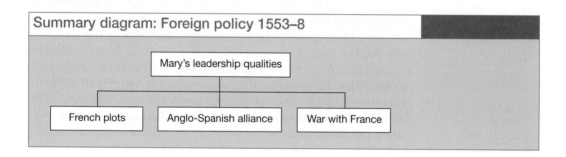

Summary diagram: Foreign policy 1553–8

- Mary's leadership qualities
  - French plots
  - Anglo-Spanish alliance
  - War with France

5 | Mary Tudor 1555–8

As expected, Mary's successful bid for the throne once again placed England securely in alliance with the Holy Roman Empire. Her proposed marriage with Philip of Spain, Charles V's eldest son, meant that England would be firmly allied with the most powerful country in western Europe. Moreover, as the Netherlands were to form part of Philip's inheritance, England's main commercial outlet would be secure. However, in spite of these apparent advantages, many Englishmen feared that the alliance would lead to a renewal of the war with France.

Key question
Why was Mary's marriage alliance with Spain and the Habsburgs unpopular?

Painting of Mary with her new husband Philip II of Spain. How are Mary and Philip depicted in this painting?

Key question
Why did the French try to prevent an Anglo-Spanish alliance?

Key date

Mary married Philip II of Spain: July 1554

French plots to prevent an Anglo-Spanish alliance

There were similar fears in France, so the French ambassador, Noailles, worked hard to promote opposition to the marriage. He was certainly involved in the conspiracy to marry Courtenay, Earl of Devon and descendant of English kings, to Princess Elizabeth and place them both on the throne. The conspiracy was planned by Sir Thomas Wyatt, Sir Peter Carew, Sir James Croft and the Duke of Suffolk (see pages 138–9). The conspirators planned to raise rebellion in four different parts of the kingdom but, in the event, only Wyatt actually rebelled. That the government was well aware of these plots and their implications is clear from a report in November 1553 to Charles V from his representative, Simon Renard (the official ambassador of the Holy Roman Empire in England), about a conversation between Mary, Lord Paget and Renard concerning the English succession. The rival claimants were:

- Mary, Queen of Scotland, the promised bride of the Dauphin (heir to the French throne), who had a claim by right of descent.

- Lady Frances, wife of the Duke of Suffolk, and niece of Henry VIII. She would have a claim if the Queen of Scotland were excluded because of having been born abroad, being a Scotswoman and married to the Dauphin of France.
- Lady Elizabeth, daughter of Henry VIII and half-sister of Mary I.

The failure of the French plot, the defeat of Wyatt in Kent and the failure of his fellow conspirators to rebel, ended French hopes of preventing the Anglo-Spanish alliance. Although the marriage agreement appeared to safeguard England against being involved in Philip's wars, there was a clause which stipulated that Philip should aid Mary in governing her kingdom. This provided a loophole which Philip could use to draw England into the continental conflict.

War with France

By July 1555 it was clear that Mary was not going to bear any children and that her health was deteriorating, ending Philip II's hopes of an heir to rule in England. In October, still plagued by ill-health, Charles V abdicated his titles and went into retirement at the age of 55. His brother Ferdinand succeeded to his German lands, while Philip became King of Spain and ruler of the Netherlands, Naples, Sicily, Milan and the New World. Philip left England to assume his new responsibilities.

However, Stephen Gardiner, the most trusted of Mary's English councillors, died in November 1555, which made the queen anxious for Philip to return to England to advise her. He paid little attention to her pleas until March 1556, when the war with France broke out again. Philip came to England to enlist support, but the Privy Council was totally opposed to any involvement in the war. England was still in a weak military position in spite of reforms to the army and navy (see page 63). Then, however, the French ambassador's plot against Mary came to light, and the Privy Council reluctantly declared war on France.

The English military campaign in France

In July 1556 the Earl of Pembroke was sent to France with an army of 7000 men. There they joined the army commanded by Philibert, Duke of Savoy, who won a decisive victory over the French at St Quentin in 1557. At the same time the English fleet attacked the French coast. These combined operations forced the Duke of Guise, commanding the main French army, to return to France from Italy. In retaliation for the English intervention he launched an attack on Calais. Unfortunately the English government had already been forced to borrow heavily to equip the army and navy sent to the continent, and were unable to afford to send reinforcements to Calais. The defences of Calais had been neglected, and Lord Wentworth, the Commander, was unable to make any real resistance. Calais fell on 13 January 1558, and the French soon occupied the remainder of the English strongholds around the port.

Key question
Why did England go to war with France?

Key dates

England and her ally Spain went to war with France: June 1557

French captured Calais: January 1558

Treaty of Cateau-Cambrensis. Peace made with France and Scotland; Calais given to France: April 1559

Profile: Philip II 1527–98

1527 – Born in Spain
1542 – Appointed regent of Spain 1542–8
1554 – Married Queen Mary I of England
1555 – Drew England into Spain's war with France
1556 – Succeeded father as King of Spain
1558 – Failed to persuade Elizabeth to marry him after the
         death of Mary
1588 – Launched the Armada against England but the invasion
         ended in failure
1598 – Died

Philip was the son of Charles V and Isabella of Portugal. Brought
up in Spain, he was appointed regent by Charles V, then became
king on his father's abdication. His marriage to Mary was political
and was intended to draw England into Spain's struggle with
France. Although he was never crowned, Philip, with his wife's
approval, took the style of King of England. In spite of
Elizabeth's refusal to accept his offers of marriage, they remained
allies against growing French power until 1569. In that year
Philip turned against Elizabeth, in part because of her detention
of Mary Stuart, Queen of Scotland, but also in response to the
hostility of the queen's advisers. Philip was a Catholic and he
supported the Pope's efforts to reconvert England to the true
faith.

In response to this humiliating defeat the government raised an
army of 7000 troops, supported by a fleet of 140 ships, to invade
France. The intention was not to recapture Calais, but to attack
Brest. Finding Brest too heavily defended the English force
captured the smaller port of Le Conquet. Meanwhile, Henry II
and Philip II were camped near Amiens with armies of 45,000
men. Instead of the expected decisive battle, the two monarchs
decided to negotiate. At first Philip demanded the return of
Calais to England as part of the settlement. Then Mary died in
November 1558, and Philip abandoned his former ally. Under
the terms of the Peace of Cateau-Cambresis in April 1559 France
and Spain signed a lasting peace treaty. Philip married Henry II's
daughter Elizabeth, and the French guaranteed not to intervene
in Philip's Italian territories. France retained Calais, the last
English possession on the continent.

Key date

Death of Mary:
November 1558

Mary's leadership qualities

Key question
Why are historians
united in their opinion
of Mary's poor
leadership qualities?

Although historians no longer agree with the opinion of Mary's
contemporaries that the loss of Calais was a national disaster, they
continue to condemn her conduct of foreign affairs. It is still
thought that Mary's stubbornness, and her almost total reliance
on her Spanish advisers, made England's military debacle
between 1557 and 1558 inevitable. There is some sympathy for
Mary over the way in which Philip II blatantly used England for

his own ends, but it is clear that she was too infatuated with Philip and the Habsburgs to take reasonable precautions to protect English interests. In 1553 the Habsburgs had serious intentions of turning England into a permanent base, to complete the 'Habsburg ring' encircling France. Philip's unpopularity in England, and the realisation in 1555 that Mary was incapable of producing an heir, is regarded as the reason for abandoning this strategy. This is what convinced Philip in 1556 to use English troops for short-term military gains, and for his desertion of his ally after the death of Mary in 1558.

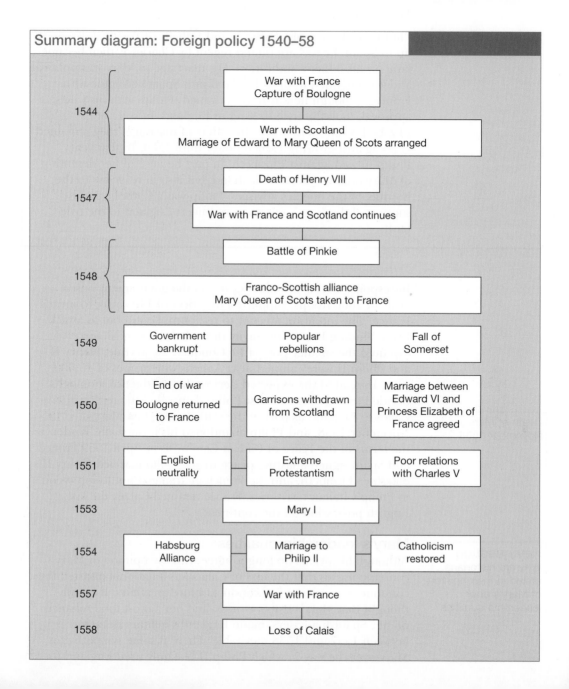

Summary diagram: Foreign policy 1540–58

| 1544 | War with France
Capture of Boulogne |
| | War with Scotland
Marriage of Edward to Mary Queen of Scots arranged |

| 1547 | Death of Henry VIII |
| | War with France and Scotland continues |

| 1548 | Battle of Pinkie |
| | Franco-Scottish alliance
Mary Queen of Scots taken to France |

| 1549 | Government bankrupt | Popular rebellions | Fall of Somerset |

| 1550 | End of war
Boulogne returned to France | Garrisons withdrawn from Scotland | Marriage between Edward VI and Princess Elizabeth of France agreed |

| 1551 | English neutrality | Extreme Protestantism | Poor relations with Charles V |

| 1553 | Mary I |

| 1554 | Habsburg Alliance | Marriage to Philip II | Catholicism restored |

| 1557 | War with France |

| 1558 | Loss of Calais |

6 | The Key Debate

Was there a crisis in foreign affairs?

The lack of political leadership between 1547 and 1558 placed England in a weak diplomatic position. However, in no way did this amount to a crisis, as the country was never in real danger of foreign invasion. Moreover, it is unlikely that even strong leadership would have improved the diplomatic situation. Mid-century foreign policy was largely dictated by the culmination of the Valois–Habsburg rivalry and the tactics of Henry VIII.

Elton

"*evil inheritance*"

Somerset and Northumberland inherited a war against France and Scotland which Henry VIII, arguably, had already lost. Faced with an impossible military situation and a bankrupt Exchequer, Northumberland's decision to make an inglorious peace in 1550 was sensible. In any case, the evidence suggests that the Privy Council favoured peace to avoid any further economic problems.

Mary I's deep Catholic convictions and her attachment to Philip II of Spain made it inevitable that she would support the Habsburgs in the final, indecisive stage of the Habsburg–Valois wars, which ended in 1558. The loss of Calais severed England's final link with the continent. When Elizabeth came to the throne she was faced with a completely different diplomatic situation.

Mid-Tudor foreign policy is still seen as being largely dictated by the broader aims of western European diplomacy which had dominated the first half of the sixteenth century. England's diplomatic position was further complicated by fears over the succession and religious reform. In the past, historians such as A.L. Rowse made considerable use of official papers and the correspondence between ambassadors and their courts to reconstruct events and policies.

More recently, historians, particularly David Loades, have begun to think that over-reliance on this type of evidence had produced a one-sided view of the issues. Official documents only state what governments wish to be left on record, while the views of ambassadors such as Renard are bound to be partisan. For this reason, much greater attention is being paid to the correspondence and family papers of the many lesser diplomats involved in foreign affairs. These men were drawn from a wide range of families among the élites, and such research increases not only the understanding of the intricate nature of diplomacy, but also its relationship with domestic politics.

However, it is still unlikely that historians will be able to probe much more deeply than the official versions of the growing number of plots and intrigues with foreign powers, because families were very careful to destroy such incriminating evidence.

Study Guide: AS Questions

In the style of OCR

(a) 'Somerset's foreign policy was a total failure'. How far do you agree?

(b) Who was the more effective in conducting England's foreign affairs, Northumberland or Mary Tudor? Explain your answer.

Exam tips

The cross-references are intended to take you straight to the material that will help you to answer the questions.

(a) In question **(a)** you have to know why Somerset's foreign policy is considered to be a failure. Use your own judgement to decide the extent to which it was successful or unsuccessful. If you judge him to have been unsuccessful, you have to decide whether his failure was the result of:

- the impracticability of the policies inherited from Henry VIII (pages 71–2)
- his own shortcomings as a leader (page 79).

On the other hand, you might argue that Somerset successfully

- defeated the Scots in battle
- secured the northern frontier from attack
- safeguarded England from foreign invasion (pages 78–9).

(b) In question **(b)** you must focus on the key phrase 'more effective' and explain which of the two rulers enjoyed the greater success. You must adopt an analytical rather than a narrative approach to answering this question, e.g. you must compare and evaluate the relative merits of the conduct of foreign policy by both Northumberland and Mary rather than simply offer a descriptive list of their policies.

Northumberland:

- relations between England and the continental powers worsened
- gave Boulogne back to the French without a fight (pages 80–1).

On the other hand he

- negotiated peace treaties with foreign powers
- reduced the threat of invasion and war
- conducted a sensible policy given England's near bankruptcy (pages 82–4).

Mary:

- allowed England's interests to be subordinated to those of Spain
- lost Calais and prestige abroad (pages 86–7).

On the other hand she

- allied England to the most powerful ruling family in Europe, the Habsburgs
- secured the northern frontier from Scottish attack (pages 85–6).

4 Religious Change 1540–58

POINTS TO CONSIDER

This chapter examines the main religious changes during the reigns of Henry VIII, Edward VI and Mary. A major point of debate is, 'Were most people still Catholic during this period or did they just conform to the religion of the monarch?' In order to understand and enter into this debate you will need to consider the following key points:

- What religious legacy did Henry VIII leave his successors?
- How successful were the reformers in introducing Protestant doctrines into the Church of England during the reign of Edward VI?
- Would Mary have succeeded in permanently returning England to the Church of Rome if she had lived long enough?

These issues are examined as five themes:

- Henry VIII's religious legacy 1540–7
- The Edwardian Church under Somerset 1547–9
- The Edwardian Church under Northumberland 1550–3
- The Marian Church 1553–8
- Was there a religious crisis?

Key dates

1534	November	Henry VIII became Head of the Church in England
1536	July	The Ten Articles introduced some Lutheran doctrines
1539	April	The Great Bible in English circulated to parishes
	June	The Six Articles restored full Catholic doctrine
1547	November	Repeal of the Act of Six Articles
	December	Act for the Dissolution of the Chantries
1548	December	First Book of Common Prayer
1549	January	Act of Uniformity
1552	January	Second Book of Common Prayer introduced some Calvinistic doctrines
	April	Second Act of Uniformity

1553	September	Catholic Mass re-introduced
1554	November	Cardinal Pole returned to England as Papal Legate. England and Rome reconciled
	December	Re-introduction of the heresy laws
1555	October	Bishops Ridley and Latimer burned at the stake
1556	March	Archbishop Cranmer burned at the stake
1558	November	Death of Mary and Cardinal Pole
1559	May	Act of Supremacy restored Henrician anti-papal laws

1 | Henry VIII's Religious Legacy 1540–7

In order to see the significance of the religious changes that took place between 1540 and 1558 it is necessary to understand:

- The reasons why religion had become a political issue and the problems this caused for Henry VIII and his successors.
- The impact that religious change had on foreign affairs after 1540.
- The doctrinal position in the Church of England at the death of Henry VIII.

Religion as a political issue

There is wide agreement that Henry VIII's motives in breaking away from Rome were much more political than religious. The English Reformation put the Church firmly under the control of the State. It also removed England from the authority of the Pope, a source of outside interference which was highly resented among the English ruling élites. The resulting royal supremacy made Henry VIII more independent and more powerful perhaps than any monarch in English history. It enabled him to rule an undivided kingdom where Church and State were merged into a single **sovereign state**. Henry VIII was able to reduce the political power of the Church and exploit its vast wealth. Church wealth replenished the Exchequer for a time, which had been almost bankrupted by Henry VIII's unsuccessful wars of the 1520s.

Somerset

On the surface, the Crown was the main beneficiary of the English Reformation. Yet, once religion had come to the forefront of politics, it created problems for the monarchy. Religious differences deepened the rift between political factions at court. Henry VIII had to tread a cautious path between the conservative Catholic and reforming Protestant parties. By 1547 he had decided that the safest way to protect the succession and the royal supremacy was to give control of the Privy Council to Somerset and the reformers. However, the fall of Somerset in 1549 (see pages 49–50) triggered a renewed struggle for political power between the Catholic conservatives and the Protestant reformers.

Key question
Why had religion become a political issue and what problems did this cause?

Key date

Henry VIII became Head of the Church in England: November 1534

Key term

Sovereign state
A country in which the monarch has supreme power over the State (government, law, the economy) and the Church (doctrine, appointments and property). Foreign powers or rulers had no right to interfere in the internal affairs of a sovereign state.

Act of the Ten Articles
Passed in 1536, the Act was intended to promote Protestant religious ideas in England and Wales by stripping away many of the traditional festivals, relic-cults, shrines and parts of the Church service.

Consubstantiation
The belief that the sacramental bread and wine given by the priest to parishioners in Church were a symbolic representation of the body and blood of Christ and therefore remained unchanged at communion.

The Ten Articles introduced some Lutheran doctrines: July 1536

The Six Articles restored full Catholic doctrine: June 1539

Some of the leading Catholic conservatives, principally the Earls of Southampton and Arundel, were able briefly to influence events in the Privy Council. However, once Northumberland had consolidated his position, they were expelled.

Northumberland

The power struggle between the conservatives and reformers resurfaced again in 1553 when Northumberland attempted to change the succession. Northumberland's action was prompted not only by personal ambition, but also by the desire to prevent the Catholic faction regaining power under Mary Tudor. Even so there was still a great deal of toleration and Catholic politicians were not excluded from government purely for religious reasons. Stephen Gardiner, the leading Catholic bishop, spent most of Edward VI's reign in prison, but this was largely because he refused to co-operate with the Privy Council. Unlike the hard-line Gardiner, a majority of the ruling élites favoured moderate reform.

Mary Tudor

When Mary Tudor came to power in 1553 there was no great purge of Protestant politicians. Indeed, men like Paget were given high office. It is true that Mary did not trust such men, but neither did she have great confidence in her English Catholic councillors. Given that among the ruling élites moderate reformers were in a majority, that Mary came to the throne at all is a sign of the toleration in England. She was supported as the legitimate heir in spite of her religion. During her reign most politicians and civil servants were prepared to conform to her religious views. It was not her religion, but the ending of the royal supremacy and her marriage to Philip II of Spain that provoked most opposition.

The doctrinal position in the Church of England during the 1540s

From the time Henry had made himself Head of the English Church in 1534 he had been under pressure to formulate an acceptable doctrine. The reform party led by Cranmer had advocated the introduction of moderate Lutheran ideas. On the other hand, the pro-Catholic, conservative faction led by Gardiner had favoured a policy of minimum change to the basic Catholic doctrines.

During the period 1534–46 royal favour swung between the two groups. The first major statement of doctrine, the **Act of the Ten Articles**, came in 1536. This Act was passed when the reformers were in the ascendancy. They introduced a number of Lutheran doctrines into the Church of England, e.g. belief in **consubstantiation**. Three years later the conservatives regained royal favour and the Act of the Six Articles (see page 45) was passed to remove many of the Lutheran beliefs. Such shifts of policy meant that by 1547 the doctrines of the Church of England were a compromise and contained many inconsistencies which were unacceptable to reformers and conservatives alike.

Catholic doctrines in the Church of England

When Henry VIII died the main articles of faith in the Church of England were in line with traditional Catholic orthodoxy:

- The Eucharist was clearly defined in the Catholic form of transubstantiation. The Lutheran form of consubstantiation was no longer accepted in the Church of England.
- Only the clergy were permitted to take communion in both the bread and the wine, while the **laity** were again restricted to taking only the sacramental bread.
- The Catholic rites of confirmation, marriage, holy orders and extreme unction had been re-introduced, alongside the previously recognised sacraments of the Eucharist, penance and baptism.
- The laity were still required to make regular confession of sins to a priest, and to seek absolution and penance.
- English clergy were no longer allowed to marry, and those who had married before 1540 had to send away their wives and families, or lose their livings.
- Although there was no specific statement on the existence of purgatory, the need for the laity to do 'good works' for their salvation had been reinstated.
- The singing of masses for the souls of the dead was held to be 'agreeable also to God's law'. It was for this reason that the chantries, where a priest sang masses for the souls of the founder and his family, were not closed down at the same time as the monasteries.
- Paintings and statues of the saints were still allowed in the churches, although the laity were instructed not to worship them.

Many of the processions and rituals of the Catholic Church were still practised, because it was maintained that they created a good religious frame of mind in those who witnessed them.

Key terms

Laity
The non-clerical general population, the parishioners as opposed to the priests.

Litany
Recital of religious teachings contained in the Book of Common Prayer.

Protestant practices in the Church of England

Although the Church of England remained fundamentally Catholic in doctrine, it had adopted a number of Protestant practices by 1547:

- Services were still conducted in Latin, but Cranmer's prayers and responses of the **litany** in English had been authorised in 1545.
- Greater importance was attached to the sermon, and the Lord's Prayer, the Creed and the Ten Commandments had to be taught in English rather than Latin by parents to their children and servants.
- Similarly, the Great Bible of 1539 was the authorised English translation which replaced the Latin Vulgate Bible. Moreover, the élite laity were allowed to read the Great Bible in their own homes, unlike on the continent where often only the Catholic clergy were allowed to read and interpret the Bible.

Key question
What were the key Protestant practices in the Church of England?

The Great Bible in English circulated to parishes: April 1539

Key date

- The practice of the Church of England with regard to some Catholic doctrines was ambiguous. Saints could be 'reverenced for their excellent virtue' and could be offered prayers, but the laity were forbidden to make pilgrimages to the shrines of saints or to offer them gifts, because it was maintained that grace, salvation and absolution of sins came only from God.
- At the same time, the number of Holy Days – days on which, like Sundays, the laity were expected to attend church and not to work – had been reduced to 25.
- Finally, in sharp contrast to Catholic countries, there had been no monasteries in England since 1540. They had been closed by royal order and their possessions had been transferred to the Crown.

Key dates

Repeal of the Act of Six Articles: November 1547

Act for the Dissolution of the Chantries: December 1547

First Book of Common Prayer: December 1548

Act of Uniformity: January 1549

Attempts between 1534 and 1546 to establish a uniform set of articles of faith for the Church of England had succeeded only in producing a patchwork of doctrines that often conflicted. Until 1547 this ramshackle structure was held together by the Henrician treason and heresy laws. Anyone breaking, or even questioning, the statutes and proclamations defining the doctrines of the Church of England was liable to confiscation of property, fines, imprisonment or execution. Similarly, the censorship laws prevented the printing, publishing, or importation of books and pamphlets expressing views contrary to the doctrines of the Church of England.

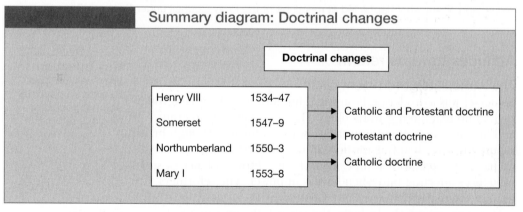

Summary diagram: Doctrinal changes

Doctrinal changes	
Henry VIII 1534–47	Catholic and Protestant doctrine
Somerset 1547–9	Protestant doctrine
Northumberland 1550–3	Catholic doctrine
Mary I 1553–8	

Key question
How far did the Edwardian Church move from Catholicism to Protestantism under Somerset?

2 | The Edwardian Church under Somerset 1547–9

The accession of Edward VI, who had been educated as a Protestant, roused the hopes of English reformers that there would be a swing towards more Lutheran, and possibly Calvinist, doctrines. Somerset's appointment as Lord Protector in 1547 established the reform party firmly in power, as intended under the terms of Henry VIII's will (see pages 37–8).

The death-bed of Henry VIII together with Edward VI and the Pope c1548. What were the probable aims of the artist in painting this picture? How reliable is this painting as a source of information about what happened at meetings of the Privy Council under Somerset?

Attitudes towards reform

The immediate government circle

Somerset was a moderate Protestant, but although he was devout, he had no real interest in theology. He was religiously tolerant, and favoured a cautious approach towards reform. Although he is reputed to have had Calvinistic leanings and, certainly, exchanged letters with John Calvin, there is little evidence of such influences affecting him when he was in power. The reformers were in the majority in the Privy Council.

However, among the bishops, there was little agreement. Although the majority of them fully supported the royal supremacy and the separation from Rome, they remained hopelessly divided on the issue of religious reform.

- Nine bishops led by Archbishop Thomas Cranmer and Nicholas Ridley, Bishop of Rochester, supported reform.
- Ten bishops led by Stephen Gardiner, Bishop of Winchester, and Edmund Bonner, Bishop of London, opposed change.
- Eight bishops were undecided.

With such an even balance of opinion among the bishops, Somerset and the Privy Council moved very cautiously on matters of religious reform.

Key question
Why was the new Regime so cautious about introducing religious reform?

Outside the immediate government circle

This is difficult to assess:

- A majority of the ruling élites seem to have been in favour of (or at least, not opposed to) some measure of religious reform.
- In general, however, the lower clergy were opposed to religious change. This, it has been suggested, was largely because the English parish clergy were still relatively uneducated, and were anxious to maintain their traditional way of life without any complications.
- The same was true for the great mass of the population, who were very conservative in their outlook. Moreover, as far as they were concerned, both their popular culture, which was based on rituals and festivals associated with the farming year, and their belief in magic and witchcraft, all formed part of the ceremonies of the old Church.

Yet there were exceptions:

- In East Anglia, because of the settlement of large numbers of Protestant refugees from the continent, there was considerable support for religious reform.
- In London and the larger towns, where clergy were better educated, there were very vocal minorities demanding more rapid, and more radical, religious change.

The introduction of some reform

In these circumstances the Privy Council decided to review the state of the Church of England, and to introduce some moderate Protestant reforms. Such a policy was opposed by the conservatives, prompted by Gardiner, who maintained that under the terms of Henry VIII's will, no religious changes could be made until Edward VI came of age at 18. In spite of Gardiner's vigorous opposition, royal commissioners were sent to visit all the bishops. They were instructed to compile a report by the autumn of 1547 on the state of the clergy and the doctrines and practices to be found in every **diocese**. To help the spread of Protestant ideas, every parish was ordered to obtain a copy of Cranmer's *Book of Homilies*, and *Paraphrases* by Erasmus.

In July an injunction was issued to the bishops ordering them to instruct their clergy to conduct services in English, and to preach a sermon every Sunday. Furthermore, the bishops were to create libraries of Protestant literature and provide an English Bible for each parish, and to encourage the laity to read these books. Finally, the bishops were told to remove all superstitious statues and images from their churches.

These modest moves towards religious reform did not satisfy the more vocal Protestant activists. The amount of anti-Catholic protest was increased by the presence of Protestant exiles who had returned from the continent after the death of Henry VIII. The problem for the Privy Council was that, while it did not wish to introduce reforms too quickly for fear of provoking a Catholic backlash, it was anxious not to prevent religious debate by taking

Key question
Why did the Privy Council introduce some moderate Protestant reforms?

Key term

Diocese
A district under the pastoral care of a bishop.

repressive measures. As a result, the Henrician treason, heresy and censorship laws were not enforced and a vigorous debate over religion developed.

Radical reformers

The more radical reformers launched a strong attack through a pamphlet campaign on both the Catholic Church and the bishops, who were accused of being self-seeking royal servants and not true pastors. Other pamphlets attacked the wealth of the Church, superstitious rituals, and in particular the Eucharist. However, there was no agreement among the protesters about the form of Protestant doctrine that should be adopted. With the government refusing to take any firm lead there was growing frustration, and some of the more radical protesters took matters into their own hands.

In London, East Anglia, Essex and Lincolnshire, where large numbers of Protestant refugees from the continent were settling, riots broke out. These frequently included outbreaks of iconoclasm, in which stained glass windows, statues and other superstitious images were destroyed. In some cases gold and silver candlesticks and other Church goods were seized and sold, with the money being donated to the poor. Such incidents were often provoked by extreme **millenarianists**, who wished to see a more equal society and a redistribution of wealth to the poor. Although the Privy Council was alarmed by the violence, it refused to take any action against the demonstrators. This inaction enraged the more conservative bishops. Bishop Bonner was particularly vehement in his protests to the government, and was imprisoned for two months.

Problems over reform

When Parliament and **Convocation** were summoned in November 1547, the question of religious reform was freely discussed. Both assemblies were in favour of reform, and Convocation agreed to re-introduce clerical marriage, although this was not approved by Parliament and so did not become law. Yet the Privy Council was still reluctant to make any decisive move towards religious reform. The reason for this was that the new regime still felt insecure, fearing that any major changes to doctrine might provoke even more unrest and possibly lead to the fall of the government.

The two major pieces of legislation, the Chantries Act and the Treason Act, did little to resolve the doctrinal uncertainties:

- *The Chantries Act.* The main purpose of the Act was to raise money to continue the war with France and Scotland; the reason given was that the chantries were centres of superstition.
- *The Treason Act.* The Act repealed the Henrician treason, heresy and censorship laws (see page 47). This measure increased the freedom with which the Protestant activists could discuss and demand radical doctrinal reforms. The immediate result was a renewed spate of pamphlets demanding that the Bible should be recognised as the only true authority for religious belief.

Key terms

Millenarianists
Radical thinkers who believed in social reform whereby a kingdom's wealth would be distributed equally to all citizens.

Convocation
An assembly of clergy that resembled Parliament in that it was divided into two houses: the upper house of senior clergy and a lower house of ordinary clergy. Convocation discussed church matters, passed Church laws and regulated the way the Church was run.

Key question
Why was there indecision and confusion over religious reform?

English translations of the writings of Luther and Calvin were being widely circulated.

In January 1548 the Privy Council issued a series of proclamations to try to calm the situation. However, the proclamations indicated no clear policy, and so only added to the confusion. Justices of the Peace and churchwardens were ordered to enforce the existing doctrines of the Church of England, including transubstantiation. On the other hand, instructions were issued to speed up the removal of Catholic images from churches. Such contradictions infuriated both reformers and conservatives alike. Finally, in September, the Council forbade all public preaching in the hope of stifling debate.

Key question
Why was there a more positive move towards religious reform after 1548?

Moves towards introducing Protestant doctrine

When Parliament re-assembled in November 1548, Somerset and the Council were in a stronger position after the successful campaign in Scotland (see page 78). For this reason they felt secure enough to take a more positive approach to religious reform. Their objective was to end the uncertainty over religious doctrine. It was hoped that the new law, known as the First Edwardian Act of Uniformity, passed in January 1549, would achieve this.

Protestant practices

The Act officially ordered all the clergy of England and Wales to use a number of Protestant practices which had been allowed, but not enforced, during the two previous years:

- Holy communion, matins and evensong were to be conducted in English.
- The sacraments were now defined as communion, baptism, confirmation, marriage and burial.
- Cranmer adapted the old communion service by adding new prayers, so that the clergy and the laity could take both the sacramental bread and the wine.
- Permission was given once again for the clergy to marry.
- Many of the traditional Catholic rituals, which the Protestant reformers considered to be superstitious, disappeared. The practice of singing masses for the souls of the dead was no longer approved.

Catholic practices

- There was still no really clear statement on the existence, or otherwise, of purgatory.
- Any form of the worship of saints, although not banned, was to be discouraged, while the removal of statues, paintings and other images was encouraged.
- Cranmer's Book of Common Prayer was a mixture of Lutheran and Catholic beliefs.
- Fast days were still to be enforced and no change was to be made in the number of Holy Days.

- The new communion service followed the order of the old Latin mass, and the officiating clergy were expected to continue to wear the traditional robes and vestments.
- Most importantly, no change was made to the doctrine of the Eucharist, which was still defined in the Catholic terms of transubstantiation. This was a fundamental point that angered many of the more radical reformers, who continued to urge the government to adopt a more Protestant definition of the sacrament of communion.

The Privy Council hoped that these cautious measures would satisfy the majority of moderate reformers, without outraging the Catholic conservatives. Although any clergy who refused to use the new service were to be liable to fines and imprisonment, no penalties were to be imposed on the laity for non-attendance. This can be interpreted as a hope by the Privy Council that they could coerce the more recalcitrant minority among the parish clergy, while not antagonising the undecided majority among the laity.

The government decided to continue with its policy of educating the laity in Protestant ideas which it had introduced in July 1547. Bishops were instructed to carry out visitations to encourage the adoption of the new services, and to test whether parishioners could recite the Lord's Prayer and the Ten Commandments in English. The effectiveness of either the legislation or the education programme depended on whether the bishops and ruling élites would enforce them. There was opposition in Cornwall, Devon, Dorset and Yorkshire. However, most of the country seems to have followed the lead of the aristocracy and gentry in accepting moderate Protestantism.

Summary diagram: The Church under Somerset

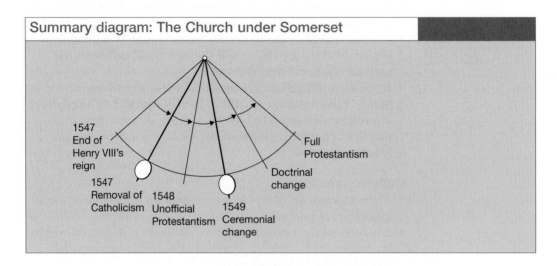

Key question
How Protestant had the Edwardian Church become under Northumberland?

3 | The Edwardian Church under Northumberland 1550–3

When Northumberland gained power in 1550 religious reform became more radical. This might suggest that the government thought there was no widespread opposition to religious change, or that they believed the recent suppression of the popular uprisings (see pages 130–6) was sufficient to prevent any further unrest. Possibly, as is thought by many historians, the changes came about because of the political in-fighting in the Privy Council that led to Somerset's fall from power. What is certain is that by 1553 the Church of England had become Protestant.

Struggle over doctrine

Key question
Why was there a doctrinal power struggle between 1550 and 1553?

After the arrest of Somerset in October 1549 it appeared that the conservative faction supported by Northumberland might seize power. They planned, with the help of Charles V, to make Princess Mary regent for the young Edward VI. However, neither Charles V nor Mary supported the scheme which, in any case, would not have been practical in view of Edward VI's support for Protestantism. Meanwhile, Northumberland, having used the conservatives to strengthen his position on the Privy Council, then switched his allegiance to the more radical Protestant reformers. This political struggle within the Privy Council continued when Parliament met in November. Attempts by the conservative faction to repeal the 1549 Act of Uniformity and strengthen the power of the bishops were defeated. In December Parliament approved measures to speed up the removal of popish images and old service books from the churches, and set up a commission to revise the procedures for the **ordination** of priests.

Key dates

The Second Book of Common Prayer introduced some Calvinistic doctrines: January 1552

Second Act of Uniformity: April 1552

By February 1550 Northumberland was firmly in control of the Privy Council, and the conservatives were driven out of office (see pages 52–3). To strengthen his position still further and to prevent a possible conservative backlash, Northumberland moved against the more conservative of the bishops.

Key term

Ordination
Ceremony in which holy orders were conferred on priests, enabling them to serve in parishes.

- Gardiner, the most able of the pro-Catholics, was already imprisoned in the Tower of London. In July he was ordered by the Privy Council to agree to the doctrines of the Church of England. He refused, and was sentenced to stricter terms of confinement.
- Bishop Bonner of London, already imprisoned by Somerset, was retried and deprived of his diocese. He was replaced by Ridley, then Bishop of Rochester, who was an enthusiastic reformer.

During the next year active reformers were appointed as bishops of Rochester, Chichester, Norwich, Exeter and Durham. These changes cleared the way for more sweeping religious reforms. The Catholic laity and clergy, deprived of their main spiritual leaders, offered little opposition, although some pro-Catholic pamphlets were circulated.

In view of his reconversion to Catholicism before his execution in 1553, many historians do not think it likely that Northumberland was a genuine religious reformer. Other historians feel that his support for such a Protestant enthusiast as John Hooper as opposed to the more moderate Cranmer and Nicholas Ridley, the newly appointed Bishop of London, in the doctrinal dispute during the autumn of 1550 (see page 101) does show that he was interested in religious reform. This is a question that, without fresh evidence, is unlikely to be resolved. Certainly the first moves towards introducing more radical Protestantism seem to have arisen from the political expediencies following Somerset's fall from power.

More extreme Protestantism

The first move to introduce more radical Protestantism was initiated by Ridley in London, where he ordered all altars to be removed and replaced by communion tables in line with the teachings of the Calvinists and other reformed Churches. In other dioceses the destruction of altars proceeded unevenly, and depended on the attitudes of the local ruling élites and clergy. At the same time the Parliamentary Commission's proposals to change the form of the ordination of priests were introduced, and instructions were issued to enforce the first Act of Uniformity (see page 95).

Key question
Why was there a swing towards radical Protestantism?

The new form of ordination, which was basically Lutheran, soon caused controversy. The major change – which empowered priests to administer the sacraments and preach the gospel instead of offering 'sacrifice and [the celebration of] mass both for the living and the dead' – satisfied moderate reformers. It removed the supposedly superstitious references to sacrifice, Purgatory and prayers for the souls of the dead. However, it did not please some of the more extreme reformers, especially because it made no attempt to remove any of the 16 ceremonial vestments, such as the mitre, cope, tippet or stole, normally worn by bishops and priests while conducting services. These were regarded as superstitious by many of the reformed Churches, whose clergy wore plain surplices.

John Hooper, who had been invited to become Bishop of Gloucester, complained that the form of ordination was still too Catholic and started a fierce dispute with Ridley over the question of vestments. As a result he refused the offered bishopric, and in July he began a campaign of preaching against the new proposals. At first it appeared that Northumberland was sympathetic and supported Hooper, but in October he was ordered to stop preaching, and in January 1551 he was imprisoned for failing to comply. Finally he was persuaded to compromise and was made Bishop of Gloucester, where he introduced a vigorous policy of education and reform. But he complained that both laity and clergy were slow to respond.

Measures to make the Church of England fully Protestant

During 1551 Northumberland strengthened his position. This cleared the way for a major overhaul of the Church of England. Cranmer was in the process of revising his Prayer Book, to remove the many ambiguities that had caused criticism. Further action was taken against the remaining conservative bishops. Gardiner was finally deprived of the diocese of Winchester in February, and in October reformers were appointed at Worcester and Chichester. These moves ensured that there would be a majority among the bishops to support the programme of religious changes that was being prepared.

Doctrinal changes

Parliament was assembled in January 1552 and the government embarked on a comprehensive programme of reform. In order to strengthen the power of the Church of England to enforce doctrinal uniformity, a new Treason Act was passed. This made it an offence to question the royal supremacy or any of the articles of faith of the English Church. At the same time, uncertainties over the number of Holy Days to be recognised were ended by officially limiting them to 25.

In March the second Act of Uniformity was passed. Under the new Act it became an offence for both clergy and laity not to attend Church of England services, and offenders were to be fined and imprisoned. Cranmer's new Book of Common Prayer became the official basis for church services, and had to be used by both clergy and laity. The new prayer book was based upon the scriptures, and all traces of Catholicism and the mass had been removed. The Eucharist was clearly defined in terms of consubstantiation (see pages 93 and 94), although there are some suggestions that Cranmer was moving towards a more **Zwinglian** or Calvinistic definition of the Eucharist as commemorative of Christ's sacrifice or the Last Supper.

Extreme reformers did not approve of the new service because communicants were still expected to kneel, and this was considered to be idolatrous. Some historians attribute such objections to the Calvinism of Hooper and another extreme reformer, John Knox, the leader of Scottish Protestantism. It is also suggested that the influence of Hooper and Knox was behind the instructions sent to bishops to speed up the replacement of altars by communion tables, and to stop their clergy from wearing vestments when conducting services.

Further attacks on the wealth of the Church

While these measures were being introduced, the government began a further attack on Church wealth. In 1552 a survey of the **temporal wealth** of the bishops and all clergy with parishes worth more than £350 a year was undertaken. The resultant report estimated that these lands had a capital value of £1,087,000, and steps were taken to transfer some of this property to the Crown.

Key terms

Zwinglian
Term used to describe the influence of Huldrych Zwingli, a Protestant religious reformer from Switzerland, who believed that local religious communities should have the right to control their own affairs without interference from either the Church authorities or State officials.

Temporal wealth
Church wealth that is calculated in land, property and goods.

The bishopric of Durham provides a typical example of this secularisation. Bishop Tunstall of Durham was arrested in October 1552 and imprisoned in the Tower of London. It was then proposed that his diocese should be divided into two parts. Durham itself was to be allocated £1320 annually, and a new diocese of Newcastle was to be given an annual income of £665. This left an annual surplus of £2000 from the income of the original diocese, which was to be transferred to the Crown. In the event, this proposal did not came into effect because of the death of Edward VI.

At the same time, commissioners had been sent out to draw up inventories and to begin the removal of all the gold and silver plate still held by parish churches, and to list any items illegally removed since 1547. The commissioners had only just begun their work of confiscation when the king died and the operation was brought to an end, but not before some churches had lost their medieval plate (see page 93).

Historical opinion
- Some historians have seen the attack on Church wealth as yet another example of the greed of Northumberland.
- Others maintain that it was necessary if the Church of England was to be thoroughly reformed.
- Recently these actions have been interpreted as an expedient to improve royal finances after the bankruptcy resulting from the wars against France and Scotland.
- To Marxist historians it is clear evidence of the growing commercialism of the aristocracy and gentry, who were pressurising the government for a further redistribution of ecclesiastical wealth.
- Yet another explanation is that it was a political move to strengthen the control of the Church by the State.

Without fresh evidence and research it is difficult to decide which one, or whichever combination of these explanations, is nearer the truth.

Assessment of the Edwardian Church
What is certain is that the death of Edward VI and the fall of Northumberland brought this part of the English Reformation to an abrupt end. The **Forty-two Articles** which had been drawn up to list the doctrines of the new Protestant Church of England never became law. It is generally agreed that by 1553 the Edwardian Reformation had resulted in a Church of England that was thoroughly Protestant. There is less agreement over whether its doctrines were basically Lutheran, or to what extent they were influenced by Zwinglian or Calvinist ideas.

However, it is clear that, although the doctrines of the Church of England had been revolutionised, the administrative structure of the Church had remained unchanged. There is equal agreement that there is insufficient evidence at present to decide whether the people of England had wholeheartedly embraced the

Key question
How Protestant was the Edwardian Church by the time of Edward VI's death in 1553?

Forty-two Articles
A list of essential doctrines drawn up by Cranmer and intended to form the basis of the new Protestant Church of England.

Key term

Profile: Thomas Cranmer 1489–1556

1489	– Born in Nottinghamshire, the younger son of a lesser gentry family
1520s	– Studied at Cambridge University where he joined the 'White Horse' group to discuss the new ideas coming from Europe, such as Lutheranism
1526	– Became a doctor of divinity
c1529	– Became chaplain to Thomas Boleyn, Earl of Wiltshire, father of Anne. Supported the case for Henry VIII's divorce
1530	– Appointed ambassador to Charles V (1530–3)
c1532	– Secretly married the niece of the Lutheran Church leader of Nuremberg in Germany
1533	– Chosen by Henry VIII to succeed William Warham as Archbishop of Canterbury
1533–4	– Presided over Henry VIII's divorce from Catherine of Aragon, promoted the marriage with Anne Boleyn and declared Henry VIII Head of the Church in England
1536	– Presided over Henry VIII's divorce from Anne Boleyn, promoted marriage with Jane Seymour
1536–8	– Worked with Cromwell in government and in turning England towards Protestantism, e.g. responsible for the 'Bishops' Book' of 1537
1539	– Unsuccessfully opposed the conservative Act of Six Articles. Forced to separate from his wife but refused to resign his offices
1540	– Took no part in the destruction of Cromwell
1541–7	– Became leader of reformist party at Court. Henry VIII's support enabled him to survive conservative attempts to destroy him
1547	– Took leading part in the Edwardian regime both in government and in the Church. Issued Protestant book of Homilies (see page 97)
1549	– Issued the blandly reformist First Book of Common Prayer
1552	– Issued the more extreme Second Book of Common Prayer
1553	– Stripped of his title as Archbishop of Canterbury
1554	– Arrested and imprisoned for heresy
1556	– Burned at the stake for withdrawing an earlier promise to accept some key Catholic doctrines

Arguably, Cranmer played a greater role than any other single Churchman in establishing and shaping the Church of England. He was fiercely loyal to the Crown and he proved to be an able government minister and Churchman. His greatest strength lay in his refusal to support religious extremism; he was willing to accept gradual change in the Church, he advocated toleration and he preached against persecution.

Contemporary illustration showing Catholics being banished from England. Why did the government believe it necessary to exile some Catholics?

Protestant religion. Research at a local level has so far provided conflicting evidence. Although a majority of the landed élites and those in government circles seemed to favour moderate Protestantism, only a few of them found it impossible to conform under Mary I.

Many of the lower clergy and a majority of the population seem to have been largely indifferent to the religious debate. Only in London and the surrounding counties does there appear to have been any widespread enthusiasm for the Protestant religion. A study of the county of Essex indicates more enthusiasm among the authorities in enforcing Protestantism than among the general public in accepting it. Earlier interpretations which indicated wild enthusiasm for either Protestantism or Catholicism are now treated with caution. It is considered that Protestantism, if not widely opposed, received only lukewarm acceptance.

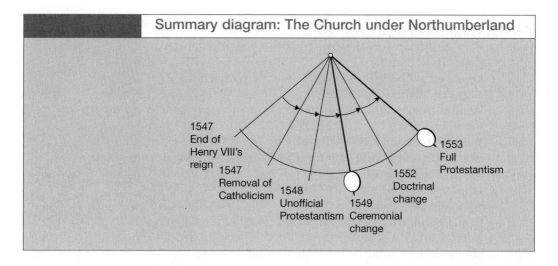

Summary diagram: The Church under Northumberland

1547
End of
Henry VIII's
reign

1547
Removal of
Catholicism

1548
Unofficial
Protestantism

1549
Ceremonial
change

1552
Doctrinal
change

1553
Full
Protestantism

Key question
How and with what
success did Mary
restore Roman
Catholicism to
England and Wales?

4 | The Marian Church 1553–8

While it is difficult to assess Northumberland's religious views,
there is no doubt about those of Mary I. Some historians have
described Mary as courageous, gentle and sympathetic. Others
see her as being proud, arrogant and stupid. These views have
not been greatly altered by recent research. However, it is agreed
that she was passionately attached to the Roman Catholic
religion.

The religious situation in 1553

In 1553 few in England doubted that Mary, after her 20 years of
resistance to the royal supremacy for the sake of her religion,
would restore Roman Catholicism. It was just as much Edward
VI's wish to preserve Protestantism, as Northumberland's
personal ambition, that led to the attempt to exclude Mary from
the throne. Mary and her Catholic supporters saw the failure of
the scheme as a miracle, and she was determined to restore
England to the authority of Rome as quickly as possible. What
Mary failed to realise was that her initial popularity sprang, not
from a desire for a return to the Roman Catholic Church, but
from a dislike of Northumberland, and respect for the legitimate
succession.

Her main supporters in England and abroad urged caution.
Both Charles V and Pope Julius III warned her not to risk her
throne by acting too rashly. Cardinal Reginald Pole, appointed as
Papal Legate to restore England to the authority of Rome, stayed
in the Netherlands for a year before coming to England. Whether
this was because Charles V refused to allow the Cardinal to leave
until the planned marriage between Philip and Mary had come to
fruition, or whether it reflected Pole's natural caution about
returning to his native land and a possibly hostile reception, is
difficult to decide. Even Gardiner, Mary's most trusted English
adviser, who had consistently resisted reform, was unenthusiastic
about returning to papal authority.

Key dates

Catholic Mass
re-introduced:
September 1553

Cardinal Pole returned
to England as Papal
Legate. England and
Rome reconciled:
November 1554

Profile: Reginald Pole 1500–58

1500 – Born a younger son of Sir Richard Pole and Margaret, Countess of Salisbury

1515 – Educated at Oxford University where he received his degree in divinity

1521 – Went to study on the continent (1521–7)

1527 – Became Dean of Exeter Cathedral

1529 – Went to study in Paris (1529–30)

1530 – Became Dean of Windsor but refused the king's offer of the Archbishopric of York

1531 – Opposed the king's divorce policy

1532 – Went abroad to study

1536 – Criticised in print Henry VIII's supremacy of the Church in England

1537 – Summoned to Rome by the Pope who made him a cardinal and papal legate to England

1538 – A furious Henry VIII had his mother and brother arrested and charged with treason. Brother executed

1541 – His 68-year-old mother was executed

1547 – Failed to persuade Somerset to return England to Roman Church

1549 – Narrowly failed to get elected Pope

1554 – Returned to England as Papal Legate and helped to restore the Church to Rome

1555 – Succeeded Cranmer as Archbishop of Canterbury

1558 – Died on the same day as Mary I

Pole was a dedicated Catholic who risked his life, and the lives of his family, to oppose Henry VIII's break with Rome. He spent most of his life abroad and was out of touch with the feelings and attitudes of his compatriots when he returned in 1554. His impact on English religious thinking was limited and he failed to turn the clock back to the 1520s. The restoration of the Pope as head of the English Church lasted for only three years and did not survive Pole's death. His greatest achievement was to maintain an English presence at the Papal Court.

Mary failed to appreciate the political implications of restoring Roman Catholicism to England. A return to papal authority would mean an end to the royal supremacy, which was strongly supported by the ruling and landed élites. Even the most ardent of the leading conservatives had been firm in their allegiance to the Crown and the Tudor State. It is agreed that the major causes of Mary's widespread unpopularity by the end of her reign, apart from the religious persecution, were the return to papal authority and the Spanish marriage. Many regarded this as interference by foreigners and an affront to English nationalism.

Key question
How successful was Mary's planned return to the Anglo-Catholicism of her father's reign?

Key term

Royal prerogative
Certain rights held by the monarchy enabling it power to make proclamations, enforce the royal will, suspend or repeal Acts of Parliament.

The restoration of Anglo-Catholicism

However, in 1553 there was no doubt about Mary's popularity and the élites rallied to her support. The aristocracy and gentry were initially prepared to conform to Mary's religious views, and the bulk of the population followed their example. But some 800 strongly committed Protestant gentry, clergy and members of the middle orders left the country and spent the remainder of the reign on the continent. Such an escape was less easy for the lower orders, and most of the 274 Protestants executed during Mary's reign came from this group. At the beginning of the reign even the most zealous of the urban radicals were not prepared to go against the mainstream of public opinion, and waited to see what would happen. Certainly, when Mary, using the **royal prerogative**, suspended the second Act of Uniformity and restored the mass, there was no public outcry.

Parliament

This lack of religious opposition was apparent when Parliament met in October 1553. Admittedly, the arrest and imprisonment of Cranmer, Hooper and Ridley, along with other leading Protestant bishops, removed the major source of opposition in the House of Lords. After a lively, but not hostile debate, the first step towards removing all traces of Protestantism from the Church of England was achieved with the passing of the first Statute of Repeal. This Act swept away all the religious legislation approved by Parliament during the reign of Edward VI, and the doctrine of the Church of England was restored to what it had been in 1547 under the Act of the Six Articles (see page 45).

Although Mary had succeeded in re-establishing the Anglo-Catholicism of her father, her advisers had managed to persuade her into some caution. There had been no attempt to question the royal supremacy, or to discuss the issue of the Church lands which had been sold to the laity. Both of these issues were likely to provoke a more heated debate.

Marriage to Philip II

Opposition to Mary's proposed marriage to Philip II of Spain and the consequent rebellion (see pages 138–41) meant that further religious legislation was postponed until the spring of 1554. Gardiner, anxious to regain royal favour after his opposition to Mary's marriage (see page 60), tried to quicken the pace at which Protestantism was removed by persuading Parliament to pass a bill to re-introduce the heresy laws (see page 46). He was successfully opposed by Paget, who feared that such a measure might provoke further disorder.

The Protestant clergy

Thwarted, Gardiner proceeded to turn his attention to Protestant clergy. The Bishops of Gloucester, Hereford, Lincoln, Rochester and the Archbishop of York were stripped of their offices, and were replaced by committed Catholics. In March 1554 the bishops were instructed to enforce all the religious legislation of the last year of Henry VIII's reign. Apart from ensuring a return to 'the old order of the Church, in the Latin tongue', these injunctions demanded that all married clergy should give up their wives and families, or lose their livings. The authorities largely complied with these instructions, and some 800 parish clergy were so deprived. Although some fled abroad, such as Richard Davies, vicar of Burnham in Buckinghamshire, the majority were found employment elsewhere in the country.

Return to the Church of Rome

Cardinal Pole's return to England in November 1554 marked the next decisive stage in the restoration of Roman Catholicism. Parliament met in the same month and passed the second Act of Repeal. This Act ended the royal supremacy, and returned England to papal authority by repealing all the religious legislation of the reign of Henry VIII back to the time of the break with Rome. However, to achieve this Mary had to come to a compromise with the landed élites. Careful provision was made in the Act to protect the property rights of all those who had bought Church land since 1536. This demonstrates that Mary had to recognise the authority of Parliament over matters of religion. It meant that she had to forgo her plans for a full-scale restoration of the monasteries. Instead she had to be content with merely returning the monastic lands, worth £60,000 a year, still held by the Crown.

Key question
How did Mary restore Roman Catholicism to England and Wales?

Religious persecution

At the same time, Parliament approved the restoration of the old heresy laws. This was the beginning of religious persecution:

- The first Protestant was burned at the stake for heresy on 4 February 1555, and Hooper suffered a similar fate five days later in his own city of Gloucester.
- In October, Ridley and Hugh Latimer, the former Bishop of Worcester, were executed at Oxford, where they were followed by Cranmer in March 1556.

Key dates

Re-introduction of the heresy laws: December 1554

Bishops Ridley and Latimer burned at the stake: October 1555

Archbishop Cranmer burned at the stake: March 1556

The death of Gardiner in November 1555 had removed a trusted and restraining influence, and thereafter the regime became more repressive. Although Gardiner had started the persecution on the grounds that some executions would frighten the Protestant extremists into submission, he was too astute a politician to fail to see that the policy was not working. Far from cowing the Protestants, he realised that the executions were hardening the opposition to Mary and encouraging the colonies of English exiles on the continent. He counselled caution, but his advice was ignored.

After his death, Mary, and Pole, who had been made Archbishop of Canterbury in December 1555, felt that it was their sacred duty to stamp out heresy, and stepped up the level of persecution. It is now estimated that the 274 religious executions carried out during the final three years of Mary's reign exceeded the number recorded in any Catholic country on the continent

The martyrdom of Cranmer and the burning of bishops Ridley and Latimer (1556), from John Fox's *Book of Martyrs* (published in 1563). How are Cranmer, Ridley and Latimer depicted in the illustration? In your opinion was Fox a Catholic or a Protestant author?

over the same period. This undermines the claim by some historians that the Marian regime was more moderate than those on the continent.

Popular reactions against religious persecution

Gardiner's unheeded warnings were soon justified, and Mary's popularity waned rapidly. There was widespread revulsion in the south-east of England at the persecution, and to many people Catholicism became firmly linked with dislike of Rome and Spain. Many local authorities either ignored, or tried to avoid enforcing, the unpopular legislation.

The number of people fleeing abroad increased, reinforcing the groups of English exiles living in centres of Lutheranism and Calvinism on the continent. They became the nucleus of an active and well-informed opposition, which began to flood England with anti-Catholic books and pamphlets. The effectiveness of this campaign is shown in the proclamations issued by the Privy Council in 1558, ordering the death penalty by martial law for anyone found with heretical or seditious literature. If before 1555 the English people were generally undecided about religion, the Marian repression succeeded in creating a core of highly committed English Protestants.

Attempts to consolidate the Marian Church

Restoring stability

Although Pole actively tried to eradicate Protestantism, his first priority appears to have been to restore stability after 20 years of

Key question
How successful were the measures to strengthen the Marian Church and eradicate Protestantism?

religious turmoil. It is widely considered that, in view of his lack of administrative experience and ability, such a formal and legalistic approach was a mistake. The reduction in Church revenues meant that there were insufficient resources available to reorganise the Marian Church effectively. Indeed, a great part of Pole's three years in office were spent in the virtually hopeless task of trying to restore the Church of England's financial position.

Reconciliation with Rome

Pole's attempts to reorganise and reconcile the Church of England to Rome were not helped by the death of Pope Julius III in 1555. The new Pope, Paul IV, disliked Pole and hated the Spanish Habsburgs. He stripped Pole of his title of Legate and ordered him to return to Rome. Pole refused to comply, and continued his work in England as Archbishop of Canterbury, but the papacy would not recognise his authority. This further hindered his work because he could not appoint bishops, and by 1558 seven sees were vacant. Such quarrels, and the blatant papal intervention in English affairs, did little to convince anyone except the most zealous Catholics of the wisdom of returning to the authority of Rome.

Certainly, such events did not help the government in its task of winning the hearts and minds of English men and women to the Roman Catholic faith. Pole's hopes that, while he struggled with his administrative tasks, the re-establishment of the old religion would lead to wholehearted acceptance of Roman Catholicism were not to be realised.

Pole was fully in favour of the educational programme which was being adopted on the continent. He appointed capable and active bishops, all of whom subsequently refused to serve in the Elizabethan Protestant Church of England.

The Twelve Decrees

In 1555 the **Westminster Synod** approved the passing of the **Twelve Decrees** that included the establishment of **seminaries** in every diocese for the training of priests, but shortage of money limited the programme to a single creation at York. This meant that the majority of the parish clergy remained too uneducated, and lacking in evangelical zeal, for the new laws to have any immediate impact on the laity. Mary's death in November 1558 came too soon for Catholic reform to have had any lasting effect. That is not to say that if Mary had lived longer, Catholicism would not have gained wider support. But the fact remains that only a significant minority clung to their faith after the establishment of the Elizabethan Church.

Key terms

Westminster Synod
Also known as the London Synod, this was a meeting of the important clergy under Cardinal Pole who wished to consolidate and promote Roman Catholicism in the kingdom and to plan the future of the Church.

Twelve Decrees
The key 12 points drawn up by Pole at the Westminster Synod. They included the need for every parish priest to be properly trained, educated and permanently resident. To help the hard-pressed clergy, Pole commissioned a newly edited Catholic New Testament and a new book of Homilies to replace Cranmer's Protestant edition. However, they were never used.

Seminaries
Religious institutions of learning designed to educate and train priests.

Key question
How Catholic was the Marian Church by the time of Mary I's death in 1558?

Assessment of the Church of England in 1558

It is just as difficult to assess the state of religion in England in 1558 as it is to measure the advance of Protestantism by 1553. It is impossible to decide whether the bulk of the population was Protestant or Catholic. While it is easy to trace the changing pattern of official doctrine in the Church of England through the acts and statutes passed in Parliament, what the general public thought about religion is difficult to determine. At present the consensus among historians is that the ruling élites accepted the principle of the royal supremacy, and were prepared to conform to whichever form of religion was favoured by the monarch.

Although the lower orders are generally considered to have had a conservative affection for the traditional forms of worship, it is thought that they were prepared to follow the lead of the local élites. Whether the religious legislation passed in Parliament was put into effect very much depended on the attitudes of the local élites, and to a lesser extent those of the parish authorities.

For this reason detailed research into parish and county communities is being undertaken in the hope of revealing the religious attitudes among the laity. Such research uses the evidence of wills, parish registers, churchwardens' accounts and court records to delve into local religious attitudes. Although such sources can be helpful, they are often difficult to use.

Case study: The churchwarden's accounts for the parish of Stanford in the Vale

The following extract illustrates some of these problems.

1552	Item.	in expences at Abingdon [a neighbouring town] going before the kings Comissioners about our church's goods.
	Item.	paid for a book of common prayer in English in the time of schism.
1553	Item.	in expences at Abingdon when the Church goods were carried to King Edward's comissioners.
	Item.	to the mason for setting up the high altar.
1554	Item.	to Henry Snodnam gent for a table with a frame which served in the church for the communion in the wicked time of schism.
	Item.	to Edythe Whayne for mending copes and vestments.
1556	Item.	in expences to Abingdon of my lord Cardinal Pole's visitation.
	Item.	in expences to Abingdon to buy images.
	Item.	for writing a bill to answer certain Articles of Religion proposed by my lord Cardinal Pole to certain of the clergy and the Justices of the Peace to discuss.

These accounts show quite clearly that religious legislation was being enforced in the parish, but the problem is to decide what this reveals about the attitudes of the local people. It might be assumed that, because the parish had complied with generally unpopular pieces of legislation for setting up communion tables and surrendering church plate, the parishioners were in favour of Protestantism. On the other hand, the speed with which the high altar was replaced in 1553 and the reference to Edward VI's reign as the wicked time of schism, might equally be interpreted as showing an attachment to Catholicism. In any case the record of religious changes might merely indicate that the local authorities were conforming to government policy, and show nothing about popular attitudes.

Death of Mary and Cardinal Pole: November 1558

Act of Supremacy restored Henrician anti-papal laws: May 1559

Key dates

Selected local case studies

This is very much the difficulty encountered in local studies. For example:

- Lancashire élites are shown to have actively resisted the introduction of reformed religion.
- In Essex, Protestantism is seen to have been enthusiastically enforced.

In neither case is much revealed about the views of the general public. Nor are historians confident that the findings for one county are typical for the surrounding region, far less for the whole country.

One recent study, based on Devon and Cornwall, does seem to have succeeded in finding out more about popular attitudes. This is an area where, because of the Western Rebellion of 1549 (see pages 130–3), historians expected to find strong religious conservatism. However, the study, while revealing no zeal for Protestantism, uncovered equally little enthusiasm for Catholicism. Indeed, by 1558 passivity and indifference seem to have replaced religious fervour in the West Country.

Religious indecision

In general, it appears that by 1558 the majority of people in England were still undecided about religion. Among the élites there was strong support for the royal supremacy, but they were willing to follow the religion of the legitimate monarch. The mass of the population do not appear to have had strongly formalised convictions, and in most cases they were prepared to follow the lead of their social superiors. Although there were small minorities of committed Protestants and Catholics, neither religion seems to have had a strong hold in England when Mary I died. When Elizabeth I came to the throne the country was willing to return to a form of moderate Protestantism. However, during her reign deeper religious divisions began to appear, and the unity of the Church of England came to an end.

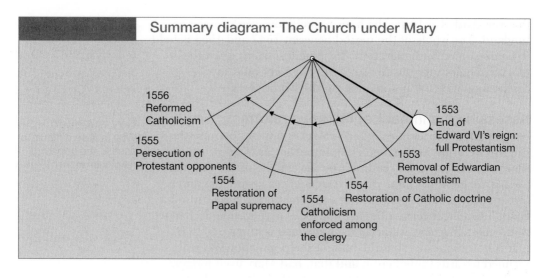

Summary diagram: The Church under Mary

1556 Reformed Catholicism

1555 Persecution of Protestant opponents

1554 Restoration of Papal supremacy

1554 Catholicism enforced among the clergy

1554 Restoration of Catholic doctrine

1553 Removal of Edwardian Protestantism

1553 End of Edward VI's reign: full Protestantism

5 | The Key Debate

How have historians' views of mid-Tudor religious attitudes changed?

Views among historians about the significance of religion in mid-Tudor England have changed during recent years. It is now felt that there was a much greater degree of religious compromise in England than on the continent, and that, as a result, religion itself was not a cause of crisis. However, religion is regarded as having a considerable influence on the political, social and economic changes that were taking place at the time. Consequently, religion can be seen as contributing directly, or indirectly, to potential crises, such as in the Western Rebellion of 1549 (see pages 130–3), or in the attempt by Northumberland to stop Mary Tudor succeeding to the throne in 1553 (see pages 136–7).

In the past, historians such as W.K. Jordan saw the Edwardian Reformation as a period of remarkable toleration during which reformed religion became firmly established in the country. They considered it to have been followed by five years of Catholic repression and persecution, which failed to stamp out English Protestantism. Such views are no longer widely held. Historians such as Christopher Haigh increasingly doubt whether Protestantism had taken much of a hold in England by 1553. Indeed, it is now suggested by historians such as David Loades that Catholicism had wide popular support among the lower orders in both the towns and the countryside.

However, some historians such as Penry Williams think that there was much less animosity between English Catholics and Protestants than was previously believed. It is true that there were extremists on both sides, just as there were individuals prepared to die for their faith. However, the vast majority of people are seen as being very moderate in their outlook, and prepared to accept whatever doctrine was held by the ruling regime. It is this that is regarded as being the basis for religious compromise in England. The whole of the period between 1547 and 1553 is held to be one of marked toleration. To some historians, even the Marian religious repression is regarded as very mild in comparison with the persecution on the continent.

Assessing the impact of religious reform

Assessing the impact of religious reform is difficult because the English Reformation was too close for either its long- or even short-term effects to be really felt by the middle of the century. Clearly religion had immediate consequences for politics and foreign policy, but in neither case can it be said to have caused a crisis. The longer term influences of social and economic change were only to become apparent over the next century.

It is now suggested that the bulk of the population was still inclined towards Catholicism, and that, had Mary lived longer, England would have remained Roman Catholic. Certainly there was religious compromise among the élites, and apathy, or even indifference, among the mass of the population towards religious change between 1547 and 1558. Zealous Catholics or Protestants were a small minority, and most people were prepared to tolerate the sudden switches of religious policy that occurred in the middle of the century. It seems likely that most people were content to follow the religion of their legitimate ruler.

It is difficult to decide whether the religious uprising in the West Country was atypical. Possibly the western rebels, like their Norfolk counterparts, were indulging in nostalgia, and protesting for what they saw as better times in the past. Certainly the majority of the people of England were ready to accept the return of Protestantism under Elizabeth I.

Key question
Why is it so difficult to assess the impact of religious reform?

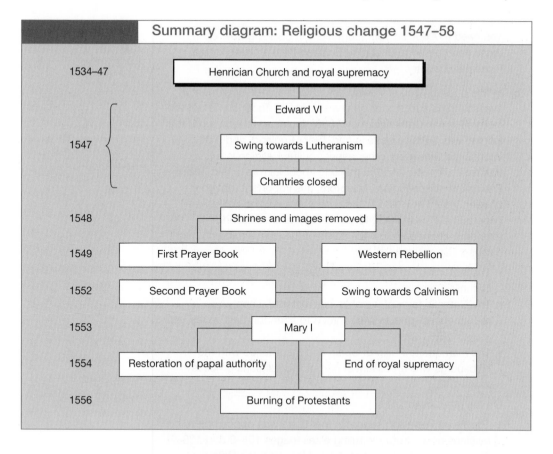

Summary diagram: Religious change 1547–58

1534–47 — Henrician Church and royal supremacy

1547 — Edward VI — Swing towards Lutheranism — Chantries closed

1548 — Shrines and images removed

1549 — First Prayer Book — Western Rebellion

1552 — Second Prayer Book — Swing towards Calvinism

1553 — Mary I

1554 — Restoration of papal authority — End of royal supremacy

1556 — Burning of Protestants

Study Guide: AS Questions

In the style of OCR

(a) To what extent had the Church in England become Protestant by 1549?

(b) How successful was Mary Tudor in her attempt to restore Roman Catholicism to England by 1558?

Exam tips

The cross-references are intended to take you straight to the material that will help you to answer the questions.

(a) In question **(a)** you should make a comparison between the state of the Church in England in 1547 and in 1549, outlining the changes that had taken place, and then assessing to what degree the Church had become more Protestant. Your answer should be analytical and not simply a description of the changes that had taken place between 1547 and 1549. For example, you should analyse and discuss the following key points:

- the closure of chantries (pages 47 and 48)
- doctrinal change (pages 96–100)
- priests allowed to marry
- iconoclasm (pages 103–4)
- freedom of religious debate (pages 92–3).

You need to exercise your judgement in deciding how each of these contributed to changing England from a Catholic to a Protestant country.

(b) In this question you are being asked to use your judgement in assessing the success or otherwise of Mary Tudor's attempt to restore Roman Catholicism by 1558. You need to remember that religion was a major issue in mid-Tudor England, and that it interlocked with every other aspect of life. Religion is a controversial topic and the thinking about its role in mid-Tudor England is still changing. Therefore, it is important that your answer should help you to indicate where religion played an important part in politics, foreign policy, and social and economic change. Below are some of the issues that you might discuss. For example:

- The restoration of the Pope as head of an English Roman Catholic Church.
- The Catholic form of worship was restored, Latin was re-introduced, priests were forced to abandon their wives, etc. (pages 109–10).
- The marriage to Philip of Spain and the alliance with the Habsburgs was an essential part of this religious process (page 109).

On the other hand:

- The Wyatt Rebellion suggests that there was opposition to her religious policy from the ruling élites (pages 108–9 and 138–9).
- The persecution of heretics made Mary (and the Catholic Church) unpopular with certain sections of the population (page 111).
- What was the reaction of the general public: did most people really care about religion or did they just conform to the views of whoever was in power (pages 113–14)?
- If Mary had not died so young would England have remained permanently Roman Catholic?

Study guide: A2 Questions

In the style of AQA

'The success of the Reformation in the years 1540–1553 owed more to the state's desire to control the Church than to the attraction of Protestant ideas.'

> **Exam tips**
>
> *The cross-references are intended to take you straight to the material that will help you to answer the question.*
>
> In this question you are being asked to discuss how far the success of the Henrician and Edwardian Reformations was driven: (i) by 'Protestant ideas' or (ii) by a the government's desire for greater

political control of the church. The question is designed, in part, to test your knowledge of the '3 Cs' (causes, course and consequences), and your ability to apply your knowledge relevantly. Your answer should include a range of political, religious and economic factors. You should:

- Begin by giving a brief introduction to the way in which views about mid-Tudor religion are changing, and the way in which religion was becoming a political and diplomatic issue.
- Discuss the importance of the spread and influence of Protestant ideas; less important before 1547 than after 1547 (pages 97–8 and 102–4).
- Demonstrate the fact that Henry VIII was no Protestant and that for him control of an essentially Catholic Church was his main aim. On the other hand, the Edwardian regime was more committed to the Protestant faith but no less determined to control the Church.
- Discuss the financial implications and benefits of controlling the Church, e.g. dissolution of the chantries. Was greed a factor in the desire to control the Church (pages 47, 92 and 98)?

In the style of Edexcel

Source 1

From: G.R. Elton, Reform and Reformation, *published in 1977.*

It has become something of a commonplace to assert that Mary Tudor was the most attractive member of her family – kind, long-suffering, gentle, considerate. The evidence of her recorded words hardly bears this out; it shows her rather to have been arrogant, assertive, bigoted, stubborn, suspicious and rather stupid. She was ill prepared to be England's first woman sovereign. She had ever been her mother's daughter rather than her father's; devoid of political skill and unable to compromise. Her persistent attachment to the papal Church and religion made her exceptional even among those who watched the Reformation with misgivings and reluctance. Humanism had passed her by as much as had Protestantism. Thirty-seven years old in 1553, she seized a power rightfully hers for the exercise of which she was utterly unsuited.

Source 2

From: R. Lockyer and Dan O'Sullivan, Tudor Britain, 1485–1603, *published in 1997.*

On at least two important occasions Mary seems to have shown political skills of a high order. The first was when negotiating with Pope Julius III at the beginning of her reign over the terms of England's return to obedience to Rome. During the bargaining – which went on for over a year – Mary showed that she was quite prepared to stand up to papal pressure. The second occasion when Mary revealed political acumen was over her marriage negotiations. Whom to marry? Mary's choice fell on Philip, son of Charles V and heir to Spain and the Netherlands. From England's point of view this was a sensible match, as Spain was still regarded as England's natural ally against France. There was some anti-Spanish feeling among a minority of Mary's subjects, as Wyatt's rebellion demonstrated, and this is where Mary's political skills were called on. By stressing the weakness of her own position in the face of an overwhelmingly nationalistic Council and House of Commons, Mary was able to obtain astonishingly generous terms for the marriage from Charles.

Source 3

From: a letter from Mary to the members of Edward VI's Privy Council, 9 July 1553.

My lords, we greet you well and have received sure information that our dearest brother the King and late sovereign lord is departed to God. Wherefore, my lords, we require you and charge you, for that our allegiance which you owe God and us, that, for your honour and the surety of your persons, you employ your selves and forthwith upon receipt [of this letter] cause our right and title to the Crown and government of this Realm to be proclaimed in our City of London and such other places as to your wisdoms shall seem good. And this letter signed with our hands shall be your sufficient warrant.

Source 4

From: a despatch from Simon Renard, ambassador to the Emperor Charles V, 1554.

She spoke to the people, and said that the objects she had in view since coming to the throne were to administer justice, keep order and protect the people's peace and tranquility. The rebel, Wyatt, had taken up arms under the pretext that she had married his Highness [Philip], but his reply showed clearly that he aimed at the Crown and meant to tyrannise and molest the people. So elegant and eloquent was her speech, that all the people cried out loudly that they would live and die in her service, and that Wyatt was a traitor; and they all threw up their caps to show their goodwill.

Source 5

From: a verse written by Sir Nicholas Throckmorton recalling the accession of Mary Tudor, 1556.

And though I liked not the religion
Which all her life Queen Mary had professed,
Yet in my mind that wicked notion
Right heirs for to displace, I did detest.

Source 6

From: David Loades, Mary Tudor, *published in 1989.*

Twelve months, almost to the day, since Mary had been proclaimed in London, and in spite of all the problems and alarms, it had been a year of extraordinary success. She had restored most of the traditional ecclesiastical order, removed the protestant bishops and married clergy, and replaced them (for the most part) with good catholics. She had survived a fairly serious rebellion and outfaced French threats of war.

(a) Using your own knowledge and the evidence of Sources 1, 3 and 4, what do you consider to have been Mary's main strengths and weaknesses as a monarch?

(b) 'Thirty-seven years old in 1553, she [Mary] seized a power rightfully hers for the exercise of which she was utterly unsuited.' Using your own knowledge, and the evidence of all six sources, explain how far you agree with this interpretation.

Exam tips

The cross-references are intended to take you straight to the material that will help you to answer the questions.

(a) In question (a) you are asked to consider Mary's main strengths and weaknesses as a monarch. It is important to note the provenance of the sources – one from a modern historian and two from contemporaries. From the evidence contained in the sources it is possible to demonstrate the conflicting opinions that exist on Mary, for example:

- the fact that two of the three sources agree on her strengths – (i) in times of danger her courage, leadership and eloquent speeches; (ii) her political skill in negotiating a foreign marriage and her manipulation of the Council and Parliament (pages 109–10)
- the third source shows her weaknesses – that she was arrogant, assertive, bigoted, stubborn, suspicious and rather stupid.

(b) In question (b) the examiner is inviting you to challenge the assumption that Mary was 'utterly unsuited' to rule. You must use your own judgement to decide the extent to which you either agree or disagree with the interpretation. You have to supply the evidence to support whichever line of argument you choose to adopt. In order to evaluate the validity of this interpretation you might begin by:

- highlighting the difficulties that affected Mary's reign (see pages 107–10), e.g. would another monarch have done any better?
- concentrating on her successes
- examining what contemporaries had to say about her and her reign – some of them might have been biased because of her femininity or Catholicism.

5 Disorder and Rebellion: A Crisis in Authority?

POINTS TO CONSIDER

This chapter is intended to guide you through the various disorders, riots and rebellions that occurred during the reigns of Edward VI and Mary. Religion, social, economic and political grievances each played a part in causing the disorder and rebellion. The sheer scale and number of the rebellions once led historians to suggest that there was a crisis in authority, but that is no longer the case. There were indeed crises but the Tudor state proved strong enough to surmount them.

These issues are examined as six themes:

- Challenging authority
- The Western or Prayer Book Rebellion 1549
- The Ket Rebellion 1549
- Lady Jane Grey and the succession crisis 1553
- The Wyatt Rebellion 1554
- Was there a crisis in authority?

Key dates

1547	July	Proclamation to remove images from churches
	December	Dissolution of the chantries
1548	April	Murder of William Body at Helston, Cornwall
	June	Enclosure Commission to enforce existing laws
	July	Tax on sheep and cloth
1549	January	Act of Uniformity and Book of Common Prayer
	June	Introduction of First Prayer Book
	June	Western or Prayer Book Rebellion
	July	Ket's rebellion in East Anglia
	October	Fall of Somerset
		Northumberland took charge of government
1553	May	Guildford Dudley married Lady Jane Grey
	June	The Devise altered the succession
	July	Death of Edward VI; Lady Jane Grey proclaimed Queen

	July	Northumberland's military expedition against Mary Tudor ended in failure
	July	Mary Tudor proclaimed Queen
	August	Northumberland executed
	December	Marriage proposal between Mary and Philip II of Spain presented to the Royal Council
1554	January	Marriage confirmed
	January	Wyatt Rebellion
	February	Wyatt enters London
		Elizabeth arrested for supposedly being involved in the rebellion
		Lady Jane Grey and Guildford Dudley executed
	July	Marriage of Mary and Philip

1 | Challenging Authority

Key question
What lay behind the challenges to the authority of the Crown, government and Church?

Although the idea of a mid-Tudor crisis has been challenged in recent years, it is difficult to escape the fact that the period between 1547 and 1554 saw a large number of disturbances. In particular, 1549 has been singled out as a notable period of crisis because it witnessed two serious rebellions – the Western and Ket rebellions – and numerous other minor disturbances, which one historian, John Guy, believes brought England close to **class war**. This idea, that there was a genuine class war between the élites and non-élites, is a controversial one and stems from the belief that from there being a respect for authority, there was a general drift towards the challenging of authority. Certainly, there were tensions in both town and country as social and economic problems reached new levels of intensity. Changes in central government and religion had not only loosened loyalty to the regime but also fuelled a growing disrespect for the clergy and the Church.

Key term

Class war
Term used by some historians to help to explain the causes of the disorder and rebellions that occurred during the reign of Edward VI. The resentment of the poor and economically vulnerable was directed towards the wealthy and powerful élites.

However, to concentrate on the idea of a class war being at the root of disorder and rebellion between 1547 and 1554 is to risk ignoring those challenges to authority which came from within the ruling class. Unlike the uprisings in 1549, the *coup d'état* surrounding Lady Jane Grey and Wyatt's rebellion (see pages 136–41) were political conspiracies among the ruling élites, and there was little popular support. Factional tensions at Court and rivalry in central government surfaced at times of crisis as in:

- 1549 when Somerset was removed by Northumberland due to his ineffective handling of the rebellions in the West Country and East Anglia
- 1553 when Edward VI's death and Mary's accession threatened to destroy Northumberland's rule
- 1554 when Mary's marriage to Philip II of Spain became the focus for opposition by men who resented their exclusion from both the Court and government.

Therefore, in order to understand the root causes of crisis and the challenging of authority, it is necessary to appreciate what constituted the forces of authority and explore the problems that affected those at the bottom of society as well as those at the top.

The forces of authority

Ruling-class views of the poor had hardened in the sixteenth century. Where once paternalism had informed the attitudes and guided the actions of the élites, now the poor were viewed with a degree of detachment that often bred disdain and fear. Casual violence and crimes of theft among the common people were thought by the élites to be on the increase while riot was an ever-present threat. The rise in poverty and its associated evil vagrancy caused alarm and led to an overreaction on the part of the authorities who enthusiastically enforced harsh measures such as the so-called **'Slavery' Act of 1547**. Coercion and persuasion were the twin means by which the Crown and government attempted to keep control but the forces of authority available to maintain law and order were limited.

Formal authority

Tudor England had no police force or standing army. The monarchy relied on its God-given power to govern and make laws. This divine right to rule enabled the monarch to command the respect of the people who were constantly reminded of the Crown's privileged status by the Church. The people were expected to abide by the law but for those who disturbed the 'King's peace' there was arrest by the Crown's officers, trial in the royal courts of justice and punishment by fine or imprisonment, or by death.

Fear of what the Crown could do was a potent weapon in the struggle to maintain law and order. The monarchy communicated its orders by means of royal proclamations that were carried by royal messengers to various parts of the kingdom. Although not everyone would be able to read these proclamations, word soon spread and the monarchy thus made its will known to a great number of people.

Royal officials

The monarchy also relied on the unpaid services of the local gentry and nobility who were expected to uphold and enforce the law by means of the powers vested in them through the offices of **Lord Lieutenant**, Sheriff and **Justice of the Peace**. The holders of these offices had no supporting forces but relied on their standing and influence in the community to exert their authority.

Only the Lord Lieutenant had the power to call musters and assemble an armed militia recruited from among the local community in times of danger such as that posed by insurrection at home or invasion from abroad. Another method employed by the monarch to enhance its prestige and, indirectly, to reinforce the power and status of its officials in the regions was to be seen on royal progresses.

Key question
What forces were available to the State to keep order?

Key terms

'Slavery' Act of 1547
Term given to the poor law passed by Somerset's government. Described by historian W.R.D. Jones as 'the most savage of all Tudor poor laws', the statute stated that sturdy or able-bodied vagrants should be branded with the letters V and S and subjected to forced labour or slavery for repeat offenders.

Lord Lieutenant
Local military officer with the power to call musters and assemble an armed militia.

Justice of the Peace
Local law officer and magistrate at shire level. He also governed the county by enforcing Acts of Parliament and acting on decisions taken by the Privy Council and other departments of central government.

Yeomen of the Guard

Unlike its counterparts on the continent, the English monarchy did not have the financial means to maintain a regular, professional army. Nor could the Crown rely on the armed retainers maintained by the nobility since Henry VII had passed laws to prevent the keeping of private armies. This was done as a result of the Crown's experiences in the Wars of the Roses when private armies had been used to defy the law. The only professional force available to the monarch was the 400 men that made up the royal bodyguard, known as the Yeomen of the Guard.

Mercenaries

In times of crisis, the monarch often employed mercenaries hired from the continent to stiffen the resistance of those forces mustered in each county by the Lord Lieutenants. However, when a county was in the grip of rebellion, as occurred in Norfolk, Cornwall and Devon in 1549, then troops had to be mustered from other counties and deployed in the affected areas of the kingdom. This is why the Crown feared a national revolt such as the one planned by Sir Thomas Wyatt in 1554 which involved four simultaneous rebellions in Kent, Devon, Leicestershire and on the Welsh border (Herefordshire and Shropshire).

Informal authority

The Crown also exercised its authority in more informal but equally effective ways. Royal imagery was used to impress both people and visitors alike. For those wealthy and influential enough to be invited to attend the monarch in one of the many palaces owned by the Crown, the sheer scale and size of the buildings themselves would have been impressive, let alone the paintings and portraits that hung within. Even the majority of the population who might be fortunate enough to view the palaces from afar would have been impressed. But if they needed reminding of the power of the Crown they had only to reach for their coins, every denomination of which carried pictures of the ruling monarch.

The Church

The most visible symbol of authority in the kingdom after the monarch was the Church. The Church exercised formal authority over its clergy and non-clerical employees, and its influence over the population at large was such that the voices of its clergy commanded respect. The Church's rituals and its moral authority helped to enforce discipline and obedience. The Church was also an effective means of reaching the people because the vast majority were expected to attend their local church on a regular basis. The Crown was well aware of the importance of the Church's role in maintaining social stability and in ensuring people's loyalty and obedience.

The Royal Supremacy ensured that, as Head of the Church, the monarch had a captive audience willing to believe what the parish

Contemporary representation of the Great Chain of Being. This shows God and the angels at the top, descending through nobility, gentry and common people down to animals and plants. What was the purpose in having the Great Chain of Being depicted in this way?

priest had to tell them. Therefore, preaching was used to guide and inform people of royal policy. For those priests who opposed the Reformation or were unwilling to preach propaganda on behalf of the Crown, the Edwardian government issued Homilies (see page 97) or printed sermons to be read in all churches. Those clerics who refused to comply with government orders were expelled from the Church.

Although the changes brought about by the Reformation weakened the spiritual authority of the Church, there is no doubt that the pulpit remained the most powerful instrument of control. The Church was able to exert so much authority over the people because of a concept known as the 'Great Chain of Being'. This conveyed the contemporary idea of God punishing those who rebelled against their monarch. It emphasised that those in authority held their power for the good of those below them, and subject to those above them.

Key question
What were the root causes of crisis and how did they contribute to the challenging of authority?

The root causes of crisis and the challenging of authority

The non-élites

The mass of the people who made up the non-élites were not prone to violent rebellion. For them it was usually the last desperate act when all other attempts to resolve their grievances had failed. They were generally uninterested in politics and reacted only to those social, economic and sometimes religious forces that affected their everyday lives. Theirs was a precarious existence living on the edge of subsistence where a drought, a bad harvest or a price rise might push them into despairing poverty. Predictably perhaps, rising crime and destitution coincided with bad harvests and hunger, which often proved the spark for riot and rebellion. Consequently, the causes of non-élite disorder and rebellion can be found mainly in the social and economic changes that occurred in mid-Tudor England.

The standard of living

There were clear links between living standards and popular discontent in the middle of the century. Even if the standard of living of the mass of the population had not fallen as dramatically as was once assumed, it had certainly not improved. For example, the rebels in Norfolk clearly felt that their economic position had declined since the end of the fifteenth century, and blamed it largely on rising rents. The groups which had generally gained from increased rents and prices were the élites, the yeomen, merchants, industrialists and some husbandmen. Consequently, part of the problem in 1549 was the general economic resentment of those who felt they were the losers, against those groups that they felt were gaining. However, it must be remembered that it is too simple to make such a clear-cut distinction. Within each grouping there were both winners and losers. Unrest in 1549 (see pages 130–6) was very localised, and a riot or rebellion might have been sparked off by one individual who thought that his neighbour had cheated him or was becoming unduly prosperous.

Rents and wages

The levels of rents and wages are regarded as another possible contributor to popular unrest, because they too had a direct effect on the standard of living. With relatively sluggish population growth up to 1540, rents and wages would remain comparatively stable.

As far as wages were concerned this is exactly what happened. In the south of England the wages for rural workers remained at 4d a day and for building workers at 6d a day until the 1550s. This meant that the level of wages obtained in the fifteenth century when population was very low was maintained in spite of the increase in population. However, because of the considerable increase in inflation, the standard of living of all wage-earners fell.

The evidence of the level of rents is less conclusive. In some areas, especially around London, rents had risen by the 1530s, and had more than doubled from 6d per acre to 13d per acre. In other areas, away from south-eastern England, they remained static, and in some places fell slightly. The pressure was heaviest on pasture land because of the demand for wool and other animal products. Enclosed land commanded higher rents, which affected levels of rent in the surrounding district.

Although the evidence is not conclusive, resentment over the level of rents and wages added to popular discontent, especially in the southern half of the country. The problem is that there is no clear distinction between smallholders and labourers. Although it is estimated that over 40 per cent of the population were wage-earners – 10 per cent working in industry – only a minority were full-time employees. Many smallholders supplemented their incomes by wages, and most workers in cottage and other industries had their own smallholdings. A large number of town labourers spent part of the year working in the countryside, especially at harvest time. This makes it very difficult to select any one particular cause for economic discontent among the lower orders, and large-scale uprisings may have been caused by groups with different grievances coming together for mutual support.

Inflation, rising prices and poverty

During the first half of the sixteenth century the price of most goods rose sharply. However, the most serious rise in prices affected foodstuffs such as grain, bread, cheese and meat. This was caused in part by a rising population because it put pressure on agriculture, which was not flexible enough to increase production to meet the growing demand. This led to hunger and anger particularly when wages failed to keep pace with rising prices. Hungry people are more inclined to riot or rebel because it is an immediate problem that cannot wait for remedy in the long term.

By 1550 the rate of inflation may have reached 200 per cent, and the very high levels of inflation reached by 1549 contributed to the widespread popular discontent. Inflation contributed to damage the economy, which led to an increase in unemployment and poverty. Ignorant of the causes of poverty and vagrancy, the government reacted ruthlessly by punishing beggars, which in turn led to resentment against authority.

The élites

The élites did not so much challenge authority as undermine it. By involving themselves in acts of rebellion they not only set a bad example for the common people but contributed to weakening the authority of the state. They did not deliberately set out to do this, because their privileged position in society, their economic wealth and political power depended on maintaining the very authority that their rebellious acts were undermining. Therefore, the élites often trod a fine line between maintaining their authority over those below them – the common people – while challenging the authority of those above them – the monarchy and central government. The dangers posed by élite rebellion were potentially more serious than those posed by popular uprisings. For example, Ket and the Western rebels (see pages 130–6) never set out to destroy the government or change the monarchy, unlike the élites who involved themselves in the *coup d'état* of Lady Jane Grey and the Wyatt Rebellion (see pages 136–41).

Political changes

The causes of élite rebellion can be found mainly in the political and religious changes that occurred in mid-Tudor England. Political change enabled factions to thrive. The shifts in the balance of power between the rival conservative and reformist factions at Court after 1540 contributed to political instability.

This instability enabled Somerset to engineer a *coup d'état* in which the terms of Henry VIII's last will and testament were ignored so that he could become Lord Protector (see page 41). However, Somerset's position was soon undermined, not by a rival faction but by a political ally turned rival. Northumberland took advantage of Somerset's indecisiveness and weak rule to organise another *coup d'état* in which he assumed the leadership of the country. In both *coups* only a minority of the élites actively participated in the change of leadership, the majority remained passive. This was principally because the position of the monarch remained unchallenged. This changed when the succession became an issue, which helps to explain why the *coup d'état* involving Lady Jane Grey and Wyatt's rebellion both failed.

Although Northumberland's rule was generally sound and progressive he lacked the authority that a monarch could claim as God's anointed. This meant that his position could more easily be challenged. His attempt to crown Lady Jane Grey failed when the élites at Court and in the government turned on him and offered their support to Mary Tudor. In challenging the dying wish of Edward VI and defying the authority of Northumberland and the Council, Mary Tudor's was the only successful rebellion of the sixteenth century. On the other hand, Mary could claim that she and the élites who supported her were championing rather than challenging the authority of the State.

Religious changes

Religion became a factor during Mary's reign because Protestant gentry and nobility feared political exclusion and economic ruin. Economically the élites had nothing to fear because the Crown did not force them to hand back monastic and chantry property. However, politically their worst fears were soon realised when Mary removed from office the majority of Northumberland's supporters and promoted those loyal to her and her faith, for example:

• Archbishop Thomas Cranmer was removed from the Council, arrested and eventually executed.

- Bishop Stephen Gardiner, who had been imprisoned under Edward VI, was released, appointed to the Council and promoted to Lord Chancellor.

Within six months of her accession Mary had turned England into a Catholic kingdom. This was reinforced by her marriage to Philip of Spain. However, the Spanish marriage and religious settlement were not to everyone's taste and men such as Sir Thomas Wyatt, Sir Peter Carew and Sir James Croft plotted to overthrow the government.

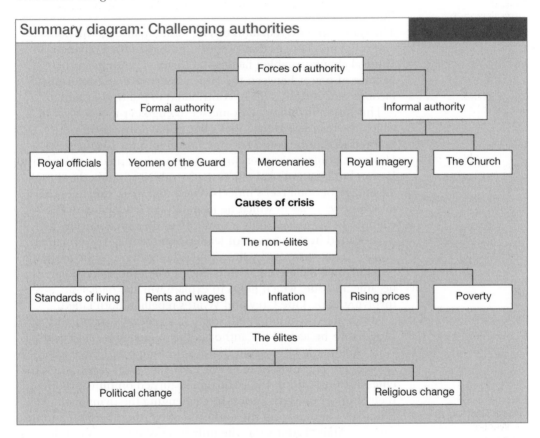

Summary diagram: Challenging authorities

2 | The Western or Prayer Book Rebellion 1549

It is difficult to judge to what extent underlying opposition to the changes in religion contributed to the rebellions of 1549 and to the fall of Somerset. Certainly, only the Western Rebellion was directly linked to religion, and even there underlying economic and social discontent played an important part in causing the uprising. To a certain extent the rebels in the west were complaining about enclosures and about the gentry, who they accused of making use of the Reformation to seize Church land for their own enrichment. Such views were held in other areas during the popular uprisings of 1549, but only in the West Country was direct opposition to the new Act of Uniformity (see page 95) the central issue.

Key question
What were the causes of the Western Rebellion?

Cornwall

The popular discontent began in Cornwall in 1547, when the local archdeacon, William Body, who was disliked both for his Protestant views and for his personal greed, began to try to introduce religious reforms. He was mobbed by a hostile crowd at Penryn and fled to London. In April 1548 he returned to Cornwall to supervise the destruction of Catholic images in churches. At Helston, Body was set upon and killed by a mob led by a local priest. Since the troublemakers dispersed quickly the authorities made only a few arrests. But they hanged the 10 ringleaders.

In 1549 the Cornish lower orders, fearing that the Act of Uniformity was going to be imposed on them, rose in rebellion and set up an armed camp at Bodmin. Because of the hostility expressed by the rebels towards landlords, only six of the pro-Catholic local gentry joined the uprising. However, the West Country élites were very unwilling to take any action against the rebellion on behalf of the government. The main leaders of the rebels were local clergy, and it was they who began to draw up a series of articles listing demands to stop changes in religion.

Devon

In Devon there was an independent uprising at Sampford Courtenay. By 20 June, the Devon and Cornish rebels had joined forces at Crediton, and three days later they set up an armed camp at Clyst St Mary. Local negotiations between the authorities and the rebels broke down, and the rebels began to blockade the nearby town of Exeter with an army of 6000 men. Lord Russell, who had been sent to crush the rebellion, was hampered by a shortage of troops and a lack of local gentry support. Crucially, the rebels were led by a prominent local gentleman, Humphrey Arundell, who was a skilled tactician and able commander. As a result it was not until August that the rebels were finally defeated. It has been calculated that the rebels lost as many as 4000 killed.

Figure 5.1: Map of the Western Rebellion.

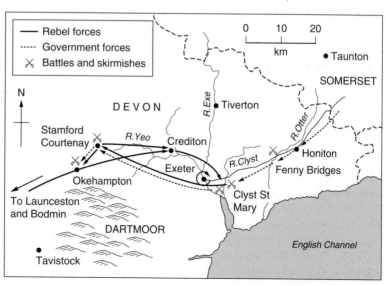

The demands of the rebels

Some of the demands put forward in the final set of articles drawn up by the rebels clearly illustrate their religious conservatism and other grievances felt in the West Country. For example, they wanted:

- to end the changes that they claimed were taking place in baptism and confirmation
- to restore the Act of Six Articles (see page 45)
- to restore the Latin Mass and images
- to restore old traditions such as holy bread and water
- to restore the concept of transubstantiation and purgatory (see page 93)
- the return of Cardinal Pole from exile and for him to have a seat on the king's ruling council.

Government reaction

The government clearly saw these articles as ultra-conservative demands for a return to Catholicism, and they were vigorously repudiated by Cranmer and the leading theologians among the reformers. It was claimed that the rank and file had been misled by, as Somerset put it, 'seditious priests, to seek restitution of the old bloody laws' for their own purposes. It was the manner in which the articles were phrased, just as much as their content, that offended the government. Unlike the usual wording of petitions to the Crown by rebels, such as the 'We pray your grace' used by Robert Ket in the same year (see page 135), each of the Western rebels' articles began 'Item we will'. Such lack of deference and respect, along with denials of the royal supremacy in the articles themselves, was seen as a greater threat to the stability of society and the State than the rebellion itself.

Cranmer was particularly enraged by such insubordination, and by the rebel demand that no gentleman should have more than one servant. It was this that enabled the government to accuse the rebels of being dangerous troublemakers, and so distract attention from their attack on religious change. In any case the government found no difficulty in pouring scorn on the lack of doctrinal knowledge in the articles. Their demands for the return of images and the old ceremonies were dismissed as idolatrous, and the old mass was described as being more like games held during the Christmas season. Even greater scorn was poured on the rebel suggestion that they rejected the new services in English because as Cornish speakers, it was a language that they did not understand.

Assessing the Western Rebellion

Historian Philip Caramani claims that the Western Rebellion was 'the most formidable opposition to the Reformation that England saw'. Historians agree that the rebels showed little knowledge of either Protestant or Catholic doctrines, but suggest that such ignorance in the West Country probably reflected similar confusion among the great mass of the population. Whether this

Key question
What were the consequences of the Western Rebellion?

is true or not, these demands do show that, in the West Country at least, many of the laity were still strongly attached to the familiar traditions of the old Church.

Although religion is acknowledged to be a key cause of the rebellion, some historians have drawn attention to the social and economic causes. For example, historian A.F. Pollard suggested that social tension lay at the heart of the rebellion and, according to historians A. Fletcher and J. Stevenson, there is evidence to suggest that the rebels considered the gentry to be their enemies. Even the leader of the royal army, Lord Russell, referred to the unfair exploitation of the common people by the local gentry and nobility, whom he claimed were taxing and raising rents excessively. The rebels were particularly angry at the new sheep tax which they wanted withdrawn, but they failed to mention it in their list of final demands. Historians tended to ignore the social and economic grievances in favour of the religious. This is no longer the case, for as historian Nicholas Fellows has suggested it is possible to make a link 'between the rebels' religious grievances and their attack upon the gentry: it was after all the gentry who had gained from the Reformation'.

Some key books in the debate

Philip Caramani, *The Western Rebellion* (Tiverton, 1994).
Nicolas Fellows, *Disorder and Rebellion in Tudor England* (Hodder Murray, 2001).
A. Fletcher and J. Stevenson, *Order and Disorder in Early Modern England* (Cambridge, 1985).
A. F. Pollard, *England Under Protector Somerset* (London, 1900).

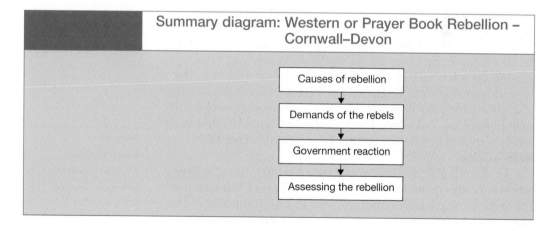

Summary diagram: Western or Prayer Book Rebellion – Cornwall–Devon

- Causes of rebellion
- Demands of the rebels
- Government reaction
- Assessing the rebellion

Key question
What were the causes of the Ket Rebellion?

3 | The Ket Rebellion 1549

East Anglia was the most industrialised part of the country. Norwich was the second largest town after London, and was a major textile centre. The causes of the rebellion are symptomatic of the confused nature of lower order discontent with the economic changes. The rising was triggered by unrest over enclosures, high rents and unsympathetic local landlords.

East Anglia had a large number of independent small farmers, who were being adversely affected by the enclosing of fields and commons by the gentry and yeomen. The collapse of textile exports had thrown large numbers of clothworkers in Norwich and the surrounding countryside out of work. In June there were riots at the neighbouring market towns of Attleborough and Wymondham, and some new fences that had been put up by Sir John Flowerdew were pulled down.

Sir John Flowerdew

Flowerdew was a lawyer who had bought up Church property in the area. This made him unpopular with the locals, who resented him as an outsider. Furthermore, he was in dispute with the townspeople of Wymondham over the local abbey, which he had bought and was demolishing. The townspeople had bought the abbey church for use by the parish, and were incensed when Flowerdew began to strip the lead from the roof. Given the truth of historian Anthony Fletcher's opinion that the gentry were 'detaching themselves in manners and values' from the mass of the people, Flowerdew's apparent insensitivity is perhaps not surprising. This detachment seems to have coloured ruling-class views of the poor and of the danger they posed to society, law and good order.

Robert Ket

Flowerdew was also in dispute with a local yeoman, Robert Ket, over land. Ket was a tanner and small landowner who had enclosed much of the common at Wymondham. Flowerdew tried to turn the rioters against him but Ket turned the tables by offering to act as their spokesman. In fact, Ket showed more organisational skill and decisive leadership than is usually found in the leaders of peasant risings. He quickly gathered an army of 16,000 men, set up camp for six weeks on Mousehold Heath just outside the town and, in July, was able to capture Norwich, the second largest town in England. The rebellion is notable for the discipline which Ket imposed, electing a governing council and maintaining law and order. Every gentleman apprehended by the rebels was tried before Ket and his council at the **Tree of Reformation**.

Like the popular uprising in the West Country, the rebellion was eventually crushed when John Dudley, Earl of Warwick (later the Duke of Northumberland) was sent to take command of the Marquis of Northampton's army of 14,000 men. Northampton had succeeded in taking Norwich but had been forced to abandon it after only a day. Unlike Northampton, Warwick was able to bring the rebels to battle at Dussingdale, just outside the city, where nearly 4000 rebels and royal troops were killed. Ket was captured and eventually hanged for **sedition**.

Key dates

Ket's rebellion in East Anglia: July 1549

Fall of Somerset: October 1549

Northumberland took charge of government: October 1549

Key terms

Tree of Reformation
The location of Ket's council of justice, which sat under an old oak tree.

Sedition
Action or speech that incites rebellion.

Figure 5.2: Map of the Ket Rebellion.

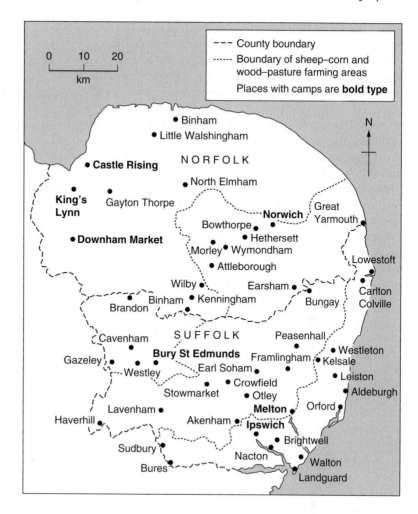

The demands of the rebels

The rebels drew up a list of 29 articles covering a range of topics. For example, they wanted:

- landowners to stop enclosing common land
- rents to be reduced to the levels they were under Henry VIII
- rivers to be open to all for fishing and fishermen be allowed to keep a greater share of the profits from sea fishing
- all **bondmen** to be given their freedom, 'for God made everyone free with his precious blood shedding'
- corrupt local officials 'who have offended the commons' to be punished 'where it has been proved by the complaints of the poor'
- incompetent priests to be removed from their churches, particularly those who were 'unable to preach and set forth the word of God to their parishioners'.

Key term

Bondmen
Peasant farmers who had no freedom to choose where they lived and worked. They were tied to the manor on which they were born and brought up.

Assessing the Ket Rebellion

Unlike the West Country rebels who seemed to wish for religion to be returned to the good old days of Henry VIII, the Norfolk insurgents supported the Protestant religious changes.

Ket encouraged Protestant ministers to preach to the rebels on Mousehold Heath and to use the new Prayer Book.

Although enclosure has been cited as the primary cause of the rebellion, in truth it was just one among many agricultural demands made by the rebels. Indeed, apart from local examples such as at Wymondham and Attleborough, there had been relatively few enclosures in Norfolk during the previous 50 years. Similarly, the requests that bondmen or serfs should be made free is strange because there is no evidence that there were many unfree tenants in sixteenth-century Norfolk.

The major demands were for commons to be kept open and free for husbandmen to graze their livestock, and that rents should not be increased excessively. The Norfolk rebels appeared to yearn for the favourable economic conditions that had existed under Henry VIII. This supports the notion that the major cause of the popular unrest in 1549 was the harsh economic conditions that prevailed in that year.

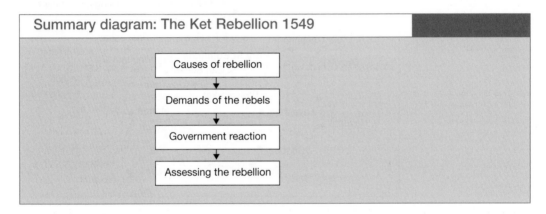

Summary diagram: The Ket Rebellion 1549

Causes of rebellion
↓
Demands of the rebels
↓
Government reaction
↓
Assessing the rebellion

4 | Lady Jane Grey and the Succession Crisis 1553

Key question
What were the causes and consequences of the succession crisis of 1553?

By 1552 Northumberland seemed to be firmly in control. Even the rapid swing towards Calvinism in the Church of England (see page 103) did not appear to be provoking any serious opposition. However, his power depended upon the support of Edward VI. By the end of the year the king's health was obviously deteriorating quickly, and the problem of the succession became a central issue once again. In accordance with Henry VIII's will, Mary was to succeed if Edward died childless. Mary's strong Catholic sympathies made her unpopular with the reform party and with Edward himself. Moreover, it was feared that Mary might renounce the royal supremacy.

To prevent a return to Catholicism, and to retain power, Northumberland, with the full support of the king, planned to change the succession. As the Succession Acts of 1534 and 1536 (see page 37) making Mary and Elizabeth illegitimate had not been repealed, it was decided to disinherit them in favour of the

Key dates

Guildford Dudley married Lady Jane Grey: May 1553

Death of Edward VI; Lady Jane Grey proclaimed Queen: July 1553

Northumberland's military expedition against Mary Tudor ended in failure: July 1553

Mary Tudor proclaimed Queen: July 1553

Northumberland executed: August 1553

Wyatt Rebellion: January 1554

Wyatt entered London: February 1554

Elizabeth arrested for supposedly being involved in the rebellion: February 1554

Lady Jane Grey and Guildford Dudley executed: February 1554

Marriage of Mary and Philip: July 1554

Suffolk branch of the family. Frances, Duchess of Suffolk, was excluded as her age made it unlikely that she would have male heirs and her eldest daughter, Lady Jane Grey, was chosen to succeed. To secure his own position Northumberland married his eldest son, Guildford Dudley, to Jane in May 1553.

Unfortunately for Northumberland, Edward VI died in July before the plans for the seizure of power could be completed. Jane Grey was proclaimed Queen by Northumberland and the Council in London, while Mary proclaimed herself Queen at Framlingham Castle in Suffolk. Northumberland's mistakes were two-fold:

- he failed to arrest Mary and keep her in custody
- he underestimated the amount of support for Mary in the country.

On 14 July he marched into Suffolk with an army of 2000 men, but his troops deserted him. The Privy Council in London hastily changed sides and proclaimed Mary as queen. Northumberland was arrested in Cambridge, tried, and executed on 22 August in spite of his renunciation of Protestantism.

Assessing Lady Jane Grey and the succession crisis

The ease with which Mary upheld her right to the throne shows the growing stability of the State and the nation. Potential political crisis had been avoided because the majority of the nation supported the rule of law and rightful succession. The direct line of descent was still considered legitimate in spite of Acts of Parliament to the contrary. A period of dynastic weakness and minority rule had passed without the country dissolving into civil war.

Two Acts were passed, one in 1553 and another in 1554, to resolve the constitutional position. This legislation was designed to confirm Mary Tudor's legitimacy, and to establish the right of female monarchs to rule in England. However, no attempt was made to make Elizabeth legitimate, although she was recognised as Mary's heir in the event of her dying childless.

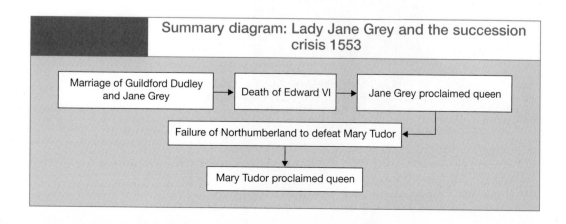

Summary diagram: Lady Jane Grey and the succession crisis 1553

5 | The Wyatt Rebellion 1554

Sir Thomas Wyatt c1521–54

Sir Thomas Wyatt was a member of a wealthy and well-connected gentry family from Kent. He succeeded to the family estates on the death of his father, also called Sir Thomas, in 1542. Sir Thomas Wyatt senior had been a courtier and diplomat, and his son was expected to follow suit. He became friendly with the influential Henry Howard, Earl of Surrey, who acted as his patron. Wyatt fought in France under Surrey in 1543–44 and in 1545 he was promoted to the English council governing English-controlled Boulogne.

Unfortunately for Wyatt, his career suffered a setback in 1547 when Surrey fell into disfavour with Henry VIII and was executed. As a committed Protestant Wyatt found favour with the Edwardian regime, which he defended in 1549 when riots broke out in Kent. He was trusted by Somerset's successor Northumberland, who appointed him to represent the English government in negotiations with the French in 1550.

Wyatt served the Edwardian regime loyally but he declared his support for Mary when Jane Grey was proclaimed queen. Wyatt's initial support for Mary soon evaporated when he heard of the Spanish marriage. As an MP he became involved in the

Key question
What were the causes of the Wyatt Rebellion?

Sir Thomas Wyatt.

opposition to the proposed marriage in Parliament but his hopes of persuading the queen to reject the marriage failed.

Conspiracy and rebellion

By the end of January 1554, anti-Spanish feelings led to rebellion. Unlike the uprisings in 1549 this was a political conspiracy among the élites, and there was little popular support. The rebellion was led by Sir James Croft, Sir Peter Carew and Sir Thomas Wyatt. These men had all held important offices at Court under both Henry VIII and Edward VI. Although they had supported Mary's accession, they feared that the growing Spanish influence would endanger their own careers. Wyatt appealed to patriotism by declaring that:

> because you be Englishmen … you will join with us, as we will with you unto death, in this behalf protesting unto you before God … we seek no harm to the Queen, but better counsel and councillors.

The conspirators planned to marry Elizabeth to Edward Courtenay, Earl of Devon (see pages 59–60), who Mary had rejected. Simultaneous rebellions in the West Country, the Midlands and Kent were to be supported by the French fleet blockading the English Channel.

The plan failed because the inept Courtenay disclosed the scheme to his patron, Gardiner, before the conspirators were ready to act. In any case, Carew, Croft and the Duke of Suffolk bungled the uprisings in the West Country and the Midlands. Wyatt succeeded in raising an army of 3000 men in Kent, and this caused real fear in the government because the rebels were so close to the capital. The situation was made worse because the troops sent to Kent under the aged and semi-retired Duke of Norfolk deserted to the rebels. Realising the danger, the Privy Council quickly raised forces to protect London.

An over-cautious Wyatt, meanwhile, took his time in making for the capital. He wasted a day besieging Cooling Castle and capturing his enemy Lord Cobham. Wyatt then wasted more time by agreeing to consider the queen's offer to discuss his grievances, but this was a calculated plan on Mary's part to gain time. By delaying his advance too long, Wyatt allowed the government time to appeal to the citizens of the capital for support, see to the defence of the city and organise its troops. Although Wyatt enjoyed some initial success as he skirted the city walls, when the main assault on London came, the rebels were trapped and defeated at Ludgate.

Government reaction

Key question
What were the consequences of Wyatt's rebellion?

The administration had had a bad scare, and Paget suggested leniency for the rebels for fear of provoking further revolts. Fewer than a hundred executions took place among the common people and most were pardoned. As for the rebels among the élites, apart from Wyatt and the Duke of Suffolk, only Jane Grey and Guildford Dudley were executed. Croft was tried and imprisoned

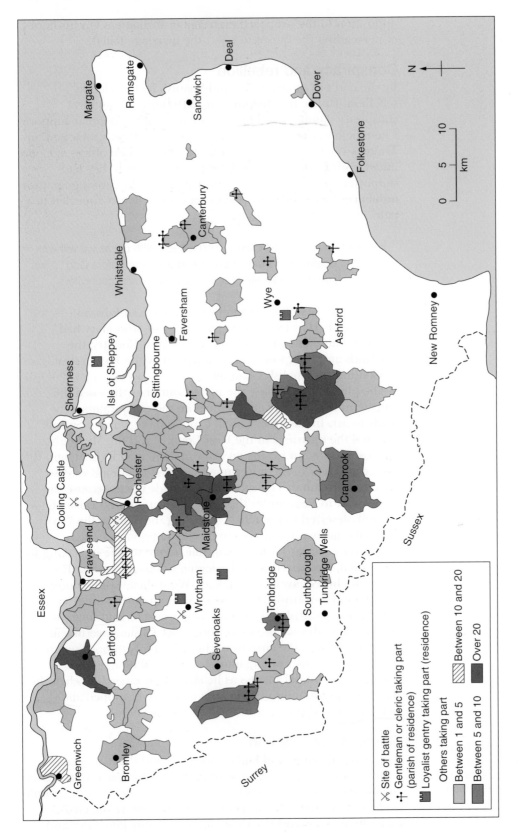

Figure 5.3: Map of Wyatt's rebellion.

A woodcut showing the execution of Lady Jane Grey. Why has the illustrator referred to the victim as Lady rather than Queen Jane?

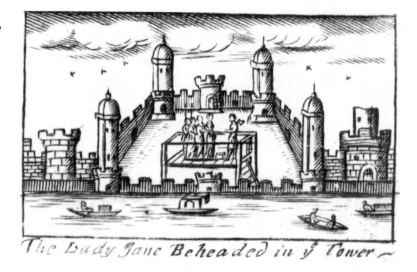

The Lady Jane Beheaded in ye Tower

but his release followed after less than nine months in the Tower of London. Carew fled to France but he was pardoned on his return in 1556. After a short imprisonment Elizabeth and Courtenay were released, and Elizabeth remained next in line to the throne. Even so, anti-Spanish feelings remained high. Philip's proposed coronation was postponed, and he only remained in England for a few months before returning to Spain.

Assessing the Wyatt Rebellion

The Wyatt Rebellion came as close as any to overthrowing the monarchy. Wyatt benefited from the proximity of Kent to the capital and from his own work in improving the muster in the county. A rapid advance on London might have met with success but hesitation and delay gave Mary and the government vital time to prepare. According to historian Paul Thomas, 'Mary's new regime was pushing its luck, not so much with a policy of Catholic restoration, as with the Spanish marriage and the provocation of those who members of the court élite who either felt excluded or feared imminent exclusion'. Historian Anthony Fletcher has stated that 'the resort to rebellion by the excluded arose because of the ineffectiveness of the constitutional methods of opposition to the royal marriage policy'. Frustrated and increasingly desperate, men like Wyatt felt compelled to act in a way calculated to end in their deaths unless they succeeded in overthrowing the monarch. In the opinion of historian Diarmaid MacCulloch, the fact that Wyatt failed demonstrates 'the bankruptcy of rebellion as a way of solving' political crises.

Some key books in the debate
Anthony Fletcher and Diarmaid MacCulloch, *Tudor Rebellions* (Longman, 1997).
Paul Thomas, *Authority and Disorder in Tudor Times 1485–1603* (Cambridge University Press, 1999).

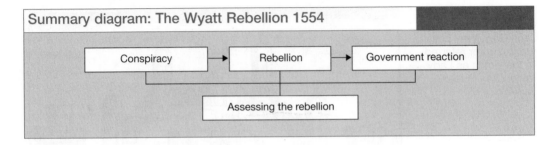

Summary diagram: The Wyatt Rebellion 1554

5 | The Key Debate

Was there a crisis in authority?

If there was a crisis in authority in the mid-sixteenth century it was in 1549, and was created by a range of misfortunes. For example:

- There was a weak, insolvent government, over-stretching its resources by trying to fight a war on two fronts.
- The government was attempting to introduce drastic religious reforms.
- Government aroused the hostility of the élites and non-élites by its social and economic policies.
- Prices, fuelled by currency debasements and increasing population levels, had doubled since the beginning of the century.
- A run of good growing seasons was brought to an end by a wet summer, and the harvest in 1549 was poor. This came at a time when agriculture was already struggling to feed the higher level of population (this had peaked at three million in 1549), and so grain prices rose.

Lesser risings

Under these circumstances it is not surprising that underlying discontent came to the surface in the form of popular rebellions. Indeed, unrest in 1549 was widespread, with some 25 counties affected by disturbances.

The causes of these minor risings were two-fold: enclosure and religious change. Although the majority of these disturbances were local protests or were stopped before they could cause serious harm, taken together they presented the government with a major challenge.

If Somerset had not been so arrogant and unwilling to withdraw troops from Scotland and France, and if there had not been a power struggle developing in the Privy Council, it is unlikely that the situation would have got out of hand. Once the government had mobilised sufficient troops, the rebellions were suppressed with comparative ease.

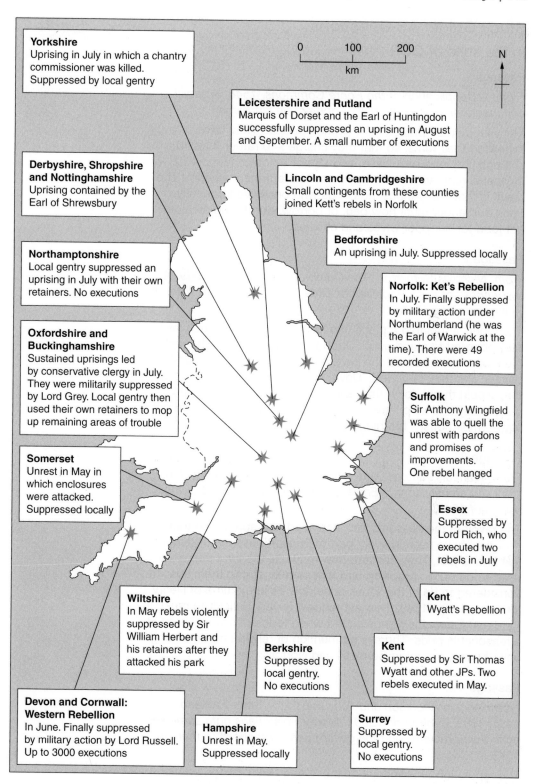

Yorkshire
Uprising in July in which a chantry commissioner was killed. Suppressed by local gentry

Leicestershire and Rutland
Marquis of Dorset and the Earl of Huntingdon successfully suppressed an uprising in August and September. A small number of executions

Derbyshire, Shropshire and Nottinghamshire
Uprising contained by the Earl of Shrewsbury

Lincoln and Cambridgeshire
Small contingents from these counties joined Kett's rebels in Norfolk

Bedfordshire
An uprising in July. Suppressed locally

Northamptonshire
Local gentry suppressed an uprising in July with their own retainers. No executions

Norfolk: Ket's Rebellion
In July. Finally suppressed by military action under Northumberland (he was the Earl of Warwick at the time). There were 49 recorded executions

Oxfordshire and Buckinghamshire
Sustained uprisings led by conservative clergy in July. They were militarily suppressed by Lord Grey. Local gentry then used their own retainers to mop up remaining areas of trouble

Suffolk
Sir Anthony Wingfield was able to quell the unrest with pardons and promises of improvements. One rebel hanged

Somerset
Unrest in May in which enclosures were attacked. Suppressed locally

Essex
Suppressed by Lord Rich, who executed two rebels in July

Wiltshire
In May rebels violently suppressed by Sir William Herbert and his retainers after they attacked his park

Kent
Wyatt's Rebellion

Berkshire
Suppressed by local gentry. No executions

Kent
Suppressed by Sir Thomas Wyatt and other JPs. Two rebels executed in May.

Devon and Cornwall: Western Rebellion
In June. Finally suppressed by military action by Lord Russell. Up to 3000 executions

Hampshire
Unrest in May. Suppressed locally

Surrey
Suppressed by local gentry. No executions

Figure 5.4: Lesser risings in 1549.

Study Guide: AS Questions

In the style of OCR

Passage 1

From: A Supplication of the Poore Commons, 1546. A social commentator attacks the rise of oppressive landlords.

Many landlords oppress the common people. They have increased their rents, so that they charge £40 rather than 40 shillings [£2] for a new lease, and £5 not 5 nobles [almost £2] for its annual rent, so we now pay more to them than we earn. The result is that many thousands of us who once lived honestly upon our labour must now beg, or borrow, or rob and steal, to get food for our poor wives and children.

Passage 2

From: Nicholas Sotherton, The Commotion in Norfolk, 1549. An eye witness of Ket's Rebellion of 1549 writes an account from the viewpoint of the gentry.

The rebels appointed a place of assembly by an oak tree which they boarded to stand upon. Upon this came Ket and the rest of the leaders and warned the people about their robberies and evil doings. But they still cried, 'Down with the gentlemen' and that they would throw down their enclosures. Within two or three weeks they had so pursued the Gentlemen that these dared not stay in their houses but hid in the woods.

Passage 3

From: Francois van der Delft, letter to Emperor Charles V, July 1549. An ambassador in England writes a brief account of the risings of 1549.

The revolt of the peasants has increased and spread, so that now they have risen in every part of England, asking for things just and unjust. They demand they may use the land that once used to be public property, and that land leased to them shall be considered to be of the same value now as in the time of Henry VII, who died in 1509. This last request is very difficult to meet. In Kent and Essex the risings ended when foodstuffs were taxed at a reasonable price. There is no mention of religion made among any of them, except in Cornwall and Norfolk.

Passage 4

From: Angela Anderson and Tony Imperato, Tudor England, 1485–1603, *published in 2001. Modern historians note some key economic problems and the government's reactions to them in 1549.*

The reputation of Somerset as the 'Good Duke' rested on his apparent desire to help those in economic difficulties. By seeming to be sympathetic he raised the hope of reform without being able to deliver it. Somerset's government chose enclosures as the crusading issue. In fact, it was more important to tackle inflation if real economic improvements were to be made, but Somerset shied away from this because the policies needed to control inflationary pressures would have reduced the taxes he needed to fight the Scottish war. A commission was established to investigate the legality of recent enclosures. Government inspectors toured the country. There was a real expectation that the commissioners would order a reversal, and bitter disappointment when they did not.

(a) **Study Passages 1 and 3**

How far do these sources agree in blaming financial hardship for causing the conflict between the common people and the gentry?

(b) **Study all the passages**

Using all these passages and your own knowledge, assess the view that enclosure was the main reason for the social unrest and rebellion in England between 1540 and 1558.

Exam tips

The cross-references are intended to take you straight to the material that will help you to answer the questions.

(a) In question **(a)** you are invited to compare the information in two passages in order to highlight the similarities between them. You should note the dates of the passages and who was responsible for them. You should also note the fact that both passages suggest that financial hardship was at the root of the conflict. The complaints include:

- increased rents
- increased cost of foodstuffs
- being forced to beg or steal in order to live (page 127).

(b) In question **(b)** you are asked to assess the validity of the statement that enclosure was the main reason for the social unrest and rebellion. You will note that all but one of the passages refer to enclosure as a factor. You should group the passages so that their evidence is used thematically to provide a focused answer.

Although enclosure was a cause of rebellion there were other equally significant factors such as:

- religious discontent (pages 129–30)
- inflation, unemployment and price rises (pages 127–8)
- increase in poverty and vagrancy (pages 127–8)
- the unfair treatment of the poor by the noble and gentry landowners (pages 128–9)
- the belief that the government under Somerset sympathised with the common people (pages 35–6).

You will need to offer a balanced answer where the social, economic and religious factors are discussed and measured against the contribution of enclosure.

Study guide: A2 Questions

In the style of Edexcel

Source 1

From: N. Fellows, Disorder and Rebellion in Tudor England, *published in 2001.*

Although the concept of a mid-Tudor crisis has been challenged over recent years, it is difficult to escape the fact that the years 1547–53 saw a large number of disturbances. In particular, 1549 saw two serious rebellions and numerous other minor disturbances, which some historians believe brought England close to class war.

There were tensions in both town and countryside as economic problems reached new levels of intensity. Changes in central government and religion had loosened loyalty to the regime so that those discontented by the hard times were ready recruits for those who wished to overturn Tudor rule.

Source 2

From: Paul Thomas, Authority and Disorder in Tudor Times 1485–1603, *published in 1999.*

When Henry VIII died in 1547, the official position of English religion may be summed up as the continued existence of an English Catholic Church in which the sacraments were largely untouched, clerical marriage was not tolerated, the monastic orders had been swept away, the royal supremacy had superseded that of the pope and the old Mass was largely retained, but one in which service and Bible gave the worshipper access to the word of God in the vernacular [language of the people].

However, this to understate the position at court, where the dying king seems to have accepted the rise of the Protestant faction led by the Seymour brothers by banishing the conservative Gardiner from the council and imprisoning the duke of Norfolk.

Source 3

From: T.A. Morris, Tudor Government, *published in 1999.*

Fundamental differences of opinion existed within the Council on the subject of the restoration of catholicism. In this case, it was Gardiner whose views were more in tune with the Queen's, advocating a ruthless response to heresy, while Paget hoped for a more sensitive restoration that would avoid social conflict and safeguard the interests of those who held former church lands. These differences resulted in the most serious example of governmental breakdown in the reign when they spilled over into the parliamentary session of 1554.

Source 4

From: an eye-witness account written by Baptista Spinola, a Genoese merchant in London, 1553.

Today I saw Lady Jane Grey walking in a grand procession to the Tower. She is now called Queen, but she is not popular, for the hearts of the people are with Mary, the Spanish Queen's daughter. She walked under a canopy, her mother carrying her long train, and her husband Guildford walking by he, a very tall strong boy who paid her much attention. Many ladies followed, with noblemen but this lady is very heretical and has never heard Mass, and some great people did not come into the procession for that reason.

Source 5

From: a report by Giovanni Micheli, Venetian ambassador, to the Venetian Senate, 1555.

Respecting the government and public business, she [Mary] is compelled (being of a sex which cannot becomingly take more than a moderate part in them) to refer many matters to her councillors and ministers. The truth is that, knowing the divisions which exist among them, her Majesty, in order not to be deceived and for the prevention of scandal, willed that Cardinal Pole should hear and have everything referred to him, it being evident that, whilst having the utmost confidence in him, she distrusts almost all the others.

Source 6

From: Edward Towne, The Tudor Years, *published in 1994.*

The crisis theory overlooks the fact that the government never lost control, even in 1549. This may have been partly because the two rebellions in 1549 had limited aims and did not intend to topple the government. The Council functioned effectively from 1540 despite undoubted factional turmoil from time to time. The governing élites survived the most dangerous moment in 1553 when they decided to back Mary's legitimate descent.

(a) Using your own knowledge and the evidence of Sources 1, 3 and 4, say what you consider to have been the main causes of rebellion in the period between 1547 and 1558.

(b) 'The monarchy was in crisis in the reigns of Edward VI and Mary because the political and religious divisions in mid-Tudor England were so serious.' Using your own knowledge, and the evidence of all six sources, explain how far you agree with this interpretation.

Exam tips

The cross-references are intended to take you straight to the material that will help you to answer the questions.

(a) In question **(a)** you are asked to consider the main causes of rebellion. It is important to note the provenance of the sources – two from modern historians and the third from a contemporary. From the evidence contained in the sources it is possible to suggest that the main causes of rebellion were due to:

- tensions in town and countryside because of economic problems (pages 127–9)
- changes of monarch, not all of which were legitimate (pages 123–4)
- changes in religion and the tension this caused among the ruling élites (pages 123–4 and 129–30)
- the socially discontented being ready recruits for those who wished to overturn Tudor rule.

(b) In question **(b)** the examiner is inviting you to challenge the assumption that the monarchy was in crisis. You must use your own judgement to decide the extent to which you either agree or disagree with the interpretation. You have to supply the evidence to support whichever line of argument you choose to adopt. In order to evaluate the validity of this interpretation you should identify the key issues raised by the sources, the counter views expressed and the support for them contained in the source package. On the other hand, you might take issue with the quotation by suggesting that the idea of crisis is no longer fashionable among historians especially as the problems that affected the mid-Tudor monarchy were not as serious as was once thought.

6 A Crisis in Society?

POINTS TO CONSIDER

In order to understand the political and religious changes taking place it is important to know something about mid-Tudor society at all levels. Although political decisions were made by the élites, popular reaction and lower order uprisings were important issues, especially in 1549. This chapter examines the ways in which the social structure changed between the late Middle Ages and the mid-sixteenth century, and assesses whether this process had created a mid-Tudor social crisis. You will need to take note of the various social theories and decide whether they are a useful way to study social changes.

These issues are examined as five themes:

- Theories of social change
- Social structure and social mobility
- Contemporary views of mid-Tudor society
- Mid-Tudor society and the theory of social crisis
- Was there a crisis in society?

Key dates

1349	Black Death and the beginning of recurrent bubonic plague epidemics drastically reduced the population
1390s	Serfdom among the lower orders was coming to an end
1400–1500	Low population, low prices, low rents and high wages created 'golden age' of lower order prosperity
1470s	Loss of political and economic power by the aristocracy and growth in royal authority
1500s	Increasing population growth and inflation forced up prices and rents and created unemployment
1500s	Growing commerce helped to increase the influence of the gentry and yeomen
1530s	Growing shortage of land created competition among the élites
1536–40	Closure of the monasteries enabled large-scale redistribution of land among the élites

| 1540 | Rapid population growth caused hyper-inflation and rising unemployment |
| 1549 | Poor harvest and widespread popular discontent led to Ket's rebellion in Norfolk |

1 | Theories of Social Change

Key question
How do Marxist and revisionist theories of social change differ?

The sixteenth century was a highly significant period because major changes were taking place within English society. However, because social change is usually such a slow, long-term process, it is virtually impossible to measure it over short periods of time such as the period between 1540 and 1558. Instead, historians have to try to assess what stage the series of complicated structural changes which had begun in the fourteenth century (see pages 18–21) had reached by the middle of the sixteenth century. At the same time they have to consider what effects particular events, such as the Reformation, were having on society. Only then is it possible to reach any conclusions about whether there was a mid-century social crisis, or the extent to which social change contributed to any of the problems facing Tudor governments at that time.

It is widely agreed that by the middle of the sixteenth century, although the actual shape of the social structure had altered very little, the changes that were taking place were causing stresses within society. However, the extent to which any such tensions contributed to the popular unrest in 1549 is not clear. This uncertainty reflects the lack of agreement about the nature of the changes taking place.

Alternative theories of social change

Many social and economic historians have stressed the importance of religious change, the variations in population levels, and the effect of inflation or **deflation**, in creating movements within and between social groups.

Deflation
The reduction of the amount of money in circulation in order to increase its value.

Key term

Religion and social change

The Reformation used to be regarded as being particularly important in the process of social change. It was considered that the break from Rome and the introduction of Protestantism were important in promoting the spread of individualism, capitalism and competition. It was suggested that many members of the élites and commercial groups adopted moderate Protestantism so that they could benefit from the increase in prices. Equally the seizure of Church lands was seen as helping the élites to build up their wealth, and to recover from the losses resulting from the breakdown of the late medieval economy. It was claimed that the Western Rebellion of 1549 (see pages 130–3) provides evidence of such developments. Certainly, the rebels were hostile towards the local gentry who, they claimed, were using the Reformation to enrich themselves.

At the same time, the adoption of Lutheran and Calvinist ideas during the reign of Edward VI was seen as introducing into England the Protestant work ethic, with its stress on thrift, sobriety and hard work. This, along with the attack on superstitious rituals and Holy Days, was considered to have begun to break down the seasonal life of the lower orders. It was the threat to their lifestyle as much as their attachment to the Catholic religion that provoked the rebels in the West Country in 1549.

However, there is considerable scepticism about the whole concept of the Protestant work ethic. It is also pointed out that the Catholic rural and urban élites were just as adept at acquiring confiscated monastic property and money-making as their Protestant counterparts. In any case, the apparent religious apathy of the majority of the population makes it difficult to decide whether religion had any long-term or short-term effects on social change.

Population and social change

Many social and economic historians have not been completely convinced by any of these general theories of social change. They have considered that variations in the levels of population and the consequent inflation or deflation were the major influence on the social structure. For them the deflationary period following the Black Death of 1349, caused by falling population levels, created a period of lower order prosperity. Many smallholders gave up their land and became wage labourers in order to benefit from the high wage levels.

On the other hand, deflation caused economic problems for the landed élites. However, when the population numbers began to recover at the beginning of the sixteenth century the situation was reversed. Landowners now began to benefit from increased prices caused by inflation. They were able to push up rents because more people were looking for land to lease. This forced many of the remaining husbandmen and cottagers from the land because they could not afford the higher rents. As more people were available for work, wages did not increase at the same rate as prices. Consequently, the living standards of both smallholders and wage labourers fell, while most of the élites were prospering. It has been suggested that it was the effect of this change that was being fully felt by 1549, and was a cause of the popular unrest.

New research

Although these ideas still remain a good starting point for thinking about social change in early modern England, they, like all general ideas, are now considered to be far too restrictive. Continued research, particularly at local level, has revealed an English society too varied to be explained by any theory. There were great differences between regions, counties and even neighbouring villages. Equally, convenient labels such as 'capitalism' or 'bourgeoisie' are no longer thought appropriate for the sixteenth century. Similarly, concepts such as 'the Protestant work ethic' are thought to be inappropriate.

While society at all levels was becoming more fluid and individualistic, and there was an increase in commercialism and competition, this is no longer seen as a cause of conflict. Indeed, it can be maintained that popular discontent was always close to the surface in pre-industrial societies where so many people lived near the poverty line. Only in times of severe hardship, such as famine or widespread unemployment, did grievances erupt into violence. So it might well be said that the mid-century problems were more economic than social.

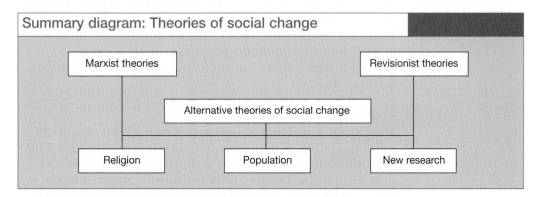

Summary diagram: Theories of social change

2 | Social Structure and Social Mobility

English society underwent an important period of evolution between 1350 and 1550. Mid-sixteenth-century society is regarded as being more competitive and individualistic than it had been during the Middle Ages. Even so, it is considered that it was still overwhelmingly rural, and retained many of the characteristics of feudal society. One of the most important signs of change is thought to be the amount of social mobility existing between the various classes or social groups.

Social mobility

The pace of social change quickened in the century and a half after the Black Death. However, there had been little structural change by the middle of the sixteenth century. The three social hierarchies of monarchy, nobility and gentry stayed broadly unaltered in size and in their relationship to each other. The late medieval economic decline adversely affected both the towns and the Church in economic terms, but had no impact on their social structure. It was rural society that changed both economically and socially.

Key question
How significant were the signs of social mobility?

The rural élites

A consequence of the economic decline of the great landowners was that during the fifteenth century some of them had to sell part of their land, and lease out much of the remainder on long leases of up to 99 years. The immediate impact of this was the temporary

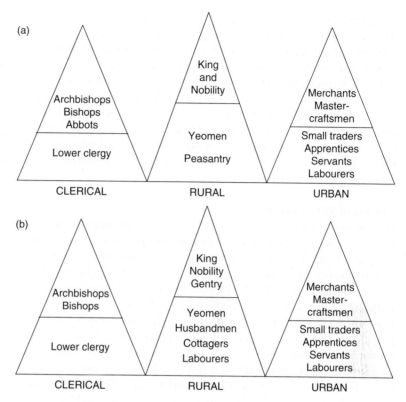

Figure 6.1: Social hierarchy. (a) Feudal social hierarchy c1350. (b) The early Tudor social hierarchy c1550.

(a)

CLERICAL: Archbishops Bishops Abbots / Lower clergy

RURAL: King and Nobility / Yeomen Peasantry

URBAN: Merchants Master-craftsmen / Small traders Apprentices Servants Labourers

(b)

CLERICAL: Archbishops Bishops / Lower clergy

RURAL: King Nobility Gentry / Yeomen Husbandmen Cottagers Labourers

URBAN: Merchants Master-craftsmen / Small traders Apprentices Servants Labourers

lowering of the social prestige of the nobility. They could no longer afford to maintain their great households, and service to the Crown became more attractive to the ambitious among the lesser élites. Likewise, the sale and leasing out of the great estates created a very active land market, which widened the availability of land. This was the beginning of the rise of the gentry.

The major change was that there had been a significant redistribution of land to the new gentry. When prices and rents began to rise after 1500 it was the gentry who benefited from such increases, and from the improving industrial and commercial conditions. The aristocracy were unable to reap any real profit from their estates until the long leases, often 99 years long, ran out towards the end of the sixteenth century and they were able to repossess their land.

The Renaissance

Another highly significant development which is considered to have altered the pattern of social mobility, particularly among the élites, was the spread of the **Renaissance** and **Christian humanism** in England at the end of the fifteenth century. The Renaissance is seen as weakening the influence of the Church. Apart from causing a growth in **anti-clericalism** by attacking the wealth and abuses in the Church, Renaissance thought encouraged the spread of secular education. Previously a clerical career was seen not just as an opportunity to obtain high office in the Church, but as a means of gaining important governmental positions.

Christian humanism

The spread of Christian humanism, with its emphasis on education for the laity, promoted universities, the legal **Inns of Court** and secular schools as an alternative for political careerists. Thomas Wolsey, the son of a Suffolk cattle dealer who rose to become a cardinal, the Archbishop of York, and Lord Chancellor under Henry VIII, is seen as the last of the great English clerical careerists. His successors, such as Thomas Cromwell and William Cecil, came to power through a university and legal education. Increasingly this became the route taken by those aspiring to a political and administrative career.

Inns of Court
Located in London, the Inns of Court provided a university-type education for those wishing to study and practise law.

Key term

The rural lower orders

Equally significant changes were taking place among the rural lower orders. The decline in economic and political power among the great landowners is considered to have brought about the disappearance of serfdom and labour services in England during the fifteenth century. All the peasantry were now theoretically free (although there were still serfs in some parts of England until the end of the sixteenth century), and so could move about the country as they chose. This is seen as ending, or at least drastically altering, the structure of peasant society. Peasant smallholders were generally described as husbandmen. Customary tenures were being replaced by a new form of tenancy for the lifetime of the holder called copyhold, for which rent was paid in cash. Many of the former peasants took advantage of the availability of land and amassed holdings of some 200 acres or more. They became commercial farmers, and joined the ranks of the yeomen.

Now that the new copyhold tenancies no longer carried the stigma of being unfree, many of the former yeomen and new gentry were also prepared to acquire this type of land. However, many husbandmen preferred to remain self-sufficient smallholders, with about 30–40 acres of land. At the same time some improved their position by acquiring enough land to become self-sufficient. Others preferred to continue to supplement the produce of their smallholdings by working for wages on the commercial farms and in rural industry. A significant number decided to take advantage of the higher wage levels created by the fall in the size of the labour force, and abandon their land to work full-time for wages. The lower orders enjoyed much greater geographical mobility, so that many more people could take advantage of them.

Assessment

By 1558 it appears that there had been little alteration to the social structure at any level. The monarchy had established its position of social and political superiority. By making good their economic losses the nobility had consolidated themselves as the major landowning group below the monarch. The gentry had established themselves as the rank immediately below the nobility. Yeomen were recognised as the most important landowners below the gentry. The urban and clerical hierarchies remained unchanged. Self-sufficient husbandmen were still the most numerous group in the rural communities. The number of wage-earners had increased and they were forming a growing rural and urban working class.

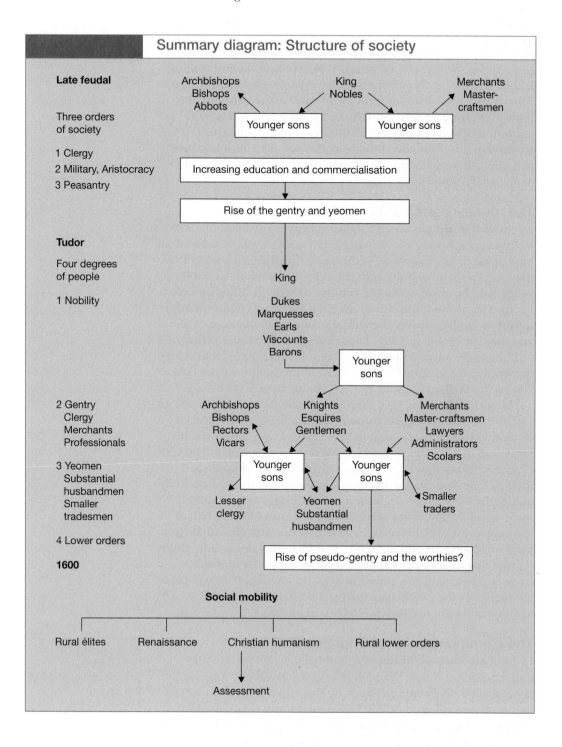

Summary diagram: Structure of society

Late feudal

Three orders of society

1 Clergy
2 Military, Aristocracy
3 Peasantry

Archbishops
Bishops
Abbots

King
Nobles

Merchants
Master-craftsmen

Younger sons

Younger sons

Increasing education and commercialisation

Rise of the gentry and yeomen

Tudor

Four degrees of people

1 Nobility

King

Dukes
Marquesses
Earls
Viscounts
Barons

Younger sons

2 Gentry
 Clergy
 Merchants
 Professionals

Archbishops
Bishops
Rectors
Vicars

Knights
Esquires
Gentlemen

Merchants
Master-craftsmen
Lawyers
Administrators
Scolars

Younger sons

Younger sons

3 Yeomen
 Substantial
 husbandmen
 Smaller
 tradesmen

Lesser
clergy

Yeomen
Substantial
husbandmen

Smaller
traders

4 Lower orders

Rise of pseudo-gentry and the worthies?

1600

Social mobility

Rural élites   Renaissance   Christian humanism   Rural lower orders

Assessment

3 | Contemporary Views of Mid-Tudor Society

Key question
How did the Tudors themselves view their own society?

The idea of a static medieval peasant population with the vast majority of families living for generations in the same village has been disproved; the early Tudor lower orders were more geographically mobile than was once thought. Similarly, it has been shown that not all towns were in economic decline. Some, particularly London, were prospering, while others were passing into obscurity. It is important to stress the localised nature of early Tudor society. The emphasis is now put on the importance and differences between counties and even neighbouring villages. There was a keen sense of local loyalty and interference by the central government was resisted. Tudor MPs were much more interested in matters relating to their own locality than in national events. Similarly, local societies had their own loyalties and interests, which were not necessarily the same as those of their social counterparts elsewhere in the country.

The muster certificates of 1522

A remarkably full picture of English society is provided in 1522. In that year the King's Council ordered a survey to be made of all men fit for military service. At the same time the government used the survey to enquire into the value of land and movable goods held by everyone in the country in order to draw up new tax lists. As a result, the survey provides the most comprehensive census of English society between the Domesday Book of 1086 and the first census in 1801. Unfortunately, the muster returns for 1522 have not survived for all counties. However, sufficient numbers remain for historians to have used them over the past 20 years to analyse the state of early Tudor society.

The picture that emerges from the muster returns is of considerable underlying continuity, but there are clear signs of increasing commercialisation by the 1520s. England was mainly rural, and most of the population lived in small villages. The Church continued to be the largest single holder of land, and there is little evidence of any marked changes in the composition of urban society. However, although the villages were mainly made up of communities of husbandmen, most of them had at least one commercial farmer, or yeoman. It is also clear that the number of servants and labourers had increased noticeably, and it is estimated that 40 per cent of the lower orders were wage-earners. The rise of the gentry as a group was clearly well advanced. By the 1520s they held some 30 per cent of the manors, and were the leaseholders of many more.

The Commonwealth of England 1565

Key question
How reliable is Smith's description of the structure of English society?

In 1565 Sir Thomas Smith, who had been Secretary of State under Somerset, wrote the book *The Commonwealth of England* (*De Republica Anglorum*), in which he described English society as he saw it. According to Smith Tudor society was divided into four groups or classes: gentlemen, urban élite, yeomen and labourers.

The value of lands & property there
The Abbot of Abingdon is chief lord there & his lands are in value by
  the year over all charges £40 0s 0d
Thomas Unton Gent. in lands 6s 8d
John Elyotte in lands 5s 8d
Sir William Craddock Clerk is parson there & his parsonage is in
  value by the year over all charges £13 0s 0d

The value of goods & other movable property there
John Wyse senior householder £22 0s 0d
John White servant 12s 0d
John Yate h. £5 0s 0d
Robert Barteley servant £1 0s 0d
Thomas Abday h. £7 0s 0d
Thomas Seuernake £2 0s 0d
John Bowell H. £4 0s 0d
William Badnoll h. £13 6s 8d
Robert Ryve servant £1 6s 8d
Thomas Carter servant £1 0s 0d
William Browne h. £1 0s 0d
John Cowley h. £2 0s 0d
John Chirchey h. £3 0s 0d
John Tayllor h. £12 0s 0d
William Yate h. £14 0s 0d
Thomas Yate his son £2 0s 0d
William Somner servant 10s 0d
Harry Harne h. £1 0s 0d
Phillippe Smythe h. £2 0s 0d
John Smythe h. £5 6s 8d
Margory Chirche widow £1 0s 0d
Julyan Chirche widow £1 0s 0d
Margett of Acris widow 10s 0d

Figure 6.2: The muster certificate for Shellingford, 1522. Why are the 1522 muster certificates so useful to historians?

Gentlemen

The first of Smith's four social divisions were gentlemen. Smith had most to say about this class because he was one of them, which is why he subdivided them into two upper and lower groups. 'The first part of Gentlemen of England' were called *'nobilitas major'*. These were the members of the House of Lords and in Smith's opinion, no man was worthy of being called or created a baron unless he had an annual income of a thousand pounds. 'The second part of Gentlemen' were called *'nobilitas minor'*. The title and dignity of knighthood could not be inherited, 'knights therefore be not born but made'. Esquires 'be all those which bear arms'. Gentlemen 'be those whom their blood and race doth make noble and known'.

In further defining the upper class and separating them from the second group Smith wrote the following:

For whosoever studieth the laws of the realm, who studieth in the Universities ... and to be short, who can live idly and without manual labour, and will bear the port, charge and countenance of a gentleman, he shall be called master.

Urban élite

Second were the urban élite, the citizens and **burgesses** of the large towns and cities. This group included merchants, retailers and craftsmen who had made their wealth by trade. Smith had little to say about this group, perhaps because he understood them the least, having been brought up and educated in a rural world.

Yeomen

Third were the yeomen, who were 'next unto the nobility, knights and squires'; a yeoman was a 'freeman born English' and had the means to enjoy an annual income of 40s (£2). Smith considered them a more significant group than the urban élite, who he felt did not fit easily into his rural framework.

Labourers

'The fourth sort or class amongst us' were the day labourers, poor husbandmen and all 'artificers' (wage labourers). 'These have no voice nor authority in our commonwealth, and no account is made of them, but only to be ruled.'

As historians Anthony Fletcher and Diarmaid MacCulloch have pointed out Smith was 'not making a sociological analysis; he was describing power'.

It must be remembered that this was an élite viewpoint, and it is not possible to be sure of the author's motives for writing the book. It may be that he was depicting society as he thought it should be, rather than showing it as it actually was in the middle of the sixteenth century. Again, he might, like the Norfolk rebels, be nostalgically looking back to a society that he thought was vanishing.

Burgesses
The most powerful members of a town's citizens. They were often descended from the town's original founders and they also tended to hold the most important offices in the town's administration.

Key term

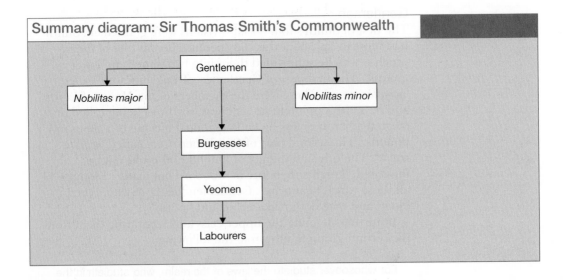

Summary diagram: Sir Thomas Smith's Commonwealth

Key question
Is there any evidence
to support the theory
that mid-Tudor
society was in crisis?

4 | Mid-Tudor Society and the Theory of Social Crisis

It was once thought that the popular rebellions and the élite power struggle in 1549 indicate a social crisis at all levels of society. In view of the apparent stability in all the social hierarchies this conclusion is no longer considered valid. In social terms neither the urban nor the clerical hierarchies displayed any signs of pressure. The clergy and urban élites appear to have supported the Crown and the maintenance of order and stability. Furthermore, no drastic change can be seen in the pattern of social development among the lower orders.

Conflict among the élites?

A number of suggestions have been put forward to support the contention that competition among the élites had reached crisis point by the middle of the sixteenth century. Revisionists have modified or re-interpreted this traditional viewpoint.

Traditional interpretation

1. The numbers of the élites was increasing more rapidly than the rest of the population, particularly after 1500, because the economic conditions favoured them and their diets and health improved. There is certainly evidence to suggest that the size of élite families was increasing by the middle of the century. For example, William Hyde esquire of Denchworth in Berkshire, who died in 1557, had 13 children, and his eldest son had 10 children. Land and office had to be found for the offspring of the upper classes, which led to greater competition.

2. There were signs of increasing competition for land between the rising gentry and the aristocracy. For example, the demand for land among the élites had begun to exceed supply. This competition for land was not caused just by the increased numbers of gentry and yeomen but by the improving commercial opportunities available to landowners. Many of the great estate owners, whose land was still tied up with long leases, wished to obtain additional land so that they could take advantage of the upturn in the economy. In addition, leaseholders were anxious to convert their leases into freehold. This situation is seen as being potentially dangerous for the Crown, as it was causing instability among the élites.

3. The English Reformation and the redistribution of Church lands had a significant impact on élite society. This was the largest redistribution of land since the Norman Conquest and would have a considerable impact on the structure of élite society. It has been estimated that in 1500 the nobility had an average annual income of £1000 compared with £130 for knights, £58 for esquires and £14 for gentlemen. However, the market in Church lands caused wide disparities of wealth within each rank. For example, by 1548 Somerset had an annual income of £7400 from his estates, much of which came

from his success in acquiring ecclesiastical property. Fellow members of the Privy Council – Northumberland, Herbert, Paget, Russell, Rich and Wriothesley – had similarly enriched themselves with Church lands. The unequal acquisition and distribution of Church property led to envy and conflict.

4. The rivalry for power between the rising gentry and the aristocracy had intensified. Henry VII and Henry VIII were accused of deliberately trying to change the social composition of the aristocracy by promoting new families at the expense of the ancient nobility. Former gentry families such as the Seymours and Dudleys, through a combination of military careers, public office, the seizure of Church lands and royal favour, had risen rapidly to the top ranks of the social hierarchy.

Revisionist interpretation

1. Doubts have been expressed about the effects the increasing numbers of élites would have had on society by 1558. It has been estimated that:

   - in 1500 there were 55 nobles, 500 knights, 800 esquires and 5000 gentlemen
   - by 1550 the number of nobles and knights had not changed.

   Although the numbers of esquires and gentlemen had risen, it is thought unlikely that the rate of increase greatly exceeded the general population growth of one per cent per year.

2. The competition between the gentry and the aristocracy is now seen in terms of traditional élite rivalry for land and power. The buoyant land market, fuelled by the availability of Church property between 1536 and 1554, more than met the needs of the land-hungry élite. On the other hand, many gentry did not compete for or acquire Church lands. For example, the ancient family of Pusey in Berkshire demonstrated that in the favourable economic conditions it was possible to prosper even without acquiring additional lands. In 1522 Thomas Pusey's wealth had been estimated at £8. When his grandson Philip died in 1573 he left £238 in his will. This represents an increase of over 2300 per cent in 50 years, whereas the rate of inflation was only 200 per cent over the same period. The increase was due in part to converting long leases (99 years) to shorter ones (20 years) and in taking advantage of greater commercial opportunities.

3. By 1558 the secularisation of Church property had had very little effect on the structure of élite society. With the exception of the immediate vicinity of London, where city merchants were very active in the land market, the land had gone to consolidate the position of the existing aristocracy and gentry. Only a small amount of land appears to have passed into the possession of new owners from the towns or industry. Success or failure was by no means dependent on the ability to buy Church property. For example, the Essex family from north Berkshire was perhaps the most successful in the county in accumulating Church lands. Their annual landed income increased from £160 in 1522 to

£238 by 1553, but further land speculation and changes in land value led to their bankruptcy by 1600.

4. The idea that the early Tudors deliberately tried to change the social composition of the aristocracy by promoting new families at the expense of the ancient nobility is now thought to be unfounded. Old noble families such as the Percys, Nevilles and Poles had fallen through royal disfavour. Others, such as the Howards, survived the displeasure of the monarchy to rise again. The Brandon family, which had risen rapidly through royal marriage, fell back into obscurity because it failed to produce male heirs. Among the lesser élites a gap was starting to develop. Some of the 'greater' gentry began to rival the aristocracy for wealth, while many of the 'parish' gentry became barely distinguishable from yeomen. This is regarded as part of the traditional pattern of success or failure – a 'wheel of fortune' with families rising, falling and stagnating.

Lower order discontent?

Key question
What evidence is there to support the theory of lower order discontent?

If there was social conflict and crisis in mid-Tudor England, the popular uprisings of 1549 suggest that it was caused by problems among the lower orders. The difficulty is to decide whether the problems were caused by social tensions. There is no reason why the comparatively stable, non-élite society of the late fifteenth and early sixteenth centuries should have radically altered by the middle of the century. The problem is considered to lie in the economic conditions, which no longer favoured the lower orders. Rising population and inflation brought prosperity to the élites, but eroded the standards of living for the masses – a situation on which R.H. Tawney, one of the early pioneering social historians, commented in 1912: 'Villeinage [serfdom] ceases but the poor laws begin'.

Population pressure

There is ample evidence to support such an interpretation of the problems in 1549. It is estimated that the population was rising at the rate of one per cent per year, and possibly faster, up to the middle of the century. This would have meant that the population level of 2.3 million in the 1520s may have reached some three million by 1550. This, it is thought, might well have put a strain on food production and created a Malthusian crisis (see pages 172–3), which was made worse by the harvest failure in 1549. The greater number of people enabled landowners to push up the level of rents, while employers were able to keep down wages.

In contrast, inflation, which is estimated to have run at four per cent per year over the whole country during the 1520s and 1530s, was made worse by the debasements of the coinage in the 1540s (see page 174) and may have reached over 200 per cent by 1550. For the growing number of cloth workers the decline of the Antwerp cloth market (see pages 185 and 186) resulted in heavy job losses in the country's largest industry. Furthermore, the comparative lack of popular unrest in the 1550s can be explained by heavy mortality caused by severe epidemics of plague and

'sweating sickness' in 1551 and 1552, and of influenza
between 1556 and 1558, which relieved population pressure
(see pages 169–71).

Social conflict?

Did the popular rebellions of 1549 (see pages 130–6) offer clear
proof of social conflict directed particularly against the gentry? It
is true that in the West Country and in Norfolk the rebels were
antagonistic towards the local gentry. The Privy Council described
both uprisings as social conflict which threatened to undermine
the whole fabric of society. However, historians now regard such
statements as government propaganda intended to unite the
élites behind an increasingly unpopular administration.

Much of the resentment towards the gentry centred on the
accusation that they were using the Reformation to enrich
themselves and to exploit their tenants. But there is little reason
to see why the sale of Church lands should have had any great

Illustration showing families forced to become vagrants in search of work. Are the poor depicted in a sympathetic way?

effect upon the tenants. Another major cause of resentment was that the rebels, like the government, mistakenly blamed enclosure for the adverse economic situation (see below). It is difficult to see how this could have had an immediate effect in 1549. The great bulk of enclosures had taken place before 1520, and most of these were in the Midlands, where there were no popular uprisings.

Clearly, enclosure did alter the pattern of community life in the villages, but is was part of the changes that had been in progress since the end of the fourteenth century. In any case, much of the enclosure had been carried out by mutual consent among the husbandmen, to improve agricultural production.

Adverse economic conditions

Social conflict was really the reaction of the masses to economic hardship. It is estimated that during the sixteenth century at least 50 per cent of the rural and urban non-élites lived on, or below, subsistence level, even in good years. Discontent, therefore, was always just below the surface, and broke into revolt at times of widespread unemployment and food shortages, such as in 1549. On such occasions the ruling élites were always accused of economic and political exploitation.

Of course, it can be argued that this was a social crisis because the élites were responsible for maintaining a social structure that placed them in a highly privileged position. It is suggested that the rural rebels were largely illiterate and inarticulate, and relied on rumour and hearsay to explain problems that they did not understand. For this reason local issues and grievances became of paramount importance, and they judged the past to have been a vanished 'golden age' of prosperity to which they wished to return. Consequently, many of the grievances of such uprisings belonged more to a 'folk memory' of past events rather than to current issues. Ket's rebellion in Norfolk (see pages 133–6) is a good example of this interpretation.

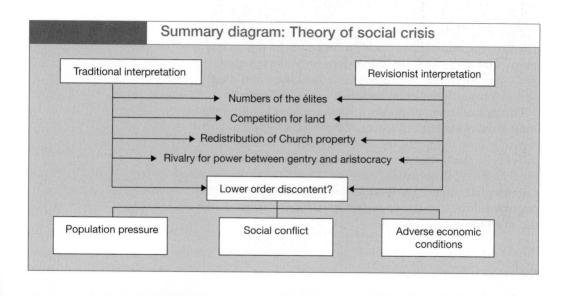

Summary diagram: Theory of social crisis

5 | The Key Debate

Was there a crisis in society?

The process of social change, although controversial, is generally easy to trace. Both the élites and the lower orders had been affected by change.

- Among the élites the emergence of the gentry from the ranks of the feudal aristocracy is still seen as a highly significant development. By the middle of the century the new structure had been strengthened by the sale of monastic and other Church lands.
- Among the lower orders there had been considerable change over the same period. The servile, feudal peasantry had disappeared, to be replaced by a new hierarchy of yeomen, husbandmen, cottagers and labourers.

Although a great gulf existed between the élites and the non-élites, the majority of the lower orders were freer and more prosperous than they had been 200 years before. There were already signs of increasing commercialism and competition at all levels of society. However, in the middle of the sixteenth century there still seems to have been considerable social stability, and little sign of social crisis. It was over the next century, when continued rise in population added to social pressures, that real signs of tension within society began to emerge.

Mid-sixteenth-century England was still an unruly nation, and violence was present at all levels of society. The government and the élites expected and feared outbreaks of popular rioting during the summer months as part of the normal course of events. These might be caused by village sports or quarrels between neighbours. A bad harvest, local enclosure or unpopular taxation might cause more widespread disorder, as in 1549 (see pages 130–6).

Nevertheless, there appears to have been a considerable degree of co-operation between social groups, particularly at local levels. The growing number of county studies and the research into gentry and noble families is revealing the different motives governing social relationships among the élites, and their attitudes towards the lower orders.

The lack of evidence makes it harder to investigate opinions among the non-élites. However, the official keeping of parish registers after 1538, and the growing number of wills and inventories left by people of relatively low social status helps historians to gain an insight into the lives of the ordinary people. Considerable attention continues to be given to the study of popular culture and disorder, and in particular to the family and the role of women in society.

At all levels mid-Tudor society appears to have been more in a process of fairly stable evolution than in a state of crisis and conflict. There was considerable underlying continuity, although significant differences had emerged. Society appears to have reached a point where the changes taking place over the previous two centuries had been consolidated. English society was about to enter the next phase of its development, which was to bring even greater structural change.

Study Guide: AS Questions

In the style of OCR

Passage 1

From: Articles of the Norfolk Rebels, 1549. Some of the demands presented by Ket and his fellow rebels to Lord Protector Somerset.

We pray your Grace that no lord of the manor encloses the common land.
We pray that priests or vicars that are unable to preach and set forth the word of God to their parishioners may be removed from their [churches].
We pray that no man under the status of knight or esquire keep a dovecot, unless it was an ancient custom.
We pray that all bond men may be made free for God made everyone free with his precious blood shedding.
We pray that no lord, knight, esquire, or gentleman graze or feed any bullocks or sheep if he has an income of £40 per year from his lands unless it is for the provision of his house.

Passage 2

From: Robert Crowley, The Way to Wealth, *published in 1550. One of the Commonwealth writers attacks landlords for their grasping behaviour and lack of obedience to the Crown in 1548–9.*

Contrary to the law against oppression and extortion, you have enclosed from the poor their common land, levied greater entry fees payable on new leases, excluded them from their rightful use of the common land, and raised their rents. What obedience did you show when the King's proclamations were sent forth to open up your enclosures, and yet you continued to enclose? If you had loved your country, would you have prevented the recent great destruction which followed from your incurable greed?

Passage 3

From: Paul Thomas, Authority and Disorder in Tudor Times
*1485–1603, published in 1999. A modern historian notes some
key religious and social problems that affected mid-Tudor society
between 1540 and 1558.*

Did religious change undermine the natural order of society and
the obedience and deference of the lower ranks towards the
upper ranks of society? Or were the religious changes the result
of demographic and economic developments arising out of
overpopulation and plague dating back to the fourteenth
century?
However when we examine the web of formal and informal
relationships which made up society in early modern England,
we can see that great changes were taking place which threw
any assumptions of a static and structured order of society into
disarray.

Passage 4

From: A. Fletcher and D. MacCulloch, Tudor Rebellions,
*published in 1997. Two modern historians offer their opinion on
the structure of and changes in Tudor society.*

Early modern society was an unequal society, and gloried in the
fact. The realities of sixteenth-century life increasingly disturbed
official attempts to portray a harmonious and static social order.
The flood of monastic, chantry and crown lands produced an
open and speculative land market. The growth of the London
and provincial food markets, galloping inflation and increased
commercial activity and litigation [going to law] offered
exceptional opportunities for social mobility in Tudor England. In
order to preserve the ideal of a static social structure those who
were successful in the competition for social advancement made
efforts to conceal their movement in society by inventing
pedigrees or heraldry [coats of arms].

(a) **Study Passages 1 and 2**
    How similar are the accusations levelled against landlords in
    these two passages?
(b) **Study all the passages**
    Using all these sources and your own knowledge, assess the
    view that religious change was the main reason for the social
    and economic problems between 1540 and 1558.

Exam tips

The cross-references are intended to take you straight to the material that will help you to answer the questions.

(a) In question **(a)** you are invited to compare the information in two passages in order to highlight the similarities between them. You should note the dates of the passages and who wrote them. Note also the fact that both passages are critical of the landlords, for example:

- they are enclosing land without a thought as to how this might affect the common people
- they are enclosing land contrary to the law
- they are greedy and grasping
- the landlords come almost exclusively from the ranks of the nobility, gentry and gentlemen; there is no mention of yeomen like Ket (pages 159–63).

(b) In question **(b)** you are asked to assess the validity of the statement that religious change was the main reason for the social and economic problems. You should group the passages so that their evidence is used thematically to provide a focused answer. You will note that two passages only – 1 and 3 – refer to religion as a factor and that neither is very convincing, e.g. in 1 religion is but one grievance among five. In 3 the historian only poses a question but does not fully answer it. You might wish to refer to the single sentence in Passage 4 which suggests that greed for monastic and chantry land contributed to social and economic problems.

You will need to offer a balanced answer where the social and economic factors are discussed – social mobility, competition for social advancement, inflation and increased commercial activity – and measured against the contribution of religious change.

7

A Crisis in the Economy?

POINTS TO CONSIDER

This chapter examines the extent to which the English economy had developed by 1558. In pre-industrial societies changes in population levels had a huge impact on the economy, and this chapter examines how agriculture and industry changed and developed during this period. Additionally, it will examine the causes and effects of rising prices, enclosures and trade recession. Finally, it will consider how effectively Tudor governments tackled these economic problems.

These issues are examined as six themes:

- Population and inflation
- Agriculture
- Industry
- The mid-Tudor trade recession
- Towns, unemployment and urban recession
- Was there a crisis in the economy?

Key dates

1349	Black Death and the beginning of recurrent bubonic plague epidemics
1470s	Beginning of population increase and inflation
1500	Prices started to rise more quickly than wages
1537–48	Series of good harvests
1549	Poor harvest and widespread popular discontent
1552	Plague and sweating sickness checked population rise
1552–3	Trade embargoes marked beginning of decline of Antwerp and beginning of commercial slump
1554–6	Severe harvest failures
1556–8	Influenza epidemics caused fall in population
1558	Loss of Calais

1 | Population and Inflation

The history of the middle years of the sixteenth century was shaped as much by underlying changes in society and the economy as by the actions of the ruling monarchs. The expansion in population and the onset of inflation had a profound effect on the lives of ordinary people. For some, they brought wealth and opportunity, but for others they made the difference between life and death.

Population: recovery and growth

There is considerable debate over the changing rates of population growth and its effects during the sixteenth century, particularly in the period between 1500 and 1558.

Population recovery 1470–1522

After the sharp demographic decline following the Black Death and the subsequent plague cycle (see page 12), population levels are considered to have ceased to fall by about 1470. This was followed by a slow recovery from about 1.5 million in 1470 to some 2.3 million by the 1520s.

There is broad agreement about this pattern of demographic decline and recovery, but not about the causes for the revival. There is little dispute that the bubonic plague, carried by the fleas of the black rat, was the cause of the initial catastrophic population losses. What is less clear is what caused the recovery after 1470. Bubonic plague was still endemic, along with a number of other diseases such as influenza, cholera, malaria and typhus. This makes it difficult to maintain that a fall in the rate of mortality was a major reason for a regrowth in population.

However, some historians believe that people were beginning to build up immunity to some forms of disease. Others suggest that vulnerability to epidemics varied and changed between age groups. The reason for recovery in population levels could have been that young adults were becoming less susceptible to diseases. If more young women survived, increased numbers of children were likely to be born, which would account for a rise in population. Alternatively it is claimed that there was a drop in **infant mortality**, which would have led to a rise in the demographic levels.

Population growth 1522–5

The situation between 1522 and 1550 is equally uncertain. It is estimated that the population was growing at approximately one per cent per year until 1550, when it possibly just exceeded three million. However, the rate of expansion was not even. It is suggested that there was only a very slow improvement until 1540, followed by rapid growth over the next decade, and that by 1558 population levels were falling back again.

Once again there is no single explanation for this pattern of events. A major factor was the presence of endemic disease. From the end of the fifteenth century a new virus had joined the killer

Key question
Why is there a debate over the changing rates of population growth and its effects during the sixteenth century?

Key dates

Black Death and the beginning of recurrent bubonic plague epidemics: 1349

Beginning of population increase and inflation: 1470s

Key term

Infant mortality Term used to describe the death rate among children, usually under five years of age. In the medieval and early modern periods, infant mortality rates were high owing to complications at birth, poor diet, disease and poor health and hygiene.

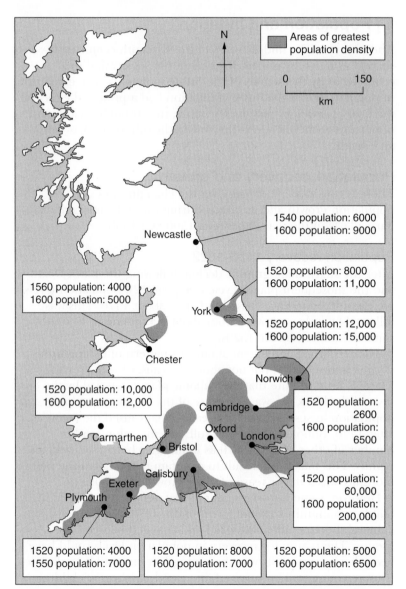

Figure 7.1:
Population distribution in the sixteenth century. What do these figures suggest about where people lived?

Map labels:

N

Areas of greatest population density

0 — 150 km

Newcastle — 1540 population: 6000 / 1600 population: 9000

1520 population: 8000 / 1600 population: 11,000

York — 1560 population: 4000 / 1600 population: 5000

1520 population: 12,000 / 1600 population: 15,000

Chester — 1520 population: 10,000 / 1600 population: 12,000

Norwich

Cambridge

Carmarthen

Oxford

Bristol

London — 1520 population: 2600 / 1600 population: 6500

Salisbury

Exeter — 1520 population: 60,000 / 1600 population: 200,000

Plymouth

1520 population: 4000 / 1550 population: 7000

1520 population: 8000 / 1600 population: 7000

1520 population: 5000 / 1600 population: 6500

diseases that were already present. The 'English sweat', a fever that spread more quickly than the plague, was particularly virulent between 1485 and 1528, and could kill within 24 hours. It struck particularly at young adults, and it is thought that this, by reducing the birthrate, slowed the rate of population increase up to 1540. Moreover there were four serious outbreaks of plague between 1500 and 1528, and another in the late 1530s, to which adolescents were especially vulnerable.

However, it is felt that the comparative absence of epidemics between 1528 and 1550 might well account for the sharp demographic increase in the 1540s. A fall in infant mortality might have been a major cause for more children surviving into adulthood.

Figure 7.2: English population change and population figures. What do these figures reveal about population change?

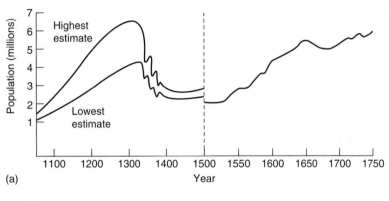

(a)

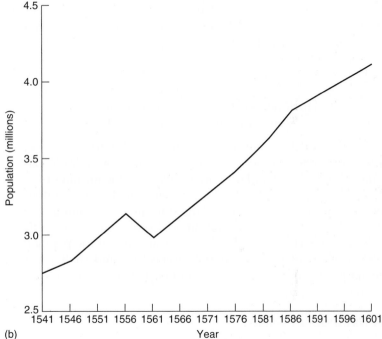

(b)

Checks to population growth 1551–8

The substantial check to population increase in the 1550s is easier to explain. In 1551 and 1552 there were fresh outbreaks of plague and sweating sickness. Even more serious was the influenza epidemic which ravaged the whole country between 1556 and 1558. It is estimated that it had a mortality rate of at least six per cent, and that the population might have been reduced to under three million.

To add to the difficulties of obtaining a clear picture, there were considerable local variations in population densities, the rate of increase or decline, and the incidence of disease. In broad terms the south-eastern section of England was more heavily populated than the north-west because of the different farming regions (see page 176).

Towns, particularly London, which had high concentrations of people, were especially susceptible to epidemics, but the rate of recovery was normally rapid. East Anglia was the most highly populated area, while the north of England had the least number of people per square mile. In sparsely settled areas epidemics were less likely, but the rate of recovery from any population losses was slower.

Variations in recovery and growth

There is ample evidence from abandoned properties and plots of land in both towns and villages that the population during the first half of the sixteenth century had not recovered from earlier losses.

- In north Berkshire the village of Hinton, even by 1573, had not recovered the level of population that it had in 1381.
- In contrast, a survey of the nearby market town of Wantage in the 1550s estimated that the town's population was 1000; a figure confirmed by calculations from the parish registers. This compares with a population of 600 in 1522 – a rise of 66 per cent over 30 years, and twice the estimated national average. The level of increase in the neighbouring villages was lower, and in some cases there was an actual decrease.

It is very difficult to pinpoint the causes of such discrepancies in the countryside, and between villages within a few miles of each other. Much of the similarly varied demographic fortunes of towns in early Tudor England can be attributed to the random outbreak of disease. The three largest towns after London – Norwich, Bristol and York – all suffered severe epidemics in the middle of the century. Indeed, it is calculated that the population of Norwich remained stationary between 1522 and 1558, which is in marked contrast to the growth of London and some other towns.

A Malthusian crisis?

Evidence in favour of a Malthusian crisis by 1549

Although the evidence for rising population levels is complicated, and often contradictory, it has been suggested that there may have been overpopulation by 1549, leading to a Malthusian crisis (see pages 172–3). The effect of the 'mini-ice age' was to introduce cooler and wetter weather, which is considered to have shortened the growing season. These conditions persisted throughout the sixteenth century, with alternating spells of good and bad weather. The result was that there were sequences of good, poor and very poor harvests.

Key question
Was there a Malthusian crisis by 1549?

There were bad harvests from:

- 1527 to 1529
- 1549 to 1551
- 1554 to 1556

There were good harvests from:

- 1537 to 1542
- 1546 to 1548

Only the exceptionally bad harvests of 1555 and 1556 were poor enough to produce an actual famine, on a wide scale. However, there were problems at a local level, such as the chronic food shortages in Coventry during the 1520s and in Norwich in 1532.

The poor harvests in the 1520s and 1550s coincided with epidemics and increased the mortality rate, while the plague epidemic of the late 1530s occurred during a run of good harvests and had less effect. Epidemics and runs of good or bad harvests affected the underlying demographic trend. The almost unbroken run of good harvests during the 1540s lowered grain prices, and so raised living standards for the mass of the population. In turn, this encouraged earlier marriage, and so intensified the upward spiral in population levels. Consequently, the poor harvest of 1549 created a subsistence crisis, which was an underlying cause of the widespread popular unrest in that year.

Evidence against there being a Malthusian crisis by 1549

On the weight of the existing evidence it is no longer considered likely that there was a Malthusian crisis in 1549. Population growth was not checked in 1549 and continued to rise until the influenza epidemics of the 1550s. Even at its height in 1550, the population level was only about half that of the early fourteenth century. Consequently, even with enclosure and increased regional specialisation (see pages 177–8), there was ample farmland to support the population. Moreover, as there had previously been a long run of good harvests, an adequate supply of stored grain remained, even in the towns.

Lower order hostility towards enclosure in Norfolk and elsewhere was not because it created local grain shortages, but because husbandmen felt that gentry competition was undermining their own agricultural specialisation (see pages 177–8). In any case, the mid-century harvest failures appear to have been caused by abnormally wet summers rather than over-cropping. The harvest failures in the mid-1550s were much more severe, but by then population levels had fallen back because of high mortality rates during the epidemics.

Causes other than food shortages must be found to explain the widespread lower order discontent in 1549. Even so, the sharp increase in population during the 1540s helps to explain the government's anxieties over enclosures, vagrancy and the need to maintain the acreage of arable land.

Inflation

Key question
Was inflation a major contributor to the economic pressures that existed by the middle of the century?

Inflation, which is estimated to have been 400 per cent over the whole of the century, is seen as another major contributor to the economic pressures that existed by the middle of the century. By 1550 the rate of inflation reached 200 per cent over the first half of the century, and the very high levels of inflation reached by 1549 contributed to the widespread popular discontent.

Causes

1. *Rising population*. A rising population, which increased demand, was the underlying cause of inflation. However, this alone does not explain the pattern of inflation during the first half of the century.

2. *Rising prices and rents*. The '**price scissors**' occurred soon after 1500. Prices and rents continued to rise until after 1550. By the 1530s grain and meat prices were increasing quite rapidly in town markets, and doubled between 1510 and 1530. Historians attribute this trend in part to the poor harvests of the 1520s, but prices showed no sign of falling even by the late 1520s after a run of good harvests. The reason for this was that commercial farmers were still concentrating on pasture for wool production rather than crops for food. This, and enclosure, are seen to be the underlying causes for the upward spiral of rents. By the 1540s population pressure added to the upward movement of inflation.

3. *Debasements of the coinage*. Other forces were at work to create high inflation by 1550. Debasements of the coinage (see page 188), which began in 1526, became very frequent in the 1540s, when the government was desperately trying to raise money to finance the wars against France and Scotland (see pages 71–2). By increasing the amount of money in circulation while devaluing the coinage, debasement caused very rapid inflation of prices.

4. *The Reformation*. At the same time the Reformation contributed to this process. Gold and silver ornaments, seized from the monasteries, chantries and churches, were melted down and turned into coins, so adding to the volume of debased coinage in circulation.

5. *Disease*. By 1553 the deaths caused by epidemics had eased population pressure and so slowed the rate of inflation. At the same time, government reforms of the currency reduced the amount of coinage in circulation (see pages 54–5). The effect was to reduce the rate of inflation still further, which might help to explain the lack of popular unrest during the bad harvests of the mid-1550s.

Key term

Price scissors
Economic term used to describe the point when prices and rents overtook wages.

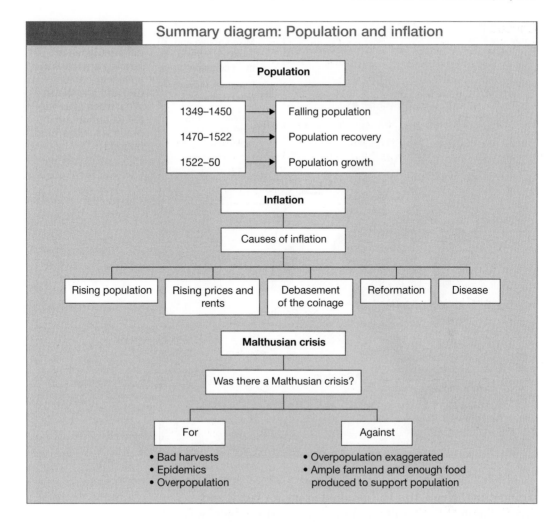

Summary diagram: Population and inflation

2 | Agriculture

Key question
Why did agriculture influence the economy?

As the largest sector in the mid-sixteenth-century English economy, and the employer of the bulk of the population, agriculture had a considerable influence on the economy. However, as agricultural development is now seen as a very slow evolutionary process, it is difficult to pinpoint precisely what stage it had reached by the mid-century.

Changes in land usage

Apart from importing food from abroad, pre-industrial farmers had two basic ways in which to increase output to feed rising populations.

- the easiest method was simply to clear and cultivate more land
- the more difficult option was to produce a greater quantity of food from the same amount of land.

During the medieval population expansion, the problem had been met by clearing more land. However, this had eventually meant cultivating increasingly marginal land unsuited to arable

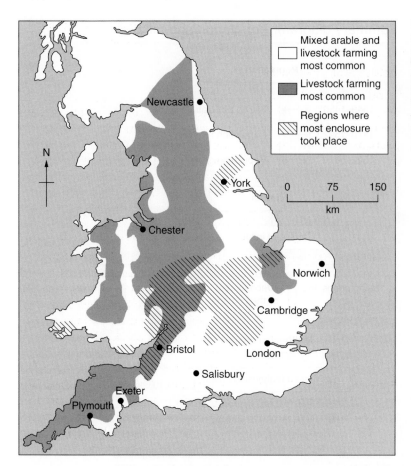

Figure 7.3: The distribution of different types of farming practices in sixteenth-century England and Wales. What does this map tell us about farming practices in the Tudor period?

farming. In the end, this had resulted in poorer yields and harvest failures. The result was a subsistence crisis – there was not enough food for the families of the poor to survive – and the breakdown of the late medieval economy.

By the fifteenth century there was no problem in feeding the drastically reduced population. This enabled farmers to abandon the poorer land, which had been made even more marginal by the change to cooler and wetter weather conditions. Whole areas, such as the Brecklands in Norfolk and Dartmoor in the West Country, were virtually abandoned. In every county many villages on the poorer or wetter soils were deserted, and were never reoccupied. This meant that large tracts of previously cultivated land reverted to grassland and pasture, which enabled more cattle and sheep to be kept.

The remaining areas of arable were on the richer soils or, at least, those soils that would support cultivation with the extra quantity of manure available. This means that English agriculture should have been able to move on to the more advanced stage of producing sufficient food from a smaller acreage of arable land. The evidence suggests that without the constant pressure to produce cereals, farming began to become more specialised. This raises the question as to why England in 1550, with a population of only just over three million, appears to have been barely able to feed this comparatively small number of people.

Changing methods

Land usage

Key question
When and why did farming methods change?

Part of the answer lies in the changes in agriculture taking place after the collapse of the late-medieval economy. One of the problems with medieval farming was that it had been largely dominated by 'peasant production methods'. A peasant smallholder had had to produce a range of foodstuffs from the land in order to meet all the needs of his family. This form of production took no account of the wide variety of soil types or their suitability for general farming. Therefore, peasant cultivation was often inefficient and wasteful.

However, even during the Middle Ages, peasants had had to adapt their farming techniques to meet the differing conditions imposed by moorlands, fens or forest. After 1350 the reduction in the number of smallholdings meant that gentry, yeomen and husbandmen could begin to specialise within the broader agricultural zones. The two major zones are divided by a line running from Newcastle in the north-east to Exmouth in the south-west. The upland area west and north of this line has thinner soils with a cooler, wetter climate, making it more suitable for pastoral farming. The lowland area to the south and east of the line has richer soils with a warmer and drier climate better suited to arable farming. Within these zones specialisations began to develop, such as dairy farming in Wiltshire or cereal production in East Anglia.

New crops and techniques

Key terms

Field rotation
System where different crops are rotated between fields.

Flexible field systems
Farmers could grow what crops they wanted where they wanted, either in large open fields or in enclosed fields.

This growing agricultural variety makes it difficult to decide how far farming had progressed by the middle of the sixteenth century. During the sixteenth century new techniques, crops and methods of **field rotation** were introduced. A number of new crops, such as clover and lucerne, were being grown to improve fodder for animal feed. Industrial crops such as saffron, woad and rapeseed were being grown to produce dyes and oils for textile manufacture. At the same time it is suggested that improvements were being made to the techniques of breeding cattle and sheep.

Enclosure

A vital part of this process of improvement was considered to be the spread of enclosure from about 1450 onwards. This, it is thought, enabled the growth of more efficient medium-sized farms, which had **flexible field systems**. These new layouts began to replace the old three-field system, where an individual farmer's land was scattered in small plots across the open fields. At the same time much of the common land was enclosed and brought under more intensive cultivation. It was these developments that are considered to have enabled the introduction of greater specialisation and new techniques.

The technique of '**up and down husbandry**' is seen to have prevented soil exhaustion, and to have maintained a better balance between arable and grazing land. Further improvements were made to grazing land by the use of floating water meadows – riverside pastures that were flooded every year with the aid of sluices so that the river silt would enhance the quality of the grass.

Up and down husbandry
A system under which land was used alternatingly over a number of years as arable and then for pasture.

Key term

Assessing mid-Tudor agriculture

The reason why enclosure and commercialisation were blamed by the government for the economic problems is that, although changes were taking place in agriculture, there had been little improvement in the level of cereal production by the mid-sixteenth century. Indeed, it is believed that enclosure was the cause of this problem.

Enclosure

In the first half of the sixteenth century, the gentry and yeomen, who were mainly responsible for enclosure, were clearly looking for the most profitable crops to gain a good return on their investment. During periods of high population grain prices rose, and so enclosed fields, which were ideal for growing cereals, were used for this purpose.

Rising population

It is thought that in response to a rising population, increasing numbers of commercial farmers converted to cereals. By the seventeenth century production was so efficient that grain prices actually fell in spite of a continued rise in population. However, population increase was almost imperceptible until after 1540. For this reason farmers were slow to shift to cereals, preferring to use enclosed land as sheep-runs, so as to profit from high wool prices.

Specialisation

Whatever type of specialism was adopted, new agricultural regions created problems for grain supplies during the first part of the sixteenth century. Not only did these new agricultural regions lower the overall national cereal output, they became increasingly dependent upon surrounding areas for grain and other farm products.

Many such areas were created by yeomen and husbandmen responding to local demands and adapting to the types of soil on which they farmed. A good example of this is Wiltshire, where the heavy soils were particularly suited to cattle-raising, and dairy farming became a speciality. Small dairy herds were attractive to husbandmen because they could be managed with family labour, and brought in a regular income from milk, butter and cheese. Larger scale cattle-rearing and fattening was usually outside the scope of the husbandmen because it required more money. For a regional farming structure to work efficiently a good infrastructure of roads and navigable rivers was needed so that produce could be moved rapidly from one part of the country to another.

The government and local authorities were aware of the problem. Attempts were made to improve river navigation, particularly on the Thames, and local landowners worked with the town authorities to improve roads. However, it is considered that little real progress was made until after the 1560s.

A contemporary view of the situation

Such a view is supported by Sir Thomas Smith in another of his books, *A Discourse on the Commonwealth of this Realm of England* (1560s) (see page 156). This takes the form of a dialogue or debate by a doctor, representing the academic view, discussing the

Everyday rural scenes depicted in a contemporary publication *The Art of Husbandry*. How reliable are the illustrations in depicting the everyday life of the lower orders?

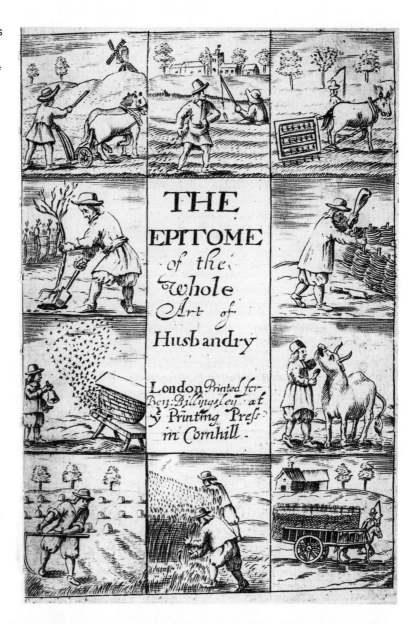

state of the economy with various members of society such as a
knight, a merchant and a husbandman. After suggesting that the
debasing of the coinage had doubled prices in his lifetime, the
doctor goes on to discuss the cost and shortage of grain. He
suggests that the best way to get more grain was either to make it
as expensive as wool, or to reduce the price of wool.

This view of the economy confirms that it was not just the
gentry and yeomen who were failing to grow enough grain, but
that husbandmen were equally to blame for any shortfalls. The
reason for this was the low price of grain in comparison with wool
and other animal products over the previous decades, which had
led to the conversion of arable to pasture. It is interesting to note
that husbandmen were just as keen to enclose their land as the
larger commercial farmers, and regarded enclosed holdings as
more efficient than the old open fields. Husbandmen clearly were
being adversely affected by increased rents and other agricultural
overheads.

At the same time they were just as ready to react as the larger
commercial farmers to market forces. This, along with rising
rents, was a major cause of popular hostility towards the gentry.
Wool was seen as the quickest way of making a profit from land,
but sheep-runs were a large-scale undertaking and outside the
scope of most husbandmen. It was such commercially based
rivalry that was an important underlying cause of the disorders in
1549.

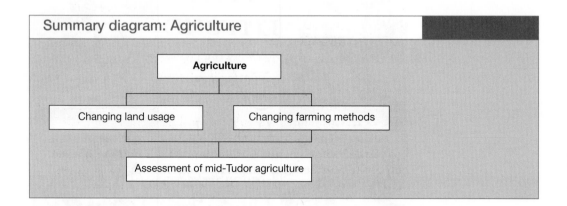

3 | Industry

Developments in industry show whether or not the mid-Tudor
economy was becoming more advanced. The agricultural sector
was just about able to feed the population, except in bad harvest
years. Less land was under cultivation so that, as the population
began to rise, surplus labour became available to work in industry.
For this to happen more jobs had to be created in both rural and
urban industries.

Key question
What were the effects
of industrial
development during
the sixteenth century?

Key question
How significant was
the development of
heavy industry?

Heavy industry

Heavy industry used to be considered the most dynamic part of the sector. It was suggested by J.U. Nef in *The Rise of the British Coal Industry* (1932) that there was a Tudor industrial revolution led by rising coal production. This idea was based on the once popular theory that there was a severe timber shortage in Tudor England, and that there was consequently a sharp increase in the use of mineral fuels. The expansion in the industrial use of non-agricultural raw materials, such as coal, was seen as being vitally important in the development of early capitalism. Such operations needed expensive equipment on a centralised site and a small, but highly skilled workforce. Mining and metal-working, along with other specialised and capital-intensive undertakings such as dyeing, brewing, glass and paper-making, are regarded as the real signs of a new, capitalistic economy.

Problems in the coal industry

These ideas are no longer accepted. It is now thought that any shortages of wood or charcoal were purely local. No sudden rise in demand for coal can be seen until the end of the sixteenth century. A major problem for expansion in heavy industry was the difficulty and cost of transport. Unlike raw materials from agriculture, coal and other minerals were only to be found in certain areas. Consequently, industries associated with these products were very localised because of the cost of carrying heavy materials more than a short distance. It is not considered that any great expansion was possible until real improvements to river navigation and sea transport began in the second half of the sixteenth century.

   Another difficulty preventing the expansion of heavy industry was that English technology was very backward in comparison with that of the continent. Problems of drainage and ventilation meant that mining operations had to be open cast. Coal was mined in south Wales, the Weald of Kent, the Forest of Dean and parts of the Midlands, but only for local use. The main coal-producing area was Northumberland and Durham, and increasingly large quantities were shipped to London from the end of the fourteenth century. However, this 'sea coal' was used largely for domestic fires and not for industrial purposes.

The metal industries

Before the second half of the sixteenth century only small quantities of coal were used in industry. Another important consideration was that coal was unsuitable for iron smelting. Iron ore, like coal, was mined in various places, but mainly in the Weald of Kent and the Forest of Dean, where there was a plentiful supply of timber for making charcoal to smelt the ore.

   At the end of the fifteenth century, gentry and yeomen ironmasters in the Weald began to use a new type of blast furnace, fuelled by charcoal and powered by water, which had been introduced from the continent. By the 1550s, 26 of these new furnaces were in use in the Weald, making it a major producer of cast iron, which was used particularly for making naval guns and shot. However, pig iron was still the major output. This was converted into bar iron in a forge fuelled by charcoal and driven by water. The bars of iron were then distributed on pack animals to blacksmiths in the towns and villages for making into tools and other small objects such as door handles.

Apart from the technological advance in iron production, little real progress was made elsewhere before 1560. Tin was mined in Devon and Cornwall mainly for export. Much the same can be said for lead and zinc mining in Shropshire and the Mendips. Although a new blast furnace for smelting lead, which only used half as much fuel, was introduced, the metal-working industries were on a very small scale. It was only after the 1570s that copper, pewter, brass and silver production began to become important.

Other specialist, centralised industries such as brick, tile and glass-making, bell-founding and gunpowder manufacture, were still very localised. New, sophisticated processes such as paper-making were only just being introduced.

Assessment of heavy industry

By the mid-sixteenth century heavy industry had had little impact on economic growth, and was still at the stage of catching up with continental technology. However, if this sector cannot be said to have made any positive contribution to industrial expansion, neither can it be considered to have added to the economic problems of the mid-century.

Rural industry

In the thirteenth century many urban textile and leather craftsmen had moved to the countryside to avoid the power of the guilds and the high cost of living in towns (see pages 187–8). There they set up new industries to make use of the cheap rural labour force. Crafts such as spinning, weaving, glove-making and basket-making had traditionally been carried out by peasant families in their own homes to supplement their incomes. Craftsmen were able to use this semi-skilled workforce to establish an industry outside the jurisdiction of the town guilds. This was the beginning of the rural textile industry that was to remain dominant until the eighteenth century. Unlike the guilds, which produced small quantities of high-quality, expensive goods, rural industries manufactured large amounts of less well-made, but much cheaper, products.

> **Key question**
> How important were the changes in rural industry?

The rural cloth industry

The largest branch of rural industry was textile manufacturing. The significance of this form of cloth production was that it was large scale and exported increasing quantities of semi-finished textiles to the continent. By the sixteenth century this industry was organised by clothiers. Generally these were merchants from a nearby town, or local yeomen and prosperous husbandmen. Raw materials such as wool or yarn were purchased by the clothier, who distributed them to his workforce for manufacturing in their cottages using their own tools.

There was a significant division of labour because the various stages of manufacture were separated, and only the clothiers sold the completed piece of cloth. It also meant that the clothier had no large outlay to provide buildings or equipment, as was the case in heavy industry. The only high-cost buildings required were the water-driven fulling mills to felt and thicken the woollen cloth by shrinking and rolling it so that the fibres interlocked, and in most cases existing flour mills could be used for this purpose. The capital costs were the purchase of the raw materials and the wages for the workforce.

However, it is thought that many of the rural workforce, particularly the weavers, remained self-employed, and were not entirely dependent on wages. The development of a major exporting industry in England is considered to be a significant economic advance. The main areas of clothmaking were East Anglia, the West Country and parts of Yorkshire.

Competition between rural and urban industries

Although the rural textile industry is seen as the major contributor to England's economic expansion up to 1550, it did create a number of problems. As the putting-out system was free of guild regulations it was not necessary for those taking part in it to have served an **apprenticeship**. This caused resentment among the members of the town guilds who saw it as unfair competition. The situation was made worse by the government's failure to enforce regulations in the countryside. Consequently, by the early sixteenth century, apart from textiles, a variety of allied trades, such as leather crafts, had become firmly established. These also competed with the more expensive products of the urban guilds.

Government legislation

From the beginning of the sixteenth century the government repeatedly passed legislation to try to exert greater control over rural industry. In part this was in response to complaints about shoddy workmanship and poor-quality goods levelled at the putting-out industry by the towns. At the same time the State was trying to take greater control over the economy in general. However, attempts by the authorities to remedy the situation were generally crude and heavy-handed. In 1559 Sir William Cecil suggested restoring the unpopular Vagrancy Act of 1547 (see page 48). Furthermore he recommended that servants and labourers should not be allowed to leave their villages, and no one should be apprenticed unless his father was a gentleman or merchant, and owned land worth at least 10 pounds a year.

Assessing mid-Tudor industry

The poor state of industry suggests that the Tudor economy had not advanced significantly by the 1550s. Consequently, no effective transfer of labour was taking place from the agricultural to the industrial sector. The situation was made worse by the

Key term

Apprenticeship Time served by students learning a trade from master-craftsmen.

down-turn in exports, which created further unemployment in the textile trades.

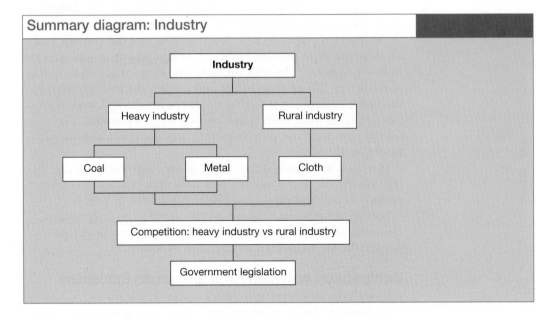

Summary diagram: Industry

4 | The Mid-Tudor Trade Recession

By the 1550s there was widespread destitution in the textile trades and in the towns. The long period of ever-rising cloth exports had ended, so bringing a sustained period of expansion from the 1460s to an abrupt halt. It is agreed that the basic cause of this problem was the decline of the Antwerp cloth market, but there were a number of other contributory factors, which need to be considered to understand the economic difficulties in mid-Tudor England.

Long-term causes
The underlying problem can be traced to developments in the fifteenth century.

1. *Exports.* By the 1440s textile exports had risen to some 55,000 cloths a year, while wool exports had fallen to an annual 9000 sacks. In the middle of the century trade was adversely affected by the general western European trade recession.
2. *Diplomatically weak.* England was in a weak diplomatic position after defeat in the war with France and the beginning of the Wars of the Roses. Consequently, English merchants lost control of their markets in central Europe and the Baltic to their main commercial rivals, the German merchants of the **Hanseatic League**. When trade recovered in the 1460s, almost half the English cloth exports were controlled by the Hanse and other foreign merchants.
3. *Merchant adventurers.* The English share of the trade had become monopolised by the Merchant Adventurers, who were

Hanseatic League
Merchants from the mainly German city ports on the Baltic Sea who came together to form a trading union and thus dominate the trade in northern Europe.

Key term

a powerful group of traders. They owed their dominant position to the large loans that they gave to the Crown, in return for which they were granted privileges denied to other English merchants. Driven out of other continental markets, the Merchant Adventurers established themselves at Antwerp in the Netherlands. This was to have a number of important consequences for English trade up to the 1550s. The Netherlands was a major centre for the dyeing and finishing of cloth, and this made it very convenient for the export of English textiles. Furthermore, at the time of the Merchant Adventurers' removal to Antwerp, the city was becoming the main commercial and financial centre in western Europe.

4. *The Antwerp–London 'funnel'.* This created what is known as the Antwerp–London 'funnel'. The monopoly of the Merchant Adventurers meant that English cloth exports came to be channelled through London, which controlled 90 per cent of the trade by the 1550s. At the same time English imports of wine, spices, manufactured goods and luxury items became concentrated on Antwerp. One beneficial effect of this commercial axis was that by the middle of the sixteenth century some 70 per cent of the country's overseas trade was controlled by English merchants. On the other hand, English ports such as Bristol, York, Hull and Southampton declined, and many merchants outside London complained that they were being excluded from the continental market.

Short-term causes

The link with Antwerp created a variety of problems through its very success.

1. Much of the rise in the volume of exports in the 1540s was the result of the repeated debasement of the English coinage. This, by reducing the value of sterling against continental currencies, artificially stimulated demand for English goods abroad by making them cheaper, and so made the slump after 1550 even deeper.

2. The importance of the trade to both England and the Netherlands made it a pawn in diplomatic exchanges and foreign policy. The early Tudors frequently used the threat of withholding cloth exports to try to force the Habsburg Empire into wars against France. Such a policy finally helped to bring about the decline of Antwerp when England's relationship with Charles V broke down during Northumberland's temporary alliance with France in 1550 (see page 81). Both sides placed restrictions on trade, and this forced English merchants to begin to look for new markets.

3. Although the Antwerp market did not finally collapse until the 1570s, its preceding decline left English trade in a very exposed position. During the first half of the sixteenth century the volume of exports to Antwerp had made English merchants disinclined to seek out alternative markets. In spite of advice, such as that given by Robert Thorne in his book

Declaration of the Indes (1530s), very little effort was made to establish new trade outlets within Europe, or elsewhere in the world. It was not until the initial slump in the trade to the Netherlands in the early 1550s that the Privy Council and the London merchants began to promote exploration in the search for new markets. The establishment of the Muscovy Company in 1553 (see pages 83–4) was the first step in this direction.

4. The underlying cause of the decline of the Antwerp market was the change in the pattern of demand. Both European and colonial buyers began to favour lighter types of fabric made of silk, cotton or linen mixed with wool, instead of the heavy English woollen cloth. This meant that during the second half of the sixteenth century English manufacturers not only had to find alternative markets, but also had to to restructure to meet the new technical developments.

Assessing mid-Tudor trade

Clearly the concentration on trade with Antwerp eventually proved disastrous for the English economy. In part, the problem was political, arising from England's reliance on Habsburg support in the wars with France. Fear of offending the Spanish Habsburgs meant that only limited attempts were made to break into their monopoly of world trade (see pages 83–4). The loss of Calais ended any lingering dreams of regaining a continental empire. Deteriorating relations between England and Spain under Elizabeth I opened the way for a more vigorous search for markets outside Europe. This was to be the basis for the expansion of world trade in the seventeenth century.

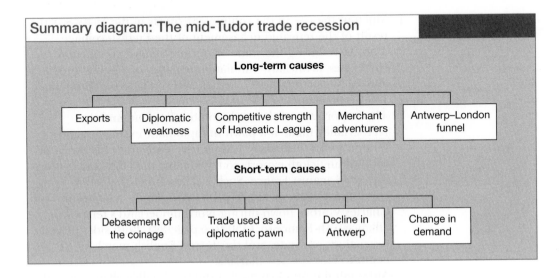

Summary diagram: The mid-Tudor trade recession

Long-term causes
- Exports
- Diplomatic weakness
- Competitive strength of Hanseatic League
- Merchant adventurers
- Antwerp–London funnel

Short-term causes
- Debasement of the coinage
- Trade used as a diplomatic pawn
- Decline in Antwerp
- Change in demand

Key question
What was the 'urban crisis'?

5 | Towns, Unemployment and Urban Recession

The commercial backbone of England's economy had long been based on three key activities: foreign trade, regional trade and the local market town trade. The last of these proved the most dynamic during the sixteenth century. The town, with its market and regular fairs, was an essential part of the rural economy because it brought producer and consumer together. Towns stimulated trade and encouraged growth in the economy.

The towns

Mid-Tudor England had many towns but few of them were large. London was six times larger than its nearest rivals, Norwich and Bristol. It has been calculated that only about seven per cent of the country's population lived in towns of over 5000 inhabitants.

The estimated populations of the largest English and Welsh towns in 1550:

London	80,000
Norwich	12,000
Bristol	10,000
York	7000
Newcastle	6000
Exeter	6000
Salisbury	5000
Oxford	5000
Carmarthen	2500

Unemployment in the 1550s was made worse by what used to be called an 'urban crisis'. In some respects this was considered to be a consequence of the development of the rural textile industry. The first stage of urban decline came from the effects of competition from the more cost-effective putting-out system. Then, in the fifteenth century, towns were adversely affected by the population losses caused by the Black Death and the continued influence of the plague cycle. Urban populations declined rapidly, especially because their crowded living conditions produced higher mortality rates.

The situation was made worse by the fall in overall population which drastically reduced the flow of migrants needed to maintain, or increase, the number of town dwellers. When population levels began to recover during the first half of the sixteenth century, the situation was reversed. Towns faced the problem of having to house, feed and employ large numbers of young and generally unskilled migrants from the countryside. At the same time, town guilds had to meet growing competition from the rural industries.

Unemployment and urban recession

Key question
How serious a problem was unemployment and the urban recession?

While some towns went into temporary eclipse, others actually expanded. In any case, the picture is distorted by the abnormal expansion of London, which was a reflection of the city's monopoly of the Antwerp trade. London was becoming recognised as the centre of government and the capital of England. Urban historians tend to see the rapid expansion of London as a positive development. London's emergence as a capital city is regarded as having become an engine for economic growth by the end of the sixteenth century.

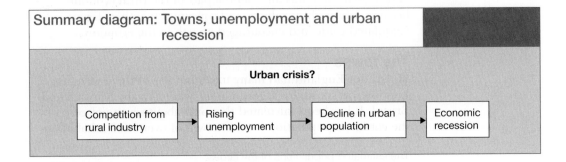

Summary diagram: Towns, unemployment and urban recession

Urban crisis?

Competition from rural industry → Rising unemployment → Decline in urban population → Economic recession

6 | The Key Debate

> Was there a crisis in the economy?

Although the mid-Tudor economy appeared to be in a weak state there is no clear evidence that it was in crisis.

Agriculture
Agriculture had become more efficient through enclosures, specialisation and commercial farming. However, because of over-concentration on wool and other animal products, it was barely able to feed the increased population by 1550, a problem that was not to be fully overcome until the next century.

Industry
There was a similar amount of change in industry. Heavy industry was still in the process of catching up with continental technology. The rural textile industry suffered temporary collapse in the 1550s after a century of expansion, but was already adapting to new demands by the second half of the century. The slump in the Antwerp cloth market in the 1550s had forced English merchants to begin to seek new markets in Europe, and to take an interest in world trade. The main difficulty was that the economy was unable to find employment for the surplus labour released from agriculture and created by a rising population.

Debasements of the coinage
Debasements of the coinage helped to increase inflation and made goods and borrowing more expensive. Rising rents, prices and unemployment, along with static wages, curtailed demand among the bulk of the population. In turn, this acted as a disincentive for people to invest in either agriculture or industry.

Taxation

The ruinously high levels of taxation from the 1520s were a further deterrent to investment. The cumulative effect of high taxation had, by the mid-century, seriously limited the cash reserves of all but the wealthiest landowners and merchants.

Political problems

It can be argued that where there were problems they were more political than economic. The two mid-century decades were characterised by almost continuous warfare, which was the culmination of the wars started by Henry VIII in the 1520s. This protracted conflict disrupted the economies on both sides of the Channel. The situation was made worse by diplomatic manoeuvrings which artificially created slumps by stopping overseas trade.

Unemployment

By the 1550s unemployment was becoming a problem in many towns. As population levels rose there were no extra jobs in agriculture, and younger people had to find employment elsewhere. They travelled to the towns to seek work, which was often not available because of the lack of urban investment. There is no real sign that rising unemployment was a key factor in the popular discontent in 1549. This is not to say that there was not widespread hardship in many areas.

Lack of investment

There was an underlying problem of a lack of investment and demand in the English economy. The rural élites favoured building country mansions and buying luxury goods to maintain their lifestyle rather than investing money to improve their estates. Similarly, the wealthy urban élites were more interested in improving their social position by purchasing country estates than expanding and improving their business interests. This situation continued until the inflationary spiral ended in the 1650s. Until then landowners and industrialists were content to live off the profits generated by rising prices without making investments.

Despite the disruptions caused by war, high taxation and debasements of the coinage, economic progress was maintained.

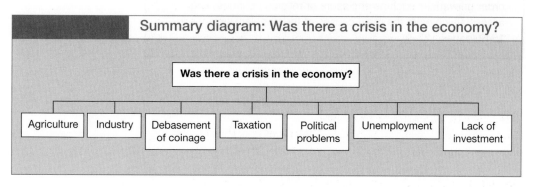

Summary diagram: Was there a crisis in the economy?

Was there a crisis in the economy?

Agriculture | Industry | Debasement of coinage | Taxation | Political problems | Unemployment | Lack of investment

Study Guide: A2 Questions

In the style of AQA

To what extent did the rise in population rather than the development of overseas trade contribute to the prosperity of England in the period between 1540 and 1558?

Exam tips

The cross-references are intended to take you straight to the material that will help you to answer the question.

In this question you must decide how far the rise in population as opposed to the development of overseas trade contributed to the prosperity of England. You might wish to challenge the assumption that England was prospering during this period, e.g. how justified are historians in considering that the mid-Tudor economy was prospering?

In order to provide a well-balanced answer you should take account of the following and conclude with your opinion based on the material used to support each of the points listed below, for example:

- familiarise yourself with the way historians study Tudor society and the economy
- note carefully why population levels had such a significant effect on the Tudor economy, and what problems were being caused by high population levels, e.g. the effects of unemployment, low wages, high rents, food shortages and inflation (which were direct results of population increase) on the living standards of the lower orders (pages 169–72)
- consider how well agriculture was coping with the need to feed a rising population (pages 175–80)
- note the varied levels of success being experienced in mid-Tudor industry (pages 181–4)
- note the contribution that English overseas trade was making to the nation's prosperity. Part of your analysis should consider the disruptive effect of wars, heavy taxation, diplomatic embargoes, English fear of offending Spain by breaking into world markets and the growing religious tensions (pages 184–6)
- analyse the importance of the same issues alongside other lower order grievances such as enclosure or religious change, and assess which were the main causes of the popular uprisings in 1549 (pages 127–9).

Further Reading

G.W. Bernard, 'Politics and Government in Tudor England', *Historical Journal*, 31 (1988), 159–82.

Philip Caramani, *The Western Rebellion* (Tiverton, 1994).

D.C. Coleman, *The Economy of England, 1450–1750* (OUP, 1977).

E. Duffy, *The Stripping of the Altars* (OUP, 1992).

G.R. Elton, *England under the Tudors* (Methuen, 1955).

A. Fletcher and J. Stevenson, *Order and Disorder in Early Modern England* (CUP, 1985).

C. Haigh, *English Reformations: Religion, Politics and Society Under the Tudors* (OUP, 1993).

N. Heard, *Tudor Economy and Society* (Hodder & Stoughton, 1992).

Christopher Hill, 'Marxism and History', *The Modern Quarterly NS 3* (1948), 52–64.

Eric Hobsbawm & T. Ranger (eds.), *The Invention of Tradition* (CUP, 1992).

W.K. Jordan, *Edward VI: The Threshold of Power – The Dominance of the Duke of Northumberland* (George Allen & Unwin, 1970).

J. Loach & R. Tittler (eds.), *The Mid-Tudor Polity, c. 1540–1560* (Macmillan, 1980).

J. Loach, *Parliament under the Tudors* (OUP, 1991).

J. Loach, *A Mid-Tudor Crisis?* (Historical Association pamphlet, 1992).

D.M. Loades, *The Mid-Tudor Crisis, 1545–65* (Macmillan, 1992).

D. MacCulloch, *Tudor Church Militant: Edward VI and the Protestant Reformation* (Penguin, 1999)

D.M. Pallister, *The Age of Elizabeth: England under the Later Tudors 1547–1603* (2nd edn, Longman, 1992).

A.F. Pollard, *England under Protector Somerset* (London, 1900).

Paul Slack, *Poverty and Policy in Tudor and Stuart England* (Longman, 1988).

Alan G.R. Smith, *The Emergence of a Nation State 1529–1660* (Longman, 1984).

Paul Thomas, *Authority and Disorder in Tudor Times 1485–1603* (CUP, 1999).

R. Tittler, *Mary I* (Longman, 1983).

P. Williams, *The Later Tudors: England, 1547–1603* (OUP, 1995).

John Warren, *The Past and its Presenters* (Hodder & Stoughton, 1998).

Glossary

Abdication When a monarch gives up the throne either by force or by retirement.

Absolution The act of being forgiven for committing a sin or sins after confession to a priest in the Catholic Church.

Absolutist/authoritarian Similar to dictatorship, where the ruler has absolute power, i.e. unchallenged rule.

Act of Six Articles Passed in 1539, the Act was intended to protect and promote Catholic religious ideas and prevent the further spread of Protestantism in England and Wales.

Act of the Ten Articles Passed in 1536, the Act was intended to promote Protestant religious ideas in England and Wales by stripping away many of the traditional festivals, relic-cults, shrines and parts of the Church service.

Anglo-Catholicism Used to describe the English Catholic Church set up in 1534 with the King as its head rather than the Pope.

Anti-clericalism Used to describe the hostility to, and unpopularity of, the Church and its priests.

Apprenticeship Time served by students learning a trade from master-craftsmen.

Arable Farming land set aside for the growing of crops.

Atlantic trade The triangular trade route between Europe, America and Africa.

Barbary coast Coast of North Africa, mainly Morocco and Algeria.

Bondmen Peasant farmers who had no freedom to choose where they lived and worked. They were tied to the manor on which they were born and brought up.

Bourgeoisie Used by Marxist historians to describe the middle class of lawyers, landowners and merchants.

Burgesses The most powerful members of a town's citizens. They were often descended from the town's original founders and they also tended to hold the most important offices in the town's administration.

Calvinism A term used to describe the influence and religious ideas and teachings of John Calvin of Geneva, a radical Protestant religious reformer who attacked the Catholic Church's wealth and privileges.

Calvinist doctrines Religious rules and instructions developed by the Protestant leader John Calvin.

Catholic Inquisition Organisation empowered by the Pope to defend the Church by rooting out enemies such as heretics.

Chancellor Senior minister in the royal government who had control of the Great Seal used to authenticate and give legal force to laws.

Chantries Small religious houses endowed with lands to support one or more priests whose duty it was to sing masses for the souls of the deceased founder or members of the founding organisation.

Christian humanism The teaching of the original classical texts in their original Latin and Greek, and the study of the humanities as the basis of civilised life.

Class war Term used by some historians to help to explain the causes of the disorder and rebellions that occurred during the reign of Edward VI. The resentment of the poor and economically vulnerable was directed towards the wealthy and powerful élites.

Commonwealth A community of shared interests where everyone, in theory, worked for the common good.

Commonwealth men A group led by John Hales, who was an MP and government minister, concerned with the economic and social welfare of the citizens of the State, especially its poor.

Constitution The rules and regulations that determine how a country is governed.

Constitutional monarchy A system whereby a monarch governs the kingdom within the limits of an agreed framework of rules that includes institutions such as the Privy Council and Parliament.

Consubstantiation The belief that the sacramental bread and wine given by the priest to parishioners in Church were a symbolic representation of the body and blood of Christ and therefore remained unchanged at communion.

Convocation An assembly of clergy that resembled Parliament in that it was divided into two houses: the upper house of senior clergy and a lower house of ordinary clergy. Convocation discussed church matters, passed Church laws and regulated the way the Church was run.

Cottagers Poorer peasant farmers who were obliged to work on the landowner's land either for free or for a fixed sum of money.

Council in the North Regional council of nobles and gentry based in York to govern northern England on behalf of the monarch.

Counter Reformation Catholic reaction against the spread of Protestantism. Led by the Pope, the Catholic Church attempted to reconvert Protestants and bring them back to the Catholic faith.

Country party Made up of those among the élites who did not hold office or enjoy royal favour, and generally lived on their estates in the countryside.

County militias Non-professional military force raised from among the able-bodied local population that lived within the bounds of a county.

Court party Seen as consisting of the members of the Privy Council, government officers and courtiers, all of whom held office and enjoyed royal patronage.

Craft guild Similar to a trade union formed to protect and promote the particular trade of its members.

Custom and excise Taxation imposed on the import of goods.

Debasement of the coinage A process whereby the government tried to preserve its gold and silver reserves by reducing the amount of precious metal that went into making coins.

Deflation The reduction of the amount of money in circulation in order to increase its value.

Diocese A district under the pastoral care of a bishop.

Dissolution of the monasteries The closure of the monasteries of England and Wales by Henry VIII between 1536 and 1540.

Doctrinal orthodoxy The traditional or long-held beliefs of, in this instance, the Catholic Church and religion. Because these beliefs and practices (doctrine) had been followed for hundreds of years they had become an accepted (orthodox) part of worship in the Catholic Church.

Dowry A sum of money paid by the bride's father on her marriage.

Edict A royal decree having the force of law.

Enclosure The enclosing of land by fences or hedges in order to divide large open fields into smaller, more manageable units.

Exchequer The centre of the Crown's financial administration since the twelfth century. It had two functions: (1) to receive, store and pay out money and (2) to audit the Crown's accounts.

Extreme unction   The act of being anointed with oils as part of a religious rite or ceremony.

Feudal crisis   The breakdown in the relationship between lord and vassal. The relationship changed from one based on rewards of land for service to one based on money payments.

Feudalism   The political and social system of medieval England. The system was based on the relationship between lord (master) and vassal (servant): in a ceremony known as homage the vassal promised to serve his lord in war and peace in return for land. The most important lord was the king and his vassals were the nobles. The nobles were lords to their vassals, the knights and esquires.

Field rotation   System where different crops are rotated between fields.

Flexible field systems   Farmers could grow what crops they wanted where they wanted, either in large open fields or in enclosed fields.

Forty-two Articles   A list of essential doctrines drawn up by Cranmer and intended to form the basis of the new Protestant Church of England.

General Warden of the North   Nobleman charged with overall responsibility for the defence of the northern frontier with Scotland.

Habsburgs   Family name of the ruling family of Spain and Austria. The head of the family from 1519 until his retirement in 1555 was Charles V who, as Holy Roman Emperor, also ruled Germany, the Netherlands and parts of Italy.

Hanseatic League   Merchants from the mainly German city ports on the Baltic Sea who came together to form a trading union and thus dominate the trade in northern Europe.

Heresy laws   Laws to punish those people who reject the State religion and the teachings of the Church.

Higher clergy   The bishops and two archbishops of England and Wales.

Holy orders   The clerical population, people who had taken oaths of loyalty and service to God and the Church on being made priests, monks or nuns.

Holy Roman Empire   Collection of states of varying sizes that covered central Europe (Germany and Austria) and northern Italy, which was governed by an elected ruler, the Emperor.

Hundred Years War   Fought between England and France for control of France between 1338 and 1453.

Husbandmen   Peasant tenant-farmers who rented their land from the local landowners.

Iconoclasm   The act of breaking, destroying or defacing religious images such as wall paintings or stained glass, and statues such as those depicting Christ and the Virgin Mary.

Impotent poor   Those who were too old, too young or too sick to work.

Infant mortality   Term used to describe the death-rate among children, usually under five years of age. In the medieval and early modern periods, infant mortality rates were high owing to complications at birth, poor diet, disease and poor health and hygiene.

Injunction   A law or decree issued by the Crown to compel the clergy in the Church of England to follow a particular order or practice.

Inns of Court   Located in London, the Inns of Court provided a university-type education for those wishing to study and practise law.

Intercursus Magnus   Treaty agreement on trade negotiated by Henry VII between England and the Netherlands.

Justice of the Peace   Local law officer and magistrate at shire level. JPs also governed the county by enforcing Acts of Parliament and acting on decisions taken by the Privy Council and other departments of central government.

Laity The non-clerical general population, the parishioners as opposed to the priests.

Legislative programme The key points of a government's plan to govern the country by passing laws, deciding levels of taxation and controls on trade.

Litany Recital of religious teachings contained in the Book of Common Prayer.

Lord Lieutenant Local military officer with the power to call musters and assemble an armed militia.

Lutheran princes Those rulers of the northern states of the Holy Roman Empire (Germany) who had converted to the Protestant faith established by Martin Luther.

Lutheranism The influence, religious ideas and teachings of Martin Luther of Wittenberg in Germany. His protest against the corruption and wealth of the Catholic Church and criticism of the Pope led to his being thrown out of the Church (1520s), after which he set up his own Protestant Church.

Malthusian crisis Socio-economic theory of T.R. Malthus (d. 1834), an English clergyman and economist who argued that when a country's population outstrips food production the result is famine.

Marian government Term used to describe the government of Mary I.

Marxists Historians who see historical change as a series of events caused mainly by social and economic tension leading to conflict between the poorer and richer classes.

Mercenary army Professional troops who serve for pay.

Millenarianists Radical thinkers who believed in social reform whereby a kingdom's wealth would be distributed equally to all citizens.

Minority government Government by councillors when the ruler is a child or minor.

Monopoly Total control of trade by one country to the exclusion of others.

Muscovy Company Company set up to trade with Russia.

Nationalistic People who are particularly proud of their country and who might distrust or even hate foreigners.

New World Used to describe all America.

Office of Crown Lands Department set up to manage the estates (most of which had been inherited from previous monarchs) that belonged to the reigning monarch.

Ordination Ceremony in which holy orders were conferred on priests, enabling them to serve in parishes.

Ottoman Empire Islamic empire centred on Turkey that threatened Christian Europe and control of the Mediterranean.

Pasture Farming land set aside for the rearing of animals.

Paternalistic The idea that a monarch would govern his kingdom and rule his subjects as a father would his house and family.

Patron A wealthy and powerful individual who uses his influence to promote the career of a supporter.

Penance When a person acknowledges their guilt or sin and seeks forgiveness.

Pilgrimage of Grace Popular rebellion in northern England (1536–7) caused by distrust of Cromwell and discontent over religious changes, particularly the closure of the monasteries.

Plague cycle Regular occurrences of plague. For example, the Black Death of 1348–51 was followed by plague outbreaks in 1361–2, 1369 and 1393.

Poor laws   Laws to deal with the poor and vagrant in society. Because government did not understand the causes of poverty and vagrancy and they feared rebellion, many of the early poor laws were designed to punish and control the poor. By mid-century some attempt was made to assist the poor by promoting charity and providing work.

Price scissors   Economic term used to describe the point when prices and rents overtook wages.

Privateers   Professional seamen who sailed for profit by means of trade or piracy, or, if employed by the State, war.

Privy Council   Élite body of councillors drawn from the nobility and more powerful gentry who met the monarch on a regular basis to offer their advice, frame laws and govern the country.

Proclamations   The Crown had the power to issue proclamations, which were official or public announcements that included the right to make new laws, especially when Parliament was not in session. The Proclamations Act of 1539 stated that royal proclamations had the same right and power as Acts of Parliament.

Protestant   Used to describe those who had protested against and separated from the Roman Catholic Church.

Protestant Lowlanders   Scots who lived in the border region with England and were among the first to be converted to English Protestantism.

Purgatory   A place of temporary suffering between heaven and hell where the dead are spiritually cleansed of sins committed in life.

Putting-out system   Manufacturing system whereby the raw material is sent out for others to finish off.

Recession   A fall in the demand for goods which leads to a drop in prices and to unemployment.

Reformation   The religious changes of the sixteenth century in England and continental Europe. What began in England as a modest reform of the organisation and teachings of the Roman Catholic Church led eventually to their merger with or replacement by more Protestant forms.

Regency Council   A select group of noble councillors who govern the kingdom on behalf of a ruler who is a child. Between 1547 and 1549 the Council was headed by Somerset to rule on behalf of Edward VI.

Regency government   Government by a regent, usually a powerful noble, appointed to rule if the monarch is either unable or too young to do so.

Renaissance   Rebirth of learning and the arts, which encouraged writers and artists to become part of what was called the spirit of new learning.

Repeal   The procedure in Parliament whereby laws are cancelled and removed from the book listing current laws, known as the Statute Book.

Revisionists   Historians who believe that older or more traditional interpretations and ideas in history should be regularly reviewed and changed if necessary.

Rough wooing   Contemporary term to describe the method used by Somerset to woo or persuade (as one would a lover) the Scots to agree to his marriage proposals.

Royal Household   The living arrangements of the monarch. It consisted of servants who looked after the monarch's person and his financial and political affairs.

Royal prerogative   The rights and privileges that traditionally belonged to the monarch. For example, the monarch had the right to appoint to public office, dispense justice and regulate trade. In emergencies the monarch also had the power to make war, raise armies and negotiate peace.

Royal supremacy   The Crown's headship and control of the Church in England.

Salic Law   A law originating in France and dating from the eleventh century which excluded females from succeeding to the throne.

Sedition   Action or speech that incites rebellion.

Seminaries   Religious institutions of learning designed to educate and train priests.

'Slavery' Act of 1547   Term given to the poor law passed by Somerset's government. Described by historian W.R.D. Jones as 'the most savage of all Tudor poor laws', the statute stated that sturdy or able-bodied vagrants should be branded with the letters V and S and subjected to forced labour or slavery for repeat offenders.

Sovereign state   A country in which the monarch has supreme power over the State (government, law, the economy) and the Church (doctrine, appointments and property). Foreign powers or rulers had no right to interfere in the internal affairs of a sovereign state.

State papers   Documents drawn up by ministers that record the decisions made and show the decision-making process undertaken by central government.

Succession Acts   Acts of Parliament passed to clarify and enforce the right of succession to the Crown of England.

Temporal wealth   Church wealth that is calculated in land, property and goods.

Tithes   Tax amounting to ten per cent of a parishioner's income (usually paid in goods) levied by the Church.

Treason Act   Law passed in Parliament to punish those who betray the State and its monarch. Political and religious disloyalty was punishable by death if convicted under the Treason Act.

Tree of Reformation   The location of Ket's council of justice, which sat under an old oak tree.

Tudor revolution in government   Theory first put forward in the 1950s by historian Geoffrey Elton to explain the changes that took place in government under the guiding hand of Thomas Cromwell. Elton describes Cromwell's handling of Tudor government during the 1530s as 'revolutionary' because he supervised the emergence of a constitutional monarchy based on parliament and working through bureaucratic departments of State.

Twelve Decrees   The key 12 points drawn up by Pole at the Westminster Synod. They included the need for every parish priest to be properly trained, educated and permanently resident. To help the hard-pressed clergy, Pole commissioned a newly edited Catholic New Testament and a new book of Homilies to replace Cranmer's Protestant edition. However, they were never used.

Up and down husbandry   A system under which land was used alternatingly over a number of years as arable land and then for pasture.

Vagrancy   Term used to describe the wandering poor who had no permanent work or home.

Valois   Name of the ruling royal family of France between 1328 and 1589.

Valois–Habsburg wars   Ongoing rivalry and conflict between the ruling families of France (Valois) and Spain/Austria (Habsburg).

Wardens of the March   Nobles appointed by the monarch to defend and safeguard the eastern and western sections of the northern frontier (March) with Scotland.

Wars of the Roses   The sequence of plots, rebellions and battles that took place in England between 1455 and 1485. The idea of the warring roses of Lancaster (red) and York (white) was invented by Henry VII after he seized the throne in 1485.

Westminster synod   Also known as the London Synod, this was a meeting of the important clergy under Cardinal Pole who wished to consolidate and promote Roman Catholicism in the kingdom and to plan the future of the Church.

Yeomen   A social class of richer peasants who may have been as wealthy as some of the gentry but were below them in social class.

Zwinglian   Term used to describe the influence of Huldrych Zwingli, a Protestant religious reformer from Switzerland, who believed that local religious communities should have the right to control their own affairs without interference from either the Church authorities or State officials.

Index